Governance and Information Technology

Governance and Information Technology

From Electronic Government to Information Government

Edited by Viktor Mayer-Schönberger and David Lazer

The MIT Press
Cambridge, Massachusetts
London, England

For information about special quantity discounts, please email special_sales@mitpress.mit.edu

This book was set in Sabon on 3B2 by Asco Typesetters, Hong Kong.
Printed on recycled paper and bound in the United States of America.

Library of Congress Cataloging-in-Publication Data

Governance and information technology : from electronic government to information government / edited by Viktor Mayer-Schönberger and David Lazer.
     p.   cm.
Includes bibliographical references and index.
ISBN 978-0-262-13483-5 (hardcover : alk. paper)—ISBN 978-0-262-63349-9 (pbk. : alk. paper)
1. Internet in public administration. 2. Internet in public administration—Case studies.
3. Electronic government information. 4. Electronic public records. I. Mayer-Schönberger, Viktor. II. Lazer, David.
JF1525.A8F76   2007
352.3′802854678—dc22   2006034532

10 9 8 7 6 5 4 3 2 1

This book is dedicated to our families:
To Birgit (from VMS)
To Lisa, Liana, and Sarah (from DL)

Contents

Acknowledgments

A book has many parents and innumerous midwives. This is especially true for an edited volume like this. These acknowledgments therefore cannot mention all the people who have helped bring it about.

We would like to thank our colleagues at the Dubai School of Government (DSG), especially Nabil Ali Alyousuf and Yasar Jarrar (whose energy is contagious), who have been advocates of this project from the beginning. The Dubai School of Government under Dean Tarik Yousef has provided invaluable financial support and generously hosted an international conference on information government in May 2005 in Dubai, which provided the genesis of this volume. We are also grateful for the support of the Belfer Center of Science and International Affairs (BCSIA) at Harvard and its director Graham Allison. We have had the fortune to work with three outstanding executive directors of the center: John Reppert, Robert C. Orr, and Juliette Kayyem. We are also grateful to Arwa Al-Ali and Fadi Salem at DSG and Ginger Dagli, the executive director of the Dubai Initiative at Harvard's Kennedy School of Government, who have been helpful at every step of the way.

We are grateful for those colleagues and practitioners who joined us in our information government conference in May 2005, and whose insights provided the basis for a number of our case illustrations: Chong Yoke Sin, William Piatt, Michael Armstrong, Salem Al Shahir, Chris Newby, Richard Otis, and Kuno Schedler. We also gratefully acknowledge the help of James Yong and Jeff Tan in understanding the development of electronic government in Singapore. We owe a special thank you to our colleague and contributor Bob Behn, who helped us settle on the term "information government."

Malte Ziewitz and Alexander Schellong have provided helpful research assistance; Susan M. Lynch ably edited the first round of manuscripts. At MIT Press, we would like to thank our editors Clay Morgan and Kathy Caruso.

As with most academic publications, this one, too, took more time than we initially envisioned. As academics, we are drawn to the spark of an interesting idea, in the hope that it can be developed into something that provides illumination and insight. Our success depends in no small part on the willingness of our families to tolerate and even embrace our academic obsessions. Dedicating this book to them is a reflection of both our love for and our debts to our families.

Viktor Mayer-Schönberger
David Lazer
Cambridge, Massachusetts
May 2007

About the Contributors

Robert D. Behn, a lecturer at Harvard University's John F. Kennedy School of Government, is always comparing the performance of the Boston Red Sox with the performance of the evil New York Yankees.

Maria Christina Binz-Scharf is assistant professor of management at the City College of New York (CUNY).

Herbert Burkert is professor of public law, information, and communication law at the University of St. Gallen, Switzerland.

Lorenzo Cantoni is professor of eGovernment and eLearning at the University of Lugano (Switzerland) and president of I.Re.F., the Lombardy Region Institute for Education and Training of Public Administration.

Cary Coglianese is the Edward B. Shils Professor of Law and professor of political science at the University of Pennsylvania Law School, where he is also the director of the Penn Program on Regulation.

Martin J. Eppler is professor of information and communication management at the School of Communication of the University of Lugano (USI), Switzerland.

Jane E. Fountain is professor of political science and public policy and director of the National Center for Digital Government at the University of Massachusetts, Amherst.

Monique Girard is associate director of the Center on Organizational Innovation at Columbia University.

Åke Grönlund is professor of informatics in the Department of Economics, Statistics and Informatics, Örebro University, Sweden.

Matthew Hindman is assistant professor of political science at Arizona State University.

Edwin Lau is project leader of the E-Government Project at the Organisation for Economic Co-operation and Development (OECD).

David Lazer is associate professor of public policy and director of the Program on Networked Governance at the John F. Kennedy School of Government, Harvard University.

Viktor Mayer-Schönberger is associate professor of public policy at the John F. Kennedy School of Government, Harvard University.

Ines Mergel is a postdoctoral fellow at the John F. Kennedy School of Government, Harvard University, and the research director of the Program on Networked Governance.

Gopal Raman, a 2006 graduate of the John F. Kennedy School of Government at Harvard University, is currently working as a management consultant in Sydney, Australia.

David Stark is Arthur Lehman Professor of Sociology and International Affairs at Columbia University and a member of the External Faculty at the Santa Fe Institute.

Sandor Vegh received his Ph.D. in American studies from the University of Maryland and is currently a consultant for the World Bank.

Darrell M. West is the John Hazen White Professor of Public Policy and Political Science and director of the Taubman Center for Public Policy at Brown University.

1

From Electronic Government to Information Government

Viktor Mayer-Schönberger and David Lazer

Information is the foundation of all governing. Information guides decisions and processes large and small—from matters of war and peace to garbage collection. The last decade has witnessed unprecedented attention to the machinery of information in government—often categorized as "electronic government." Information and communication technologies have been touted as the cure for everything from the rigid, silo-based architecture of government to the sagging rates of participation in our democracy. However, too often the focus of electronic government has been on technology—on the technically possible—rather than on the flows of information. This volume seeks to explore a deeper understanding of the role of information flows within government, between government and citizens, and (to a lesser extent) among citizens regarding government. Technology can only make certain types of information flows *possible*—it does not mean, as individual chapters in this book make clear, that they will or should occur. Given current technologies, the elasticity of human institutions and cognition is far less than that of bits.

This chapter first lays out the current state of understanding of electronic government, because most of the attention to information and government in the last decade has come under this rubric. We then present our vision of an "information government" paradigm, which focuses on the flow of information within, to, and from government. We conclude with an overview of the contributions to this edited volume.

Electronic Government

Over the last two decades, computing power has spread to businesses and citizens in all developed countries. The availability of affordable networked hard- and software by the early 1990s made it possible for these computers to become connected to a global information infrastructure most commonly referred to as the "Internet." Combined with drastically reduced telecommunication costs, these developments have provided the foundation for delivering public services electronically.

Frequently termed "electronic government," this online delivery of public services has been seen as the next step—following "electronic commerce"—toward the creation of an information society. By the late 1990s, many governments had devised electronic government strategies. Consultants busied themselves, helping governments implement ambitious strategies and benchmarking implementation successes. Electronic government, it was suggested, would evolve swiftly through defined stages, beginning with a web presence of public agencies ("information") to a means for citizens to communicate with these agencies ("interaction") to offering public services online to citizens around the clock seven days a week in the convenience of their homes ("transaction") (Netchaeva 2002). This in turn would lead to a transformation of the public sector (Rais Abdul Karim and Mohd Khalid 2003). The sequence of stages was depicted as inevitable, fueled by technology, citizen demand, and economic realities in the public sector.

Electronic government so defined focuses on the interface between citizens and government, and on how it changes due to technology (Silcock 2001; West 2005). This flavor of electronic government promised to make it easier, faster, and cheaper for citizens (as customers) to transact with public agencies, responding to customer demand to "build services around citizens' choices" (Curthoys and Crabtree 2003).

The attention given to this transaction-oriented view of electronic government has translated into a significant increase in public online services (although see chapter 2).

In the United States, for example, the U.S. Post Office contracted with a for-profit company to develop a one-stop shopping website for people moving from one location to another. The website—moving.com—offered citizens a way to file a change-of-address form, to notify utility companies of their move, and to buy packaging material and hire moving trucks from private-sector partners. Moving.com provided a customer-centric front office solution that reduced transaction costs for citizens by eliminating the need to go to the post office, file a change-of-address form, and notify separately utilities and others of the move.

Similarly, Singapore has integrated its online public services into an easily accessible web portal, through which citizens using a smart card can transact securely with their government, reducing citizen search and data entry costs (Ke and Wei

2004; Yong 2005). Electronic government services offered in Dubai's Internet City make it possible to incorporate companies or get a work permit in a matter of hours—a drastic cost savings for the private sector compared with the paper-based process.

Facilitating interaction with government lowers the cost of dealing with public authorities in terms of time and money—for citizens and the private sector. This benefits society at large by reducing overall transaction costs. As Edwin Lau describes in chapter 3, the OECD has highlighted this contribution of electronic government to economic policy objectives in its electronic government report, followed recently by another report on how electronic government is contributing to overall economic competitiveness (OECD 2003).

Such a transactional perspective on electronic government requires that citizens be willing to transact with their government online. Not surprisingly, electronic government so conceived faces two kinds of challenges. First, just as is the case with electronic commerce, a prerequisite to its success is that citizens have the equipment and skills and feel comfortable and safe transacting online. General ease of use, but also security, integrity, and privacy of transactional and personal data have to be maintained, as well as the authenticity of the transactional partners (Bannister 2005; Dutten et al. 2005; Holden and Millet 2005). Successful implementation may therefore require significant engineering, marketing, and education efforts. Second, the online provision of public services requires governments to address equity questions between the digital haves and have-nots in a way that is not true of private actors (Warschauer 2003). The position of the government to mandate certain behaviors by its citizens creates a reciprocal obligation on the government to not make those behaviors onerous. Thus, while it may be acceptable for firms to abandon brick-and-mortar outlets for cheaper online distribution channels, such a limited benefit-cost calculation is not appropriate for government agencies.

In contrast with this "narrow" perspective of electronic government that is focused on citizen-government transactions online, many commentators have suggested a much broader definition of electronic government, covering the entire use of information and communication technologies in the public sector (Janssen, Rotthier, and Snijkers 2004).

According to this view, electronic government is yet another step in a continuous process of achieving public-sector efficiencies through the use of technology, a process that began with filing cabinets, typewriters, and calculators and continued with the introduction of copy machines and word processors. In this sense, electronic government is an extension of the long history of office automation in the public sector.

From this perspective, the purpose of electronic government is similar to the use of all information-handling technologies before: to save public resources and to make public-sector activity more efficient. Electronic government is seen as a mechanism with which a given level of service can be offered with a reduced budget, or an increased amount of work may be achieved with a constant budget. Either way, electronic government is the tool to "achieve better government" (OECD 2003).

While this broader definition of electronic government encompasses online public services—the "narrow" view of electronic government—the focus shifts from the interface between government and citizens to the inner workings of government. This shift reflects the belief that efficiency gains through the use of the Internet and related information and communication technologies are realized primarily within government rather than directly by citizens. Not surprisingly given this impetus, such a conception sees electronic government as a tool of or closely related to new public management, with its aim to improve performance of given public objectives at reduced cost (Osborne and Gaebler 1992).

In contrast to the narrow definition, the hurdles encountered when implementing electronic government writ large are not primarily about citizen privacy, security, user-friendliness, or equity, but track the more general hurdles of organizational and structural reform of the public sector, from rethinking hierarchies to cross-agency collaboration (Peters 2001). Such a perspective emphasizes the challenge to institutional change (cf. Steinmo, Thelen, and Longstreth 1993; March and Olsen 1989), highlighting the path-dependent nature of technology adoption and focusing on the role that existing institutions play in how technology is utilized within government (Fountain 2003; chapter 4; also see Orlikowski 2000).

Others characterize electronic government as explicitly incorporating democratic processes (Bekkers 2003; Esterling, Neblo, and Lazer 2005; Janssen, Rotthier, and Snijkers 2004; West 2005), asking, for example: How does technology create the potential for citizens to become more involved in the policymaking process (Thomas and Streib 2003)? How does the realization of that potential then exacerbate or ameliorate existing biases in the political participation (Bimber 2003; Mossberger, Tolbert, and Stansbury 2003; Norris 2001)?

Taken together, these views of electronic government are helpful in drawing attention to particular elements of the use of information and communication technologies in the public sector, from the online interface between government and citizens to technology's role in reforming public administration. What the useful labels obscure, however, is the fact that commentators writing about narrow or broad electronic government look at a phenomenon from very different viewpoints. Despite its many merits, electronic government has thus become a catchall tag for the practice of using technologies in the public sector. In academic literature, electronic government has frequently turned into an epiphenomenal term, covering research that utilizes the entire spectrum of methods and theories to explain and analyze technology's impact on the functions of government.

This volume suggests that the eclecticism implicit in the term *electronic government* ought to be complemented not by another, or differing, definition of the term itself. Instead, we put forward the notion that examining the flows of information within the public sector and between the public sector and the citizens—what we term information government—provides a means to better understand the significant changes of governing and governance that occur in part facilitated by new technologies. Thus, information government is not another stage of electronic government —rather, it is a conceptual lens that offers a complementary perspective to understand the changing nature of government and its relationship to the citizenry.

Information Government

Here are two images (figures 1.1 and 1.2). The first is an image of a Sumerian cuneiform tablet. It is a record of a transaction involving fresh reeds during the reign of Ibbi-Sin, approximately 2028 BCE.[1] The second is the logo the IRS has adopted for

Figures 1.1 and 1.2
Tax records: 4,000 years ago and today.

electronic filing of taxes by individuals. These two images encapsulate both the continuities and the changes with respect to information and governance over the millennia. All government is, in part, about acquiring, processing, storing, and deciding upon information—whether we are talking about the Sumerian government of millennia ago or the U.S. government of today. The premise of this volume is that it is useful to focus on *information government*, the flows of information within government as well as between government and citizens.

The need to enable particular information flows has been identified as arguably the key driver of organizational design (Mintzberg 1992; Thompson 1967). For centuries it has prompted organizations to place individuals with high levels of time-sensitive and reciprocal interdependence in close proximity to each other and to their informational tools. The private sector has long organized its structure around the necessities and constraints of information flows. The modern military, with its strict system of hierarchy, and the successful twentieth-century Weberian bureaucratic state are paradigmatic examples of organizational systems built around these informational principles, in terms of how both these flows and these authority systems are structured.

The ability to acquire and disseminate information, to control the flow of information, has often been described as a source of power. The further the nature of our society turns from industrial to informational, the stronger this source of power will become (Castells 1996, 18–22). Information government as a concept prompts us to examine these information flows, where, when, and why they change, and what the interaction is between these changes and public-sector activities.

We suggest that it is useful to examine these flows independent of the medium for the information—clay or silicon. To be sure, modern information and communication technologies frequently change the flows of information. So have many technological advances before, from the printing press to the typewriter, from microfilm to the Xerox machine. One must not, however, conflate technology and the agent of change. In fact, while technology often facilitates a change in information flows, it can happen even in the absence of technological change—for example, through institutional reorganization. Such change, too, is shaping the public sector and captured through the information government lens. This focus on information rather than technology also ensures that we are not too awed by technology and its potential capabilities, but instead keep in mind the arguably more important constraints of human information processing.

What technology-agnostic information government acknowledges is that digital information and communication technologies allow for a much greater malleability of how information might flow. Digital information and communication networks in particular have obviated several of the premises for organizational design on which many of our institutions, including government, have been based. Some tight grouping structures for certain types of informational interdependencies may always be necessary. However, in general, where organizational structure was driven by the presence of information in a particular location, that locational imperative may be much reduced.

The freeing of informational flows may thus undermine particular grouping and hierarchical principles. Organizational structures that were necessitated by a desired flow of information—grouping people together and with their information resources, as well as putting them in defined hierarchies to steer the flow of information a particular way—may lose their legitimacy as digital networks facilitate people as well as organizations to rethink the direction of their information flows. Broadly viewed, information about policy increasingly becomes a global public good (Lazer 2005; also Mossberger 2000). More concretely, people as well as organizations gain a newfound *flexibility* (Castells 1996, 62).

It is no coincidence that the availability of new technologies occurs at the same time as calls for networked governance, which involves moving functions both outside government and away from hierarchy within government (e.g., Goldsmith and Eggers 2004; Meier and O'Toole 2006). This reflects the possibility of moving from pyramidal, silo-based structures, to more decentralized, networked (in terms of information flows) systems. Commentators from Drucker to Castells have written about the fundamental consequences this change will bring for corporations (Drucker 1988). Terms such as "horizontal corporation" and "network enterprise" have been proposed (Boyett and Conn 1991, 23; Castells 1996, 168–170). As organizational units focus at least in part on processing information, government agencies, indeed government as a whole, may equally be transformed. Information government analyzes this transformation process by examining the "who," "what," "when," and "which" of information flows.

A word of caution is in order. Currently there may be a general trend to transform hierarchical structures into more networked, horizontal ones, although it may be stronger in the private sector driven by profit maximization and pressures for efficiency gains. It is not inevitable, however, that all or even most organizational change will be in this direction. The evolution of issuing passports in Austria offers a cautionary tale. For decades, citizens would apply for a new passport by filing an application together with birth certificate, citizenship record, and related documents at a local government office. A few weeks later, the passport would be available for pickup. In 2003, network technology combined with affordable printing devices facilitated the on-demand issuing of passports at numerous local government offices throughout the country. Linking previously separate government databases, citizens would not have to show birth certificates and similar documentation each time they applied for a new passport. Instead, showing the old passport was sufficient. Local government offices could validate the information through their linked database, and print the new passport on the spot, most of the time within ten to twenty minutes. Government agencies had moved from hierarchical information flows to integrated and decentralized ones, empowering the periphery of the system and increasing efficiency for citizens.

However, in 2005, these information flows were once again centralized. In the wake of 9/11 and related international trends, the Austrian federal government adopted passports with biometric identifiers. This necessitated new infrastructure to facilitate the flow of (passport) information from government databases into passports. Due to cost concerns, the government centralized this infrastructure, requiring citizens to wait weeks for their passports to be centrally produced (using linked databases) and then physically sent to the local passport agency. The decision did not simply burden citizens. It changed the flow of information, from a decentralized networked structure to a linked and centralized one. All information is available at the center, while the periphery (the local passport offices) has lost informational access—not even able to tell citizens when their passports will be ready.

As this example shows, technology-enabled flexibility of information flows does not imply development of organizational structures in only one particular direction. The case also underscores the fact that technology may facilitate change but does not cause it (Bijeker 1995; Fischer 1992; Jasanoff et al. 2001). The decision to decentralize and recentralize was a political one, based on preferences, values, and available resources, not dictated by technology. Finally, the case highlights the utility of the concept of information government; following the flows of information and looking at their changes sheds additional light on what is happening.

Information also flows between the government and citizens. Digital networks may change what kind, how much, and how easily government information is accessible to citizens, and (potentially) vice versa (Graber 2006). This has significant consequences for the balance not just between individual and the state, but also between government and society as a whole. The information government lens helps bring these changes into focus.

This volume is divided into three sections. Part I examines the interplay between technological change and evolving information flows within government over the last decade. Part II focuses on the implications of the blurring informational boundary between government and society. Part III discusses the issues in evaluating the impact of reengineering information flows. The chapters in each section are matched with illustrative cases. What follows is a brief synopsis of each chapter.

Leading off part I, Darrell M. West (chapter 2) canvasses the global electronic government landscape. He finds that the online provision of public services has not followed the impressive trajectory pundits predicted, despite the availability of basic technological resources in many jurisdictions.

Edwin Lau (chapter 3) argues that electronic government proponents have focused too much on the easily identifiable pecuniary gains for the public sector and for citizens transacting online with government. This fails to capture less visible, wider gains especially for citizens due to changed and enhanced information flows, which may yield both improved governance and greater private-sector growth.

In contrast to West and Lau, Jane E. Fountain (chapter 4) reconceptualizes the relationship between government organization and digital information and communication networks using the information government lens. Looking in particular at the issue of information flows between two hierarchical government agencies, she analyzes the hurdles that such cross-jurisdictional informational cooperation faces and examines how they may be overcome.

Building on the concept of information government, part II broadens the information government concept beyond the provision of public services to include transparency and participation—not necessarily in the form of electronic democracy envisioned by electronic government proponents. Rather, part II focuses on the role information flows play in connecting government outcomes to citizen activities.

Cary Coglianese (chapter 5) looks at electronic rulemaking, a case where the online provision of a public service (the formal commenting process in agency rulemaking) traverses into territory of electronic democracy. Contrary to some expectations, Coglianese finds that while electronic rulemaking may have lowered transaction costs for civic engagement, it has not resulted in massive democratic involvement by citizens. Instead of creating a "strong" deliberative democracy, he see the rise of a new "information class"—individuals and organizations that are particularly well suited to gathering, manipulating, and presenting information.

The net positive result of e-rulemaking, Coglianese argues, is not dramatically more citizen engagement and democratic deliberation, but better rules due to a more comprehensive and inclusive information gathering and commenting process— enhanced information flows. E-rulemaking, in short, engages a broader range of organized interests, ones with resources to overcome the costs of expertise, but not of having a presence in Washington.

Herbert Burkert (chapter 6) adds a normative dimension to Coglianese's analysis. Focusing on freedom of information legislation, he shows why conventional transaction-centered electronic government conceptions fail to capture the informational dimension. Asserting the power and importance of information flows, Burkert argues that freedom of information laws are necessary complements to the online provision of public services. Burkert discusses the historical trajectory of information access legislation, arguing that much of the existing legislation across the world does not meet certain minimum standards that he enumerates. Similar to Coglianese, he does not anticipate the emergence of strong, deliberative democracy. Instead, he underscores the necessity of civil society organizations to fulfill the role of information intermediaries, keeping government accountable through access to information about government.

While strong, deliberative democracy will likely remain an impossibility, Monique Girard and David Stark (chapter 7) show that for specific issues, carefully crafted online deliberation may work if the role of information and its flow is understood correctly. Emphasizing the interpretative dimension of information, they argue that the most important result of such processes is the creation of an information repository of shared experiences.

Matthew Hindman (chapter 8) examines the relationship between political mobilization and the evolving flows of publicly relevant information among citizens. While much of the rhetoric of electronic democracy suggests that the doors to political voice have been blown open by the gales of the information age, Hindman finds that such a view is not supported by the data. Instead, Hindman argues, we see a new (but still narrow, elite) information class that is now plugged into the information stream. For example, he finds that the most well-known bloggers in the United States represent a fairly thin slice of American society—disproportionately young, male, urban, and trained at elite private universities. The quality they share is primarily informational: they have excellent sources, process information swiftly into eloquent prose, and disseminate information faster than the organized press. In short, the civic sphere has been rewired, but not fundamentally broadened.

The three chapters in part III tackle the challenge of evaluating the consequences of changes in information flow within government and between government and citizens. As Robert D. Behn (chapter 9) points out, conventional electronic government—making services available online—can be evaluated using cost-benefit analysis most easily when there is little change in information flows, or when these changes are well aligned with changes in monetary gains or losses. Assessment, however, is much more challenging when changes in information flows cause informational gains and losses that are not easily translatable into dollars and cents.

Martin J. Eppler (chapter 10) suggests an additional evaluation framework, complementing conventional cost-benefit analysis. In addition to attempting to monetize changes in information flows, as Behn proposes, he suggests measuring the quality of information and adding changes in informational quality to the evaluation balance sheet.

David Lazer and Maria Christina Binz-Scharf (chapter 11) look at the process of evaluation from within the system. Rather than offering another method of evaluation, they examine the mechanisms and structures that may help spread evaluation information on the use of information and communication technologies in the public sector. Utilizing network theory, they highlight the role that a variety of intergovernmental organizations play in connecting otherwise distant parts of the informational ecosystem regarding information technology and government.

In chapter 12, we shift the analysis from the role that information plays in governing to thinking about the challenges of governing information. In particular, we delve into three issues: (1) the balance of individual and collective interests in the potential increase in the informational power of government; (2) the role that information from the government plays in enabling the deliberative sphere within society, and (3) the institutional (as compared to technological) limitations in reengineering information flows.

Conclusion

The objective of this chapter has been to provide an overview of *information government*—a conceptual framework focusing on the information flows within government and between government and citizens. We purposely separate the framework from particular technologies—a handwritten note may convey the same information as an e-mail—while asserting that digital networks in particular facilitate the rewiring of information flows. Most electronic government rhetoric (and research) has focused on the potential use of information and communication technology (ICT) for efficiency gains, reducing costs to the government or reducing costs (and/or increasing services) to citizens. The objective of this volume is to highlight the informational dimension, focusing on the interaction among information flows, information intermediaries, citizens, and government actors. Understanding of the informational dimension, we hope, will in turn inform the implementation of technologies and policies to structure information flows that simultaneously increase the efficiency of government and the deliberative capacity of our institutions and citizens.

Note

1. http://www.brown.edu/Facilities/University_Library/libs/hay/focus/cuneiform/.

References

Bannister, Frank. 2005. "The Panoptic State: Privacy, Surveillance and the Balance of Risk." *Information Polity: The International Journal of Government and Democracy in the Information Age* 10: 65–78.

Bekkers, Victor. 2003. "E-Government and the Emergence of Virtual Organizations in the Public Sector." *Information Polity: The International Journal of Government and Democracy in the Information Age* 8: 89, 90.

Bijker, Wiebe E. 1995. *Of Bicycles, Bakelites, and Bulbs: Toward a Theory of Sociotechnical Change*. Cambridge, MA: MIT Press.

Bimber, Bruce. 2003. *Information and American Democracy: Technology in the Evolution of Political Power*. Cambridge, UK: Cambridge University Press.

Boyett, Joseph H., and Henry P. Conn. 1991. *Workplace 2000: The Revolution Reshaping American Business*. New York: Dutton.

Castells, Manuel. 1996. *The Rise of the Network Society*. Oxford, UK: Blackwell.

Curthoys, Noah, and James Crabtree. 2003. *SmartGov—Renewing Electronic Government for Improved Service Delivery*. London: The Works Foundation.

Drucker, Peter F. 1988. "The Coming of the New Organization." *Harvard Business Review* 88: 45–53.

Dutton, William, Gerardo Guerra, Daniel Zizzo, and Malcolm Peltu. 2005. "The Cyber Trust Tension in E-Government: Balancing Identity, Privacy, Security." *Information Polity: The International Journal of Government and Democracy in the Information Age* 10: 13–23.

Esterling, Kevin, Michael Neblo, and David Lazer. 2005. "Home (Page) Style: Determinates of the Quality of House Members' Websites." *International Journal of Electronic Government Research* 1: 50–63.

Fischer, Claude S. 1992. *America Calling—A Social History of the Telephone to 1940*. Berkeley: University of California Press.

Fountain, Jane. 2003. "Information, Institutions, and Governance: Advancing a Basic Social Science Research Program for Digital Government." KSG Working Paper RWP03-004, January, pp. 5–6.

Goldsmith, Stephen, and William Eggers. 2004. *Governing by Network: The New Shape of the Public Sector*. Washington, DC: Brookings Institution Press.

Graber, Doris. 2006. *Media Power in Politics*, 5th ed. Washington, DC: CQ Press.

Holden, Stephen, and Lynette Millett. 2005. "Authentication, Privacy and the Federal E-Government." *Information Society* 21: 367–377.

Janssen, Davy, Sabine Rotthier, and Kris Snijkers. 2004. "If You Measure It They Will Score: An Assessment of International eGovernment Benchmarking." *Information Polity: The International Journal of Government and Democracy in the Information Age* 9: 124–125.

Jasanoff, Sheila, Gerald E. Markle, James C. Peterson, and Trevor J. Pinch, eds. 2001. *Handbook of Science and Technology Studies*. Thousand Oaks, CA: Sage Publishers.

Ke, Weiling, and Kwok Kee Wei. 2004. "Successful E-Government in Singapore." *Communications of the ACM* 47 (June): 95–99.

Lazer, David. 2005. "Regulatory Capitalism as a Networked Order: The International System as an Informational Network." *Annals of the American Academy of Political and Social Science* 598: 52–66.

March, James G., and Johan P. Olsen. 1989. *Rediscovering Institutions: The Organizational Basis of Politics*. New York: Free Press.

Meier, Kenneth J., and Laurence J. O'Toole Jr. 2006. *Bureaucracy in a Democratic State: A Governance Perspective*. Baltimore: Johns Hopkins University Press.

Mintzberg, Henry. 1992. *Structure in Fives*. Englewood Cliffs, NJ: Prentice Hall.

Mossberger, Karen. 2000. *The Politics of Ideas and the Spread of Enterprise Zones*. Washington, DC: Georgetown University Press.

Mossberger, Karen, Caroline J. Tolbert, and Mary Stansbury. 2003. *Virtual Inequality: Beyond the Digital Divide*. Washington, DC: Georgetown University Press.

Netchaeva, Irina. 2002. "E-Government and E-Democracy." *The International Journal for Communication Studies* 64: 467.

Norris, Pippa. 2001. *Digital Divide: Civic Engagement, Information Poverty, and the Internet Worldwide*. Cambridge, UK: Cambridge University Press.

OECD. 2003. *The e-Government Imperative*. Paris: Organisation for Economic Co-operation and Development.

Orlikowski, Wanda. 2000. "Using Technology and Constituting Structures: A Practice Lens for Studying Technology in Organizations." *Organization Science* 11, no. 4: 404–428.

Osborne, David, and Ted Gaebler. 1992. *Reinventing Government: How the Entrepreneurial Spirit Is Transforming the Public Sector*. Reading, MA: Addison-Wesley.

Peters, B. Guy. 2001. The Future of Governing, 2nd ed. Lawrence: University of Kansas Press.

Rais Abdul Karim, Muhammad, and Nazariah Mohd Khalid. 2003. *E-Government in Malaysia*. Malaysia: Pelanduk Publications.

Silcock, Rachel. 2001. "What Is e-Government?" *Parliamentary Affairs* 54: 88.

Steinmo, Sven, Kathleen Thelen, and Frank Longstreth, eds. 1992. *Structuring Politics: Historical Institutionalism in Comparative Analysis*. Cambridge, UK: Cambridge University Press.

Thomas, John Clayton, and Gregory Streib. 2003. "The New Face of Government: Citizen-Initiated Contact in the Era of E-Government." *Journal of Public Administration Research and Theory* 13: 83–102.

Thompson, James. 1967. *Organizations in Action: Social Science Bases of Administrative Theory*. New York: McGraw-Hill.

Warschauer, Mark. 2003. *Technology and Social Inclusion: Rethinking the Digital Divide*. Cambridge, MA: MIT Press.

West, Darrell. 2005. *Digital Government: Technology and Public Sector Performance*. Princeton: Princeton University Press.

Yong, James S. L. 2005. *E-Government in Asia*, 2nd ed. Singapore: Marshall Cavendish.

I
Technological Change and Information Flows in Government

2

Global Perspectives on E-Government

Darrell M. West

Electronic government offers the promise of moving beyond the use of technology to improve public-sector performance to thinking about how to employ new advances for information government and democracy itself. In this latter perspective, the technocratic vision of e-government is supplanted by a viewpoint that envisions technology empowering ordinary citizens and using digital means to bring citizens closer to leaders. In its boldest formulation, technology is seen as becoming a tool for long-term system transformation and democratization.[1]

Unlike traditional bricks-and-mortar agencies that are hierarchical, linear, and one-way in their communications style, digital delivery systems are nonhierarchical, nonlinear, interactive, and available twenty-four hours a day, seven days a week. The nonhierarchical character of Internet delivery frees citizens to seek information at their own convenience. The interactive aspects of e-government allow both citizens and bureaucrats to send as well as receive information (Bimber 1998; Garson 2003).

The fundamental nature of these advantages has led some to predict that the Internet will transform government (National Performance Review 1993). By facilitating two-way interaction, electronic governance has been hailed as a way to improve service delivery and responsiveness to citizens. Stephen Goldsmith, President George W. Bush's Special Advisor for Faith-Based and Community Initiatives, says: "Electronic government will not only break down boundaries and reduce transaction costs between citizens and their governments but between levels of government as well" (qtd. in Council for Excellence in Government n.d.). Jeffrey Seifert and Matthew Bonham (2004) argue that digital government has the potential to transform governmental efficiency, transparency, citizen trust, and political participation in transitional democracies. Using examples from Asia and Europe, these authors suggest that with proper political leadership, the power of the Internet can be harnessed for major system change.

In making these claims, proponents suggest that the pace of Internet change is consistent with the classic model of large-scale transformation. In this perspective, change is rapid and abrupt, and visible to social observers. Often spurred by either scientific breakthroughs or economic improvements that facilitate the availability of the new technology, large-scale change produces revolutions in individual behavior and organizational activities.

Not all technological innovation, however, leads to large-scale transformation (Kraemer and King 1986). An alternative model stresses incrementalism. First proposed by Charles Lindblom (1959) in regard to organizational decision making, this kind of change is characterized as a "muddling through" process. In looking at how organizations make choices, Lindblom asked whether change was rational and dictated in key respects by economic trade-offs, or was it a political process characterized by small-scale shifts constrained by budgetary and institutional processes?

In the world of government, Lindblom suggested, politics dominates and organizations are more likely to muddle through decisions and rely on small-scale change. Political dynamics affect how decisions get made. It is not always the most rational decision that emerges based on costs and benefits. Rather, choices get made based on who is best organized, strongest politically, or in control of the bureaucratic structure. The political character of public-sector decision making limits the speed of change and how quickly new technologies get incorporated into the governmental process (Wildavsky 1984).

There are a number of reasons why political change tends to be small-scale and gradual. Government actions are mediated by a range of factors: institutional arrangements, budget scarcity, group conflict, cultural norms, and prevailing patterns of social and political behavior, each of which restricts the ability of technology to transform society and politics. The fact that governments are divided into competing agencies and jurisdictions limits the ability of policymakers to get bureaucrats to work together promoting technological innovation. Budget considerations prevent government offices from placing services online and using technology for democratic outreach. Cultural norms and patterns of individual behavior affect how technology is used by citizens and policymakers. In addition, the political process is characterized by intense group conflict over resources. With systems that are open and permeable, groups organize easily and make demands on the political system.

These kinds of political constraints are so widespread that Richard Davis, Michael Margolis, David Resnick, Andrew Chadwick, and Christopher May predict in the long run that Internet technology will *not* transform democracy. If anything, technology reinforces existing social and political patterns rather than creating new realities. In regard to technology, Davis (1999) notes "that complex bureaucratic maze also has been duplicated on the Web" (137). Agency websites serve to perpetuate their own mission and do little to enhance responsiveness or citizen participation. Margolis and Resnick (2000) argue that "far from revolutionizing the conduct of politics and civic affairs in the real world, . . . the Internet tends to reflect and reinforce the patterns of behavior of that world" (vii). Chadwick and May (2003) found government websites in the United States, Great Britain, and European Union to be "predominantly non-interactive and non-deliberative" (271) and concluded that e-government was not likely to reshape governance.

In this chapter, I look at the speed of global e-government change as a way to investigate whether digital technology is producing system-wide transformation. Thinking globally about technology is useful because it broadens the scope to nations that have very different political, organizational, and financial dynamics. One of the limits of relying on any single country is the difficulty of generalizing beyond that area (Welch and Wong 2001). An international approach gives researchers a chance to see how political and institutional context affects the ability of governments to innovate in the technology area. Using a detailed content analysis of government websites in 198 different nations in 2001, 2002, and 2003, I measure the information and services that are online and discuss how e-government has changed over time.[2]

In general, I find that global electronic government is not producing a major transformation of the public sector. While some countries have embraced digital government broadly defined, a number of other countries have not placed much information or many services online, and are not taking advantage of the interactive features of the Internet. This limits the transformational potential of the Internet and weakens the ability of technology to empower citizens and businesses. Few nations appear to view the Internet as a way to empower ordinary citizens and produce fundamental change in their political systems.

Cross-National Comparisons

It is difficult to compare countries around the world because of their heterogeneity in terms of economic development, regime type, cultural patterns, telecommunications infrastructure, and Internet usage. Some countries are extremely rich, while many others lack the means to supply adequate education, housing, and health care. In terms of political structure, nations vary from presidential democracies and parliamentary systems to military dictatorships, monarchies, and authoritarian regimes. Openness to information technology varies from areas where broadband is widely available to places where television and other forms of media transmission have been banned.

Substantial research has been undertaken on why some countries feature high Internet connectivity and others do not. In Lebanon and Russia, for example, less than 10 percent of the population has any kind of access to the Internet, either through phone modems or broadband connections. These figures contrast with industrialized nations, which have Internet access levels of 60–70 percent.

In looking at the situation cross-nationally, academic scholars have reached very different conclusions concerning these disparities. One of the earliest studies was undertaken by Eszter Hargittai (1999), who compared eighteen countries that were members of the Organisation for Economic Co-operation and Development (OECD). She focused on Internet penetration and found that its best predictors were economic wealth (measured by gross domestic product, or GDP, per capita) and telecommunications policy. Countries that were wealthy and had a competitive market structure featured higher levels of connectivity.

Sampsa Kiiski and Matti Pohjola (2002) looked at Internet hosts per capita for 1995–2000 for 23 OECD countries and telephone access charges for 141 countries (including those outside the OECD). They found that GDP per capita affected growth in computer hosting, but that the competitiveness of telecommunications markets had no independent effect on Internet penetration. Economic wealth and digital access costs mattered more than market structure or regulatory approach. Investment in education did not affect the results for OECD countries, but was important for the larger sample of OECD and non-OECD nations.

Pippa Norris (2001) undertook a cross-national comparison of 179 countries. She examined the relationship between a variety of social, economic, and political factors and the number of people online in each nation. Basically, she found that economic wealth (measured by GDP per capita) and the level of research and development spending were the best predictors of Internet usage. Neither education nor the level of democratization were significantly linked to citizen usage.

Consistent with the results for Internet usage in general, there is tremendous variation in e-government participation around the world. A public opinion survey of 29,077 people in twenty-seven countries undertaken by Taylor Nelson Sofres, a consulting company (see Mellor, Parr, and Hood 2001), found dramatic variations in the percentage of each country's population that had accessed online government. The results ranged from a high of 53 percent in Norway, 47 percent in Denmark, 46 percent in Canada, 45 percent in Finland, and 34 percent in the United States to 3 percent in Turkey, Indonesia, and Russia, 5 percent in Poland and Lithuania, and 8 percent in Slovakia and Latvia. The average across the twenty-seven-nation survey was 26 percent.

Some marked differences existed across different countries in terms of how secure individuals felt about conducting online transactions. Two-thirds of people in the surveyed countries felt "unsafe" using the Internet to conduct government transactions online. These were individuals who worried about the overall confidentiality of public-sector websites. Germany was the nation having the highest percentage (85 percent) of people saying they felt unsafe, compared to 84 percent in Japan, 84 percent in France, 72 percent in the United States, and 72 percent in the Czech Republic. Countries that showed the lowest levels of unsafe feelings in regard to online government transactions were Estonia (27 percent), Canada (30 percent), Denmark (31 percent), Hong Kong (32 percent), and Finland (37 percent). Those reporting the greatest concern over Internet safety were women and people aged 25 to 44 years old.

A year later, when Taylor Nelson Sofres (Mellor and Parr 2002) completed a follow-up survey of 28,952 people in thirty-one countries, the percentage of the population in these countries that had used online government rose from 26 to 30 percent. There also was little change in what uses people made of online government. Twenty-four percent of adults reported they used e-government for information seeking, up from 20 percent in 2001. Eleven percent said they used it for downloading forms, up from 9 percent the previous year. Eight percent said they used e-government to provide information to the authorities, up from 7 percent in 2001. Seven percent indicated they provided bank account or credit card information to a government site, up from 6 percent the preceding year. Four percent said they used government websites to express a point of view. Rather than seeing dramatic changes from year to year, the report's authors concluded, "There has been very little change to the shape of the Government Online adoption curve."

There were some changes over time in perceptions of global e-government from the citizens' point of view. The percentage of people feeling it was okay to provide personal information to a government website rose from 14 percent in 2001 to 23 percent in 2002. While this demonstrates some improvement, the numbers reveal that many report feeling either unsafe or unsure about confidentiality when it comes to government websites. Indeed, in some countries, large numbers of citizens report concerns about giving personal information online at government websites. For example, 90 percent of Japanese citizens say they are concerned about providing personal information, compared to 82 percent in Germany, 76 percent in France, 75 percent in Taiwan, and 72 percent in Italy.

There are obvious reasons for the disparity in e-government performance across nations. Few nations have the financial resources, organizational capacity, and political will to make technology change a top priority. Resources vary enormously as do organizational capacity and political leadership. Countries that lack wealth have a difficult time justifying investment in new technology (Katchanovski and LaPorte 2005). Nations where citizens, organizations, and politicians doubt the potential of technology face barriers in the implementation of electronic governance.

Research by Todd LaPorte and Chris Demchak (2001), for example, found an association between a country's national income and the openness of its government websites. In particular, they found that electronic government progress is related to the magnitude of capital flows across countries. Nations that have access to capital are in a much stronger position to innovate than those that do not.

In her international study of online government, Norris (2001) found that "more affluent industrialized economies characteristically have the richest access to multiple forms of communication and information technologies . . . and this environment is most conducive to the spread of online parties as well" (1). This research demonstrates that wealth and political development matter to the incorporation of technology into political activities. Countries that rank high on economic and political indicators show much stronger commitment to e-government and are in a much stronger position to execute its implementation in the public sphere.

However, what most of these studies have not addressed is what is online at national government websites around the world and how quickly e-government has changed from year to year. For the last several years, I have supervised a team of researchers who examined the national government websites in 2001, 2002, and 2003 for all nations around the world. I looked for material on information, services, and databases, interactive features that would facilitate outreach to the public, and visible statements that would reassure citizens worried about privacy and security over the Internet. I looked at a wide variety of political and economic systems, from monarchies, federated systems, and presidential democracies to parliamentary systems, dictatorships, and communist countries.

The data for the analysis consisted of 2,288 national government websites in 2001, 1,197 sites in 2002, and 2,166 websites in 2002.[3] Sampling was based on a purposive strategy designed to reach the major departments of national government in the various countries. Among the sites analyzed were those of executive offices (such as a president, prime minister, ruler, party leader, or royalty), legislative offices (such as Congress, Parliament, or People's Assemblies), judicial offices (such as major national courts), cabinet offices, and major agencies serving crucial functions of government, such as health, human services, taxation, education, interior, economic development, administration, natural resources, foreign affairs, foreign investment, transportation, military, tourism, and business regulation. Websites for subnational units, obscure boards and commissions, local government, regional units, and municipal offices were not included in this study.

Regardless of the type of system or cultural background of a country, websites were evaluated for the presence of two dozen different features dealing with information availability, service delivery, and public access. These are features that in past research have been found to be important to citizens and ways of using technology to boost productivity and public sector performance. The website characteristics assessed included contact information, access to publications and other information, external links, a variety of multimedia features, credit card payments, and so forth (see West 2005 for detailed explanation of coding system). Numbers reported here represent the percentage of a country's websites that have online publications, databases, services, and so on.

For national government websites that were not in English, the research team employed foreign language readers who translated and evaluated national government websites where possible. Foreign languages employed in this study included French, Spanish, German, Italian, Russian, Chinese, Arabic, and Turkish. This helped insure the fullest assessment of government websites in the native language of that country.

Online Information

In looking at government websites from around the world, the research team examined how much material was available that would help citizens contact government agencies and navigate websites, and how this changed over the past few years. Many agencies have made progress at placing information online for public access. In 2003, 89 percent of government websites around the world offered publications that a citizen could access, up from 77 percent in 2002 and 71 percent in 2001. Seventy-three percent offered databases, up from 41 percent in 2001. Eighty-two percent had links in 2002 to external, nongovernmental sites where a citizen could turn for additional information, which is up from 42 percent in 2001.

As a sign of the early stage of global e-government, most public-sector websites do not incorporate audio clips or video clips on their official sites. Despite the fact that these are becoming much more common features of e-commerce and private-sector enterprise, only 8 percent of sites in 2003 (the same as in 2002, but up from 4 percent in 2001) provided audio clips, while 8 percent had video clips (up from 4 percent in 2001). A common type of audio clip was a national anthem or a musical selection.

Online Services

Fully executable, online service delivery benefits both government and its constituents. Of the websites around the world, however, only 16 percent offer services that are fully executable online, up from 12 percent in 2002 and 8 percent in 2001. These low numbers of electronic services and the fact that most sites offer no services demonstrates that global e-government remains in an early stage of development. Of the 2003 sites, 9 percent offer one service, 3 percent have two services, and four percent have three or more services. Eighty-four percent have no online services.

North America (including the United States, Canada, and Mexico) is the region of the world offering the highest percentage of online services. Forty-five percent (up from 41 percent in 2002 and 28 percent in 2001) had fully executable, online services. This was followed by Asia (26 percent), the Middle East (24 percent), the Pacific Ocean islands (17 percent), and western Europe (17 percent). Only 1 percent in Russia/central Asia, 5 percent in Africa, and 6 percent of sites in eastern Europe offer online government services.

Of the 198 nations analyzed, all show wide variance in the number of online services provided by different governments. The country with the largest number of services in 2003 was Singapore, with an average of 7.8 services across its government agencies. This was followed by the United States (4.8 services), Turkey (3.2 services), Hong Kong (3.1 services), and Taiwan (2.4 services). It is important to keep in mind that our definition of services included only those services that were fully executable online. Unlike other national surveys, which have less specific definitions for online services, my research team did not count it as a fully executable, online service if a citizen had to print out a form and mail or take it to a government agency to execute the service.

The most frequent services found included ordering publications online, buying stamps, filing complaints, applying for jobs, applying for passport renewals, and renewing vehicle licenses. Several countries had novel online services. For example, the Dominican Republic's National Drug Control office had a "drug information" link in which anonymous citizens could report illegal drug dealing. Bangladesh's National Tourism Organization offered online booking of hotel rooms. Canada offered a number of services online such as change of postal address forms, package tracking, and ordering stamps. Egypt allowed for personal and union registration online at the Ministry for Manpower and Emigration. Lithuania offered searches for stolen vehicles, invalid identity documents, and wanted persons through its Ministry of the Interior.

One of the features that has slowed the growth of online services has been an inability to use credit cards and digital signatures on financial transactions. Of the government websites analyzed, only 2 percent of websites in 2003 accepted credit cards and one-tenth of 1 percent allowed digital signatures for financial transactions (similar to 2002). Among the sites having a capacity for digital signatures are the Singapore governmental office of statistics and Denmark's portal site. Since some government services require a fee, not having a credit card payment system makes it difficult to place government services that are fully executable online and limits the transformational potential of the Internet.

The other limitation has been financial and political resources. Online services are expensive to develop. Since each country has different laws and regulations, few off-the-shelf software packages exist that are cheap and readily available. The need for unique programs obviously restricts the ability of poor nations to place services online for their citizens and business community. In addition, progress at placing electronic services online requires a strong political will. In order to overcome bureaucratic inertia and get disparate agencies to work together on cross-agency portals, leaders must be able to gain cooperation, integrate agency efforts, and marshal the financial resources necessary for improvement in this area. When a country has a very small number of its citizens with access to the Internet, it is difficult to justify the expenditure of scarce resources on online government.

Public Outreach

As noted earlier in this chapter, e-government offers the potential to bring citizens closer to their governments. Indeed, this is one of the hopes of information government: that it will decrease the gap between citizens and leaders and thereby further the democratization of political systems. Regardless of the type of political system that a country has, the public benefits from interactive features that facilitate communication between citizens and government.

In our examination of national government websites, we looked for various features that would help citizens contact government officials and make use of website information. E-mail is an interactive feature that allows ordinary citizens to pose questions to government officials or request information or services. We found that 84 percent of government websites in 2003 (up from 75 percent in 2002) offered e-mail contact material so that a visitor could e-mail a person in a particular department other than the webmaster.

While e-mail was the easiest method of contact, government websites employed other methods to facilitate public feedback. These included areas to post comments, the use of message boards, and the creation of chat rooms. Websites that used these features allowed citizens and department members alike to read and respond to others' comments regarding issues facing the department. This technology was less prevalent than e-mail, with 31 percent of websites offering this feature in 2003, while 33 percent provided it in 2002.

Twelve percent (up from 10 percent in 2002) of government websites allowed citizens to register to receive updates regarding specific issues. With this feature, web visitors could input their e-mail addresses, street addresses, or telephone numbers to receive information about a particular subject as new information became available. The information could be in the form of a monthly e-newsletter highlighting a prime minister's views or in the form of alerts notifying citizens whenever a particular portion of the website is updated. One percent allowed websites to be personalized to the interests of the visitor, and 2 percent provided personal digital assistant (PDA) access.

With the exception of e-mail, the limited use of interactive features that facilitate citizen feedback showed that technological change had not advanced very far on the global scene. Most countries had not embraced a vision of e-government as a tool for citizen empowerment. Instead, officials viewed the Internet as a billboard for one-way communications with the public. They were not taking advantage of two-way features that provide citizens with a chance to voice their opinions or personalize websites to their particular interests. In so doing, they have limited the transformational potential of the Internet and made it difficult to use digital means to transform political systems.

Regional Variation

In looking at regional differences by particular feature, the research team noted that North America and Asia were the areas showing the greatest progress on several electronic government dimensions (see table 2.1). For example, these regions ranked high in terms of the percentage of their websites offering online services. In contrast, poor countries in Africa, Central America, and South America did not provide much in the way of online services or other e-government features. As shown in the next section, these regional variations in e-government performance reflect fundamental differences in financial capacity across the regions.

Explaining E-Government Performance

To this point, I have described the extent of global e-government performance, but I have not explained variation across countries. In this section, I present an aggregate analysis of electronic government. Using a conceptual model based on organizational, fiscal, and political factors, I seek to determine what distinguishes stronger e-government countries from those that are weaker.

For my measure of e-government performance, I rely on the average number of fully executable electronic services across a nation's agencies based on the 2003 content analysis. For the independent variables, I use seven different measures of organizational, fiscal, and political attributes in each country. Organizational features include a measure of the extent of formal schooling.[4] This is designed to show how well-educated the labor force is in each country. In addition, I use a measure of the number of scientists and engineers working in research and development in each country per million residents from 1996 to 2000.[5] This measures the extent of technical expertise available in each nation. I also rely on an indicator that reveals the extent of corruption present in each country, as measured by the World Bank.[6] This shows the efficiency with which governmental agencies function, which is related to an agency's ability to incorporate new technology on its website.

Table 2.1
E-government features by region, 2003

	North America	Central America	South America	Western Europe	Eastern Europe	Russia	Middle East	Africa	Asia	Pacific Ocean
Publications	96	87	94	96	92	98	80	79	90	82
Database	87	77	83	78	74	85	56	60	78	72
Audio clip	18	10	7	6	6	4	10	6	10	7
Video clip	17	4	8	9	7	4	8	2	18	3
Privacy	57	5	1	7	0	1	7	3	26	33
Security	43	2	0	2	0	0	3	0	14	14
Services	45	9	14	17	7	1	24	5	26	17
Credit cards	17	0	0	2	0	0	3	0	2	5
Digital sign	0	0	0	0	0	0	0	0	0	0
E-mail	94	87	91	92	87	80	71	72	82	85
Comment	50	33	29	36	19	12	32	20	43	31
Updates	33	6	14	15	6	5	10	6	14	16
Personal	3	0	0	1	0	0	1	0	0	0
PDA access	0	0	0	0	0	0	16	0	2	2

Table 2.2
The impact of organizational, fiscal, and political factors on online services, 2003

	Number of online services
Education	−0.28 (0.37)
Corruption	−11.53 (13.35)
Number of scientists	−0.01 (0.01)
Gross domestic product per capita	0.003 (0.002)*
Party competition	4.44 (11.34)
Civil liberties	4.68 (5.42)
Internet usage	0.67 (0.90)
Constant	−14.03 (33.87)
Adjusted R square	0.06
F	1.93
N	113

Note: The numbers are the unstandardized least squares regression coefficients, with the standard error in parentheses. The number of asterisks indicates the level of statistical significance. Tolerance statistics show no multicollinearity problem in the model.
$* p < 0.05$; $** p < 0.01$; $*** p < 0.001$.

For financial resources, I employ a measure of each nation's 2001 GDP per capita in U.S. dollars.[7] This shows the extent of fiscal capacity and shows how rich or poor a particular nation is. Building on the Internet usage results of Hargittai (1999), Kiiski and Pohjola (2002), and Norris (2001), my hypothesis is that countries with greater wealth will be more likely to engage in electronic government than poorer countries.

Finally, for the analysis of political determinants, I examine party competition, the extent of Internet usage, and a civil liberties scale within each country. The party competition item looks at how competitive the political parties are in each nation.[8] Internet usage is measured as a percentage of the overall population in 2001 that used the Internet.[9] The civil liberties scale is a 1999 Freedom House measure of liberalism within each country.[10] The hypothesis is that the more liberal and democratic a country is, the greater is its ability to move toward the openness and transparency associated with e-government.

Table 2.2 shows the regression results for indicators of the number of online services. The only statistically significant predictor of the number of online services is gross per-capita GDP in each nation. Countries that were richer tended to have more electronic services on their websites ($p < 0.05$). This is in keeping with the results of earlier studies highlighting the relationship between e-government and per-capita GDP. There were no organizational or political factors that were important. Neither liberalism nor level of democracy was associated with e-government performance. It did not matter how competitive the party structure was or what the degree of liberalism was on civil liberties. Democratic nations were no better than nondemocratic countries at innovating in regard to technology policy.

Conclusion

The most optimistic vision of electronic government is that the integration of new information and communication technology (ICT) into government will result in a radical disjuncture of business as usual. Based on the preceding analyses, the reality falls far short of these utopian aspirations. Portal development has been weak as has placing services online or incorporating interactive features onto their websites. Even for countries that have put together portal sites for their government, inconsistencies remain in terms of design, navigation, and usability (e.g., see FirstGov case illustration). Not only are governments failing to use technology to transform the public sector, their efforts consist mostly of small steps forward (e.g., the shifting of existing resources to online). Far less effort has been expended on interactive features that would empower citizens and facilitate the gathering of information by government to improve their delivery of services. Further, only one-third of government websites are searchable, limiting the ability of ordinary citizens to find information that is relevant to them. The hope that the public sector would move beyond a technocratic vision of better service delivery to system transformation is not borne out.

A number of factors explain the lack of an abrupt transformation. Wealth (as measured by per-capita GDP) is a significant predictor of quantity of online services, where a variety of political and societal variables, notably, are not strongly related to online services. Wealthy regions, such as Europe, parts of Asia, and especially North America, thus do have a substantial number of services online. Poorer regions, especially Africa, lag far behind. Organizational factors, such as general obstacles to interagency cooperation and resistance to changing standard operating procedures are also likely key variables slowing the adoption of the more radical changes that developments in ICT might enable.

Notes

1. An earlier version of this paper was presented at the annual meeting of the American Political Science Association, September 2–5, 2004, Chicago, Illinois. Portions of this chapter are drawn from West 2005.

2. Funding for the 2001 global e-government research was provided by World Markets Research Centre, a London consulting company. Detailed reports on Brown University's annual e-government studies can be found at www.InsidePolitics.org.

4. Data developed by Pippa Norris of the John F. Kennedy School of Government at Harvard University. They are available online at her Shared Global Database (http://ksghome.harvard.edu/~.pnorris.shorenstein.ksg/data.htm).

5. These data are from the Human Development Index developed by the United Nations Development Programme (http://hrd.undp.org).

6. Data developed by Pippa Norris of the John F. Kennedy School of Government at Harvard University. They are available online at her Shared Global Database (http://ksghome.harvard.edu/~.pnorris.shorenstein.ksg/data.htm).

7. These data are from the Human Development Index developed by the United Nations Development Programme (http://hrd.undp.org).

8. Data developed by Pippa Norris of the John F. Kennedy School of Government at Harvard University. They are available online at her Shared Global Database (http://ksghome.harvard.edu/~.pnorris.shorenstein.ksg/data.htm).

9. These data are from the Human Development Index developed by the United Nations Development Programme (http://hrd.undp.org).

10. Data developed by Pippa Norris of the John F. Kennedy School of Government at Harvard University. They are available online at her Shared Global Database (http://ksghome.harvard.edu/~.pnorris.shorenstein.ksg/data.htm).

References

Bimber, Bruce. 1998. "The Internet and Political Transformation." *Polity: The International Journal of Government and Democracy in the Information Age* 31, no. 1: 133–160.

Chadwick, Andrew, with Christopher May. 2003. "Interaction Between States and Citizens in the Age of the Internet." *Governance: An International Journal of Policy, Administration, and Institutions* 16, no. 2: 271–300.

Council for Excellence in Government. N.d. "E-Government: The Next American Revolution." Washington, DC.

Davis, Richard. 1999. *The Web of Politics.* New York: Oxford University Press.

Garson, David. 2003. *Public Information Technology: Policy and Management Issues.* Harrisburg, PA: Idea Group Publishing.

Hargittai, Eszter. 1999. "Weaving the Western Web." *Telecommunications Policy* 23: 701–718.

Katchanovsi, Ivan, and Todd LaPorte. 2005. "CyberDemocracy or Potemkin E-Villages." *International Journal of Public Administration* 28, no. 7/8: 643–664.

Kiiski, Sampsa, and Matti Pohjola. 2002. "Cross-Country Diffusion of the Internet." *Information Economics and Policy* 14, no. 2: 297–310.

Kraemer, Kenneth, and John King. 1986. "Computing and Public Organizations." *Public Administration Review* 46: 488–496.

LaPorte, Todd, and Chris Demchak. 2001. "Hotlinked Governance: A Worldwide Assessment, 1997–2000." Paper presented at the annual meeting of the American Political Science Association, San Francisco, August 30–September 2.

Lindblom, Charles. 1959. "The Science of Muddling Through." *Public Administration Review* 29 (Spring): 79–88.

Margolis, Michael, and David Resnick. 2000. *Politics as Usual: The Cyberspace 'Revolution'*. Thousand Oaks, CA: Sage Publishers.

Mellor, Wendy, and Victoria Parr. 2002. "Government Online: An International Perspective." Taylor Nelson Sofres Consulting Company, November.

Mellor, Wendy, Victoria Parr, and Michelle Hood. 2001. "Government Online: An International Perspective." Taylor Nelson Sofres Consulting Company, November.

National Performance Review. 1993. *From Red Tape to Results: Creating a Government That Works Better and Costs Less*. Washington, DC: Government Printing Office.

Norris, Pippa. 2001. *Digital Divide?* New York: Cambridge University Press.

Seifert, Jeffrey, and Matthew Bonham. 2004. "The Transformative Potential of E-Government in Transitional Democracies." Available at http://www1.worldbank.org/publicsector/egov/.

Welch, Eric, and Wilson Wong. 2001. "Global Information Technology Pressure and Government Accountability." *Journal of Public Administration Research and Theory* 11, no. 4: 509–538.

West, Darrell M. 2005. *Digital Government: Technology and Public Sector Performance*. Princeton: Princeton University Press.

Wildavsky, Aaron. 1984. *The Politics of the Budgetary Process*. Boston: Little, Brown.

Case Illustration

FirstGov: The Road to Success of the U.S. Government's Web Portal

Maria Christina Binz-Scharf

FirstGov went online on September 22, 2000, representing the first portal that would allow searching of the entire federal government. It got its start when Bill Piatt, then CIO of the General Services Administration (GSA), made reference to a GSA project aimed at organizing and making available online government information in a January 2000 article for *Federal Computer Week* (Piatt 2000), which caught the attention of high-ranking government officials. Shortly thereafter, Eric Brewer, an Internet entrepreneur and professor of computer science at UC Berkeley, offered to donate a search engine to government. In June 2000, President Bill Clinton announced the gift from the Federal Search Foundation, a nonprofit organization established by Brewer, and instructed that FirstGov be launched in ninety days.

From the beginning, the objective of FirstGov was to organize the material around the user, not the organizational boundaries of government. Both the search engine and the organization by topics were innovative at the time, grounded in the philosophy that citizens do not need to know how government is organized in order to find the information they are looking for.

A Herculean Task

The fundamental difference between FirstGov and all other government web portals is the former's broad view of government, as well as the comprehensiveness of topics. One of the major challenges right from the beginning was the sheer enormity of FirstGov's scope. As Piatt stated: "No one had ever attempted to organize an institution as large and diverse as the federal government in this way before" (2005, 1). How should the millions of government web resources be organized to both make them useful to the public and provide quality government information? This question was further complicated by the fact that a lot of the information provided by different government websites was redundant—a fact that can be attributed to the evolution of the World Wide Web. In the early days of the Internet, whoever had the ability to start a website simply did so, and since there were no coordinated web policies at the government department or agency level, these websites evolved independent of each other. In addition, although the information contained on many websites was similar, it was at the same time often conflicting. This was due to the common practice of including information that was not central to an agency's operations. However, while coordinating these individual efforts so as to serve the public better seemed to be the next logical step, Piatt recounts that people involved in the early stages of FirstGov were surprised to encounter entrenched resistance by various programs and agencies to making their information easily available.

Furthermore, Piatt and his team hoped that the transparency of government information that FirstGov helped facilitate would lead to a certain degree of standardization among agency websites in terms of their quality. As Piatt explains: "We couldn't make agencies have good websites. So we did feel like if we were able to shine the light on the [good] websites and make them easy to find, in a relatively short period of time the site owners would improve their website because they would see how much better other websites were."[1] The expectation that "the [websites] that were not very good would have pressure brought on them internally to improve the way they look" eventually came true: "The overall quality of federal web sites has increased tremendously over the past five years," says Piatt. While much of this improvement can be attributed to the transparency that FirstGov created, the FirstGov team also actively addressed this challenge by enabling peer-to-peer communication. An interagency Web Content Managers Group was set up for government web managers to share ideas, challenges, lessons learned, and best practices in managing the content of government websites.

The Challenge of Getting Funded

Another substantial challenge in the beginning was funding. FirstGov was initially funded by a percentage of the IT budgets of twenty-seven agencies, including the President's Management Council, through a pass-the-hat message. This unpredictable mechanism made it difficult for FirstGov to maintain its operations, as FirstGov's director Beverly Godwin states: "It was very hard to manage when you didn't know when the money would be coming in. . . . We had a lot of contracts, and so we had the promise letters and sometimes didn't have the money yet when we needed to spend it." However, FirstGov was able to overcome this challenge when it was fully appropriated by Congress as a result of the E-Government Act of 2002, which required the maintenance of a federal Internet portal and authorized annual appropriations to the GSA for this purpose.[2] Not only did these appropriations ease the task of managing the portal, but they also gave the FirstGov team renewed confidence in their work on the portal by guaranteeing the continuity of the program.

The Key to Success: Providing What the Public Wants

The number of visitors to FirstGov has increased steadily each year since 2000, up to 85 million in 2004 and the first half of 2005 combined. To increase traffic to the portal, the FirstGov team invests significant time in search engine optimization, or efforts directed at increasing a website's rank in search results. This is intimately linked to discovering the terminology the public uses, because adopting that terminology means ranking high in search results. One of the main reasons for the surge in popularity of the portal over the years has been the fact that FirstGov concentrates on what the public wants. The FirstGov team has learned and continues to learn about how the public searches for government information on the Internet. Finding the right terminology through web statistics and search terms both on FirstGov and general search engines is one such way. A very powerful source of knowledge is given by the database behind 1-800-FEDINFO, a national telephone contact center. The public can call this number with any question about government, and questions are stored in a database. Since the database has been in existence for over twenty years, it provides a wealth of information on what the public asks; and since the call center is managed by the Federal Citizen Information Center at the GSA, the same organization that operates FirstGov, this information is readily accessible by the FirstGov team. A recent result of this learning process from e-mails and phone calls has been an FAQ database linked to the FirstGov portal, which ranks the questions according to the number of hits they receive. So while questions about passports usually dominate the list, recently the top questions have related to Hurricane Katrina, reflecting the public's interest in this topic.

Interagency Collaboration

Another important factor in providing the information the public wants is collaborating with numerous government agencies to identify what their top requests are by means of web search, e-mail, and telephone as well as to identify new services being offered at these agencies. Consequently, FirstGov can raise the visibility of topic-area portals that might otherwise be marginalized in the many big portals to which FirstGov links. Conversely, the collaboration with other agencies in this realm also allows FirstGov to detect deficiencies in the offering of online services. As Godwin recounts: "For example, parents—we built a cross-agency portal for parents because it didn't exist. [The Department of Health and Human Services] did not have any champion ready and willing to do it. So we said, 'Do you mind if we do it?' and they said, 'no'. We prefer when the experts in the agencies do [the cross-agency portals], but when they don't and it's a big group, a big audience, we'll build them here." Detecting these deficiencies in online government is possible for the FirstGov team because it constantly surveys customer analytics, market research, and market trends. The most recent result of detecting such a deficiency is the launch of Espanol.gov, a Spanish-language version of FirstGov, opening the federal government's Web portal to a potential audience of 28 million Spanish speakers.

Where FirstGov Stands Today

In the words of Piatt, "FirstGov today is still true to its original objective: an easy, fast place to find government information" (2005, 4). The information structure of the portal has largely remained unchanged, offering information organized by audience, by topic, and by organization; and there are no immediate plans to alter that structure. Current efforts are directed at improving the display of information on the site. FirstGov has just started a contract to test a new design that should enable users to find the information they are looking for with greater ease. Another improvement effort is to add popular function-alities to the portal, such as getting the local weather forecast. This feature could previously be accessed through the "Get it done online" section of the website, which linked to a box on the website of the National Weather Service. After web statistics showed that this link constantly ranked high, the FirstGov team decided to add a local weather forecast box directly to the portal frontpage. These efforts add functionality to the portal, as Godwin states: "Even though it's still not being done at FirstGov—it's being done at the page where the data is and where the expertise is, but that is not seen by the user."

Epilogue

Having overcome the initial difficulties related to FirstGov's funding as well as managing the enormity of its scope, FirstGov has provided what the public wants. The simple, but powerful philosophy of transcending traditional government boundaries to provide a citizen-friendly website has led to numerous awards for the portal over the past five years, including the prestigious Innovations in American Government Award from Harvard University's John F. Kennedy School of Government. However, staying true to this philosophy will require the FirstGov team to engage in an ongoing learning process, says Godwin: "Continuous work needs to be done, continuous improvement, based on the public influence."

Notes

1. Unless otherwise noted, the quotes from Bill Piatt and Bev Godwin are based on personal interviews conducted by the author.

2. E-Government Act (2002), section 204.

References

Piatt, Bill. 2000. "Embrace the New Economy." *Federal Computer Week* (January 24). Available at http://www.fcw.com.

Piatt, Bill. 2005. "FirstGov: Online Government in the Year 2000." Dubai Initiative I-Government Conference, paper series. Cambridge, MA: Belfer Center for Science and International Affairs (BCSIA).

3

Electronic Government and the Drive for Growth and Equity

Edwin Lau

Introduction: A Proposed Outline for Assessing Electronic Government Benefits

The burst of the "dot.com bubble" has obliged governments to become less starry-eyed about the benefits of electronic government and to raise more questions about the expected and actual returns of e-government projects. It is no longer sufficient—or even desirable—for countries to aim to put all public services online as was the objective of many Organisation for Economic Co-operation and Development (OECD) governments in the late 1990s and early 2000. Instead, such projects need to demonstrate their contribution to overall government objectives.

Increasingly, countries are using business case methodologies to demonstrate the costs, risks, and expected returns, in terms of both savings to government and benefits to citizens and businesses resulting from ICT (information and communication technology) investment. Lacking a business case, governments risk developing technology-enabled services that may not correspond to the needs of citizens and businesses. While private-sector business case methodologies can be useful in the public sector, they are primarily tailored to the decision-making needs of businesses and do not (nor are meant to) measure broader effects of these services and processes. Using private-sector business cases as guides, governments risk focusing too much on short-term financial and electronic service delivery objectives, while overlooking the overall impact of technology-enabled services (OECD 2005b).

The purpose of this chapter is to identify a broader set of these impacts, illustrate their importance, and provide some examples of how countries have sought to realise these benefits. This chapter does not provide new measures and indicators—many of which are currently under discussion in countries—but highlights some of the current approaches being tested and how the variables interact.

Table 3.1
Costs, benefits, and beneficiaries: A proposed outline

Type of benefit / Beneficiaries	Government	Nongovernment (citizens and business)
Direct financial costs and benefits	1. *Reducing costs* freeing resources for public and private innovation; increasing value of products and services	2. *Reducing burden* administrative simplification; providing higher valued and faster services; saving time and money and improving equity
Direct nonfinancial costs and benefits	3. *Capturing total benefits of investment* achieving synergies across service delivery channels; enabling the sharing and reuse of data for more proactive service delivery; promoting access as part of channel management strategy	4. *Increasing user satisfaction* 24/7 service; improving personalization and service quality; improving access and equity; addressing security and privacy concerns; transparency and choice
Indirect costs and benefits: "Good governance" as a public good	5. *Supporting legitimacy* supporting security and trust at an aggregate level; modernization and transformation of the public sector; ensuring equity; increasing responsiveness, accountability, and participation 6. *Supporting growth* improving the business environment; creating an information society; establishing an infrastructure for secure and reliable transactions	

In order to measure the impact of electronic government, one first needs to decide *what* type of costs and benefits to consider and the population to *whom* these costs and benefits will accrue. Table 3.1 presents a simple categorization of costs, benefits, and beneficiaries. There are two major groups of beneficiaries, government and nongovernment (nongovernment being citizens and businesses), and three categories of costs and benefits (see table 3.1). The term "direct" is used to specify costs and benefits that can be (1) easily identified and quantified and (2) associated with a specific user group, as compared to the provision of a public good for all. Indirect benefits, on the other hand, are those that are difficult to ascribe to a specific user group such as increased feelings of security and trust in government, greater transparency and accountability, or improved environment or business conditions.

Table 3.1 is meant to be a conceptual guide for planners, analysts, and evaluators to consider e-government investments and implementation decisions in terms of quantifiable and nonquantifiable costs and benefits for specific user groups and to also take into account the public good costs and benefits of e-government.

The three types of benefits in table 3.1 are complementary and not mutually exclusive. For example, ensuring secure online transactions is a nonfinancial benefit in terms of improving user satisfaction, but it can also promote overall trust in government and therefore be an indirect benefit. The type of benefit that one may wish to focus on depends on the time scale, the purpose of the analysis (i.e., for investment decisions or for marketing of online services), and the level of decision making as the focus of such projects can be quite different at the project, agency, and national level.

The following discussion lays out each of the three broad types of benefits: direct financial, direct nonfinancial, and indirect good governance. Particular emphasis is placed on the latter two, because direct financial costs and benefits are—as Behn argues in chapter 9—well understood and analyzed compared with the other two categories. Many studies on electronic government either look at direct costs and benefits accrued within government, applying public management theory, or utilize concepts from electronic commerce to understand direct financial costs and benefits for the citizens and customers. The remaining two categories are less well understood—it is not possible to simply "follow the money." Instead, as has been argued in this book, one is better advised to follow the information, since the analysis of informational flows aids in uncovering nonfinancial costs and benefits.

There is, however, a further difference in level of difficulty between assessing direct and indirect nonfinancial costs and benefits. For direct but nonfinancial costs and benefits, public management theory as well as concepts of the nature of the relationship between the individual citizen and government can provide useful guidance. The third category—indirect nonfinancial costs and benefits—looks at the consequences for government as a whole and for citizens as a whole of delivering public services online. At that level, theories of government legitimacy take the place of theories of public management. Concepts of the individual citizen as consumer are supplanted by concepts of the "citoyen"—the publicly engaged citizenry.

Direct Financial Costs and Benefits

Financial costs and benefits, whether they are for citizens and business or for government, are the most immediate for many e-government decision makers and form the basis for most return on investment (ROI) calculations.

Benefits to Citizens and Businesses: Reducing Burden

Direct financial benefits to the users of electronic information and services takes the form of time and money saved in finding and using public information and services and reductions of administrative burden due to the simplification or elimination of processes and requirements.

The costs that government rules and regulations impose on citizens and businesses generally fall into three categories (Deloitte Research 2003):

1. Finding which rules and regulations are needed for compliance;

2. Understanding what the regulations mean and figuring out how to comply with them;

3. Complying with rules and regulations.

The third category is typically the biggest cost driver in terms of the direct costs related to collecting required information, completing forms, and dealing with government agencies. Costs are, however, also incurred by time delays and uncertainty in the provision of either information or answers to requests.

An OECD survey of small and medium enterprises (SMEs) in ten countries found that on average, SMEs spent nearly US$27,500 per year or about 4 percent of annual turnover, complying with the administrative requirements of tax, employment, and environmental regulations. This equates to an average cost of US$4,000 per employee (OECD 2001). These findings are confirmed by a U.S. Small Business Administration (SBA) study that showed that the cost of U.S. federal regulations totalled US$1.1 trillion and that the cost per employee for all firms was US$5,663 (Crain 2005).

As a result, administrative simplification appears increasingly on government agendas, and ICT has an important role to play. A 2001 survey conducted by the OECD revealed that twenty-six of the twenty-eight countries responding had included ICT initiatives as an element of their strategy to reduce administrative burden (OECD 2003a). The U.S. Small Business Paperwork Reduction Task Force has recommended that the federal government use ICT to reduce the regulatory administrative burden.[2]

Examples of reducing burden by simplifying the electronic front-office interface include electronic one-stop shops, web-based portals, and Internet-based registers. For example, Mexico has established a Federal Register of Formalities and Services on the Internet. The register enables users to obtain all business forms online and to carry out some regulatory transactions electronically with the Ministry of the Economy. An advisory service is available to assist users. In this way, along with facilitating compliance, the register simplifies both users' access to rules and their understanding of what is required of them. Another example is the U.S. portal, Business.gov, that assists businesses in finding, understanding, and complying with laws and regulations as well as finding, filling in and submitting forms, and conducting financial transactions.

Effective use of government-held information can also enable governments to eliminate some obligations entirely. For example, through the reuse of existing data, New Zealand and many of the Nordic countries have eliminated the requirement for most wage and salary earners to file annual tax returns. Instead, the government provides a prepopulated form for a user's approval, using existing information from public databases.

One approach to measuring the benefit of e-government-related burden reduction is by adapting existing regulatory impact analysis (RIA) methodologies to look at the impact of e-government. Such methodologies are increasingly being used in countries such as the United States, Denmark, and Holland to systematically measure regulatory burden, and provide a way to focus on the broader financial benefits (in terms of time and money) of e-government for its users. For example, the Netherlands calculates burden through a standard cost model that estimates that companies face EUR 16.3 billion per year in administrative costs and that citizens face burdens of EUR 1.3 billion and 112 million hours per year. It has set a target of a 25 percent net reduction in burden by the end of 2007, and currently estimates that EUR 10 million in annual savings have already been achieved, much of it due to the use of ICT.

Benefits to Government: Reducing Costs

Generally speaking, financial savings to government can be divided into front-office and back-office savings. The "front office" refers to government as its constituents see it, meaning the information and service providers, and the interaction between government and both citizens and business. The "back office" covers the internal organization operations that support core processes and are not accessible or visible to the general public.

Front-office savings consist of the benefits of a simplified and more automated interface with users. Governments are realizing, however, that putting information and services online creates new parallel channels rather than replacing existing service-delivery channels. At least in the short term, this has led to an overall increase in government spending. In a 2002 OECD survey of Finnish government IT (information technology) offices, over 20 percent of the respondents felt that e-government had actually increased the costs of service delivery (OECD 2003c). Measuring this additional cost is difficult since, as yet, few governments have cross-cutting methodologies that allow the comparison of costs across service delivery channels (see the section of this chapter on Capturing Total Benefits of Investment). In order for government to reduce front-office costs, however, it has become clear that they will have to persuade users to migrate from traditional delivery channels to the new electronic channels as they become available (and as appropriate for a given user and/or service), in order to greatly reduce and/or eliminate the more costly channels.

One of the major challenges to measuring the impact on the internal efficiency of government relates to treatment of the potential costs and benefits of additional organizational changes, streamlining of processes, and integration of services, in addition to the ICT aspect of e-government initiatives. This is an important factor that should be considered in both individual and aggregate or comparative evaluations of e-government.

As financial savings are the most direct and measurable benefits, it is not surprising for governments to focus on them first. This may be why tax services, with their large potential for administrative savings to government through automation, have consistently been among the first and most advanced online services to be developed in OECD countries. Even when governments are able to demonstrate likely financial benefits from potential e-government projects, however, there is no guarantee that such benefits will be actually realized, or that they will be available for allocation to other priority areas, spent internally, or returned to taxpayers in the form of reduced government spending. What is done with savings has a bearing on how accurately they are recorded because of the implicit incentives created. The custodial responsibility of government to manage public resources responsibly has implications for the nonfinancial and "good governance" benefits addressed in the rest of this chapter.

To date, only two countries have attempted to move beyond the costs and benefits of individual e-government initiatives to look at the aggregate case for e-government. Australia and the United Kingdom have each developed cost-benefit methodologies in order to compare and aggregate individual business cases. Based on a survey of twenty-four Australian e-government projects, where financial benefits to the agency were claimed, the National Office for the Information Economy estimated that an investment of AU$108 million generated AU$100 million in multiyear savings for government, as well as AU$14.62 in savings per transaction for users and over AU$25 in savings for businesses as compared to the delivery of comparable services over traditional channels (NOIE 2003).

The shortage of whole-of-government studies is mainly due to the lack of a consistent methodology that covers a wide range of e-government applications, the difficulty in estimating costs and benefits for major IT projects, the problems with estimating service takeup, and the speed of government transformation of its production processes. The United Kingdom's aggregate review of the business cases for about thirty high-impact e-government services was based on a common framework for analysis. The study focused on the realization of benefits, and showed that a successful completion of the business case resulted in a high-quality proposal that identified clear and auditable benefits that could be tracked through to their realization. When business cases did not exist (or were undertaken poorly), key performance indicators were rarely identified, no baseline values were collected, no evidence of impact was sought, and efficiency and performance remained obscure.

Direct Nonfinancial Costs and Benefits

Direct nonfinancial benefits to the users of electronic information and services take the form of service quality, access to information, and confidence. Such benefits are real, but more difficult to enumerate than the direct financial benefits discussed earlier. Nonetheless, it is important to understand nonfinancial benefits in order to guide e-government projects to maximize their benefits and to make them more user-focused.

Benefits to Citizens and Business: Increasing User Satisfaction

E-government holds the potential to improve *user satisfaction*—a subjective and difficult to measure indicator that incorporates elements of accessibility, convenience, accuracy, speed, and cost. Service quality can be improved and a more personalized service provided through the use of ICT; government e-mails, portals, and better search technologies found on the Internet have the potential to make access to information and services easier and more intuitive, without any specialized knowledge of government required on the part of users. But service quality is only one element in determining user satisfaction. Evidence suggests that user satisfaction is likely to be shaped by a wide range of factors:

Customer service   Private-sector studies have highlighted that the way people are treated by staff ranks only just behind quality and price of product in determining their satisfaction.

Information   There is a strong correlation between satisfaction with different services and whether people feel that they are well informed about them.

Procedural fairness   Users are willing to revise their expectations as long as they feel that they are being treated fairly. Of equal importance is the opportunity for recourse and feedback.

Choice   There is some evidence that enhanced levels of choice can boost user satisfaction, even if it does not have a discernible impact on service outcomes.

The U.S. Federal Internet Portal, www.usa.gov for example, seeks to improve user satisfaction by making the portal more user-focused. It continuously collects statistics on the number of visitors and page views, frequency with which pages are clicked (or not), and the most common search terms in order to better understand who is using the portal and for what purpose. The site manages a customer satisfaction survey, relying on the American Customer Satisfaction Index, and uses the Nielsen Net Ratings to obtain details on customer demographics. Finally, www.usa.gov conducts one-on-one usability testing and focus group testing to verify the effectiveness of the information and services to which it is providing access.

Given the importance of nonfinancial benefits, it is essential that e-government business cases capture this dimension by at least listing the different types of benefits that will be produced and the number of people or businesses that will be affected. Successful delivery of e-government and user satisfaction can be measured, in part, by using service takeup as a proxy measure. The takeup of e-government services is steadily increasing worldwide, and the picture for growth is encouraging. While takeup is driven by a number of different variables including access, user satisfaction will also remain a key driver.

People see the Internet as an increasingly acceptable means of interacting with government. Canada, for instance, relaunched its government portal with a new user focus and improved design two years ago—a probable factor in the subsequent doubling of its unique audience numbers. In the United States, a September 2002 report commissioned by the Pew Foundation found that 71 million Americans have used government websites, up from 40 million in March 2000 (Larsen and Rainie 2002). Moreover, a survey released in April 2003 by the Council for Excellence in Government noted that 75 percent of e-government users think it has made it easier to get information, and 67 percent like doing governmental transactions online (Hart-Teeter Research 2003).

Current measures of takeup tend to be very broad. For example, Denmark measures e-government use as having visited a government website in the past month. The type of usage metric one looks at will also depend on the type of benefit one is trying to measure. For example, the number of website-based transactions may be a good indicator of the number of people taking advantage of more efficient electronic processing, but page views (i.e., a web page that has been viewed by one visitor) and site visits will continue to be useful measures of usage given the importance of the government's role in providing public information.

The boundary between financial and nonfinancial measures is permeable as new methodologies will allow social scientists and policymakers to develop new quantitative proxies and measures for qualitative and often subjective "intangible" benefits. But there will continue to be a need for a qualitative understanding of user satisfaction in order to shape service delivery and to increase takeup.

Benefits to Government: Capturing Total Benefits of Investment

A second area in which nonfinancial benefits can be achieved is the potential for e-government to benefit both front- and back-office operations regardless of the service delivery channel. This requires governments to strike an equilibrium between financial and nonfinancial objectives and to address the overall impact of e-government. While the impact of e-government on government operations may indeed have a major financial component, the broader impact on service delivery is still not well understood. The question is both theoretical as well as operational: as e-government becomes a more mainstream part of government, where does the "e" leave off and where does "government" begin?

Governments have increasingly sought to focus attention of their e-government projects on improving public-sector performance. Focusing on overall outcomes allows governments to make the business case for cross-cutting and horizontal e-government initiatives that may not show sufficient benefits for an individual governmental agency, but that either enable broader service delivery as in the case of electronic authentication and digital signatures, or that hold benefits for government as a whole. Opportunities to "cross-sell" related services to common user groups, for example, are enhanced by approaching e-government from a whole-of-government perspective and should lead to greater use of services as more personalized information is known about users and as services are better targeted.

A broader view of e-government impact, also allows government to integrate non-financial components of their e-government mandate. In the interest of equity, governments need to extend the benefits of ICT to as many as possible, and "access" was the most frequently cited out of nineteen different components of e-government strategy among twenty-five EU countries published in 2002–2003. The risk that e-government will benefit only those who already have access to ICT and the knowledge to use it is a very real one. This challenge has often been addressed in terms of the "digital divide" (the gap between those with the skills and access to use ICT and the Internet and those without), both among countries and among the diverse populations within individual countries. As this gap narrows in many OECD countries, governments wanting to provide user-focused e-services equitably will need not only to examine questions of physical access to and affordability of hardware, software, connectivity, and ICT skills, but also the extent to which the online services offered by government provide an "irresistible" incentive for individuals and businesses to use the Internet. This is particularly true if governments want to reap some of the financial benefits of e-government through a channel management strategy.

Among OECD countries, a growing proportion of the population has access to the Internet, but in many instances, the heaviest consumers of public services are among those least able to access and use the Internet or online services. Governments must strike a balance between the desire to open up new channels in order to improve efficiency and quality and the need to maintain the traditional ones for reasons of equity and effectiveness. To date, governments have emphasized that implementation of e-government will not mean that the traditional ways of interacting with government will disappear. Looking forward, when governments start to seriously seek e-government efficiency gains, they will be faced with the need to make choices among these objectives.

Governments are adopting e-government tools and practices in both the front and back office in order to remain responsive to citizens' needs. This gives rise to an "e-enabled" administration in which both traditional and electronic service delivery channels share common information resources that allow users to move seamlessly across channels. Electronic services for citizens and businesses can also be used to improve traditional modes of delivery, such as providing front line civil servants with access to information, expert tools, and forms, but this may have the unintended impact of decreasing incentives for users to migrate to online delivery channels.

The Australian government has begun work on a multichannel service delivery strategy that focuses on e-government as a system to improve data flows and coordination for all types of services, regardless of how they are delivered. A user can therefore look up information about a government service on the Internet, contact a call center with specific questions, and go into a governmental office for a final transaction, all based on seamless access to a common set of data. Such a strategy may also look to steer more people to less expensive online contacts as they become more comfortable with the Internet (OECD 2005b).

Mainly as the result of equity considerations, most governments have chosen not to force users to adopt new channels by denying them services through existing channels or imposing fees or charges that are higher offline than online (except for certain services delivered specifically to business). However, by demonstrating to users the value of electronic service delivery, governments can often increase user takeup. One way is developing incentives for users to move voluntarily to online channels—for example, by sharing administrative savings with users. If they fail to do so, front-office savings as the result of electronic delivery of information and services will not materialize (OECD 2005b).

While these choices are inherently political, it is important to recognize the dynamic nature of this situation in order to time decisions optimally. For example, as time goes by, governments can reasonably assume that more users will be willing and able to access and use online services. In some instances, it will be possible to close down traditional channels simply through a gradual erosion of demand. In others, at some point it may become economical to invest in providing skill development or mediated access to online services for the small percentage of users who are left unable to use services online without assistance. What is most important when governments reach the point of making such choices is that they and their agencies base their decisions on a common framework to measure the relative costs and benefits of different channels (OECD 2005b).

Indirect Costs and Benefits: "Good Governance" as a Public Good

E-government can result in additional indirect benefits for both government and users when it supports a government that is more transparent, accountable, responsive, and open. This is not automatic, but can only be achieved when e-government systems and practice are used to codify and reinforce the formal and informal structures, relationships and expectations that make up "good governance."

The direct benefits of more transparent and secure services that a user accrues at the point of each electronic transaction has a cumulative impact in terms of legitimacy and economic benefits for all of society that is greater than the sum of its parts. For example, expectations for fair and equitable treatment and the use of transparent criteria in the determination of public benefits as part of electronic services is the result of embedding eligibility criteria in impartial systems, the "disintermediation" of civil servants, greater ease for users to question government decisions, and simplified access to information about eligibility rules and rights. At a societal level, however, the result may create more citizen trust in public online services, and potentially in government itself.

Benefits for Citizens and Business: Supporting Growth

At an aggregate level, individual increases in trust as the result of user satisfaction and good governance (as discussed earlier) also have a broader impact on the economy as a whole in terms of creating a safe environment for investment and for doing business. The World Economic Forum (WEF), for example, includes "public trust of politicians" and "business costs of corruption" as components of its Global Competitive Index (WEF 2004). E-government can be used to reduce corruption by maintaining data on transactions, lessening individual discretion, and providing ways to trace corrupt acts, thus helping to reinforce a culture of accountability.

E-government can improve market functioning by promoting the free flow of information. By publishing information online, governments can reduce information asymmetries (the unequal possession of information by market actors) and generate economic efficiency. For example, all things being equal, increased information about health care options can improve market efficiency. Regular publishing of macroeconomic indicators on the Internet also reduces asymmetric information and can lead to more efficient and stable financial markets.

At the international level, businesses can gain access to valuable information, such as import-export processes, market information on sectors and countries, intellectual property protection, currency exchange risks, insurance, licensing rules, and country requirements. Government websites can help a country attract investment by providing a website to facilitate foreign investor access to information, laws, rules and regulations regarding doing business and investing in the country. In the European Union (EU), efforts to standardize data across the EU further promote market integration and cross-border electronic public procurement (IADBC 2005).

E-government information and services benefit from user familiarity with e-services that come from e-commerce and the Information Society in terms of building better services and drawing in more users. But can the relationship work in the opposite direction with e-government development contributing to IT diffusion in a society?

In its review of e-government in Finland, the OECD noted that in addition to ensuring access and providing more advanced, secure, and integrated electronic services, increasing adoption of electronic services requires increasing users' overall level of experience and skills with regard to both e-commerce and e-government. In a survey of Finnish ministries and agencies, the two factors that most constrained user demand for e-services were identified as "the lack of experience in using electronic services" (70 percent) and "the electronic service delivery not seen as sufficiently advanced" (60 percent). These are followed by other factors—namely, security and privacy issues, lack of access, and insufficiently joined-up/integrated electronic services in the public sector (OECD 2003c).

Experience with e-service delivery not only reinforces ICT competency and familiarity for the user, but may also serve to increase overall confidence in electronic service delivery, provided that governments ensure the privacy, security, and technical level of service that users expect. For example, greater-than-expected user demand during the rollout of the French online tax filing system, Copernic, resulted in server failures that left thousands unable to file their taxes on the eve of the deadline, obliging the government to extend the filing date for online filers.

Many citizens and businesses are leery of e-commerce and e-services (see figure 3.1). Leading by example, governments can demonstrate the positive effects of ICT use that, in turn, can increase the adoption of ICT and e-business in the economy. Furthermore, governments can promote innovation and modernization by exhibiting emerging technologies and business processes, and by promoting the

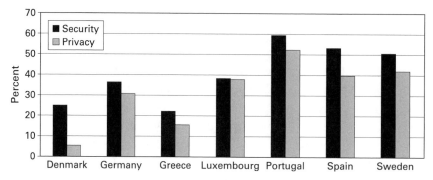

Figure 3.1
Proportion of Internet users aged 16–74 reporting security and privacy concerns as main reasons for not purchasing over the Internet, 2003. As a proportion of Internet users aged 16–74 who had never purchased over the Internet. The exact Eurostat question wording is "Security concerns/worried about giving credit card details over the Internet" and "Privacy concerns/worried about giving personal details over the Internet."
Source: Eurostat, Community Survey on ICT usage in enterprises, 2002 and 2003, October 2004.

development of Information Society skills and innovation. E-government programs can foster a culture of online security by setting security standards for the delivery of e-services. Success in this area can promote both public and government support for other e-government priorities.

As consumers of ICT goods and services, governments themselves can play a role in stimulating market demand, in particular as government ICT spending tends to be less influenced by cyclical market downturns. The OECD has identified an impact of the ICT sector on multifactor productivity growth, and since the ICT industry is characterized by high entry rates of new firms, it becomes a potential engine for growth (OECD 2003b).

E-government can also lead to new business models, using agents as intermediaries in providing information to government. The TYVI (Finnish acronym for "Information from Companies to Public Authorities") project in Finland provides an example of such new business opportunities. In 1997, the Finnish Ministry of Finance established the TYVI project in order to simplify business-to-government (B2G) reporting of financial data through private brokers. The system allows data to be reported only once to one broker, who then transmits the data to public authorities upon request. TYVI operators are paid by public authorities according to the volume of data received (along with a monthly connection fee). However, this is not their main source of income. While companies report to the brokers free of charge, there has been strong demand for complementary services, such as improving the integration of data collection into business software packages. Additional value-adding services can range from converting data into different formats and transferring data to management for monitoring and ongoing support. Business adoption of the TYVI system has grown by a factor of five in the period 1999–2002, and the system has demonstrated strong benefits for all parties: the government has improved access to business data at a low public cost, private companies have simplified their reporting relationship to government and have access to market-based complementary services where needed, and the five TYVI brokers are developing a new and expanding market (OECD 2003c).

As mentioned earlier, reduction of administrative burden for citizens and businesses is a major area of potential e-government benefits and represents one of the most apparent links between e-government and competitiveness. Empirically, decreasing the costs of interacting with government is associated with greater economic growth for the private sector. For example, EUROSTAT data analysis in an European Commission (EC) working document on benchmarking enterprise policy shows a negative correlation between level of burden (based on a six-point scale) and average annual growth of employment in startup enterprises (fewer than 9 persons) (EC 2000). While the factors related to economic growth remain quite complex, improved research on how e-government outputs such as administrative simplification affect overall economic outcomes would further strengthen the case for e-government. Electronic public procurement and regulation compliance, for example, represent some of the main areas where e-government can promote competitiveness.

Benefits to Government: Supporting Legitimacy

In the context of several decades of declining public confidence and trust in government (Holzer et al. 2004), improving service quality through e-services could have a significant positive impact on citizen confidence and satisfaction with government. If people believe that government is incompetent and cannot be trusted, they are less likely to provide such crucial contributions as taxes and voluntary compliance with laws, and government will have more difficulty recruiting talented staff. This forms a cumulative downward spiral in which government's ability to perform is continuously degraded, thereby reinforcing citizens' levels of dissatisfaction and distrust (Nye 1997).

A quantitative study of factors influencing trust and government in Belgium found that satisfaction with the federal government and the working of democracy in Belgium have an impact on the level of trust, but that the largest effect comes from satisfaction with the public administrations as service providers (Kampen, Snijkers, and Bouckært 2003). A Canadian study (Institute for Citizen-Centred Service 1998) found a similar strong positive correlation between satisfaction with services and overall opinions of government service provision. These results appear to confirm that a role exists for ICTs in improving the quality of public administrations and the services that they provide, and that this can have a positive impact in improving citizen satisfaction and trust in government services.

Conversely, a study undertaken by the Pew Research Center in the United States (1998) found that in a period where trust in federal government had fallen, satisfaction with the services provided by nineteen agencies had risen significantly. Other commentators (Bouckært 2003; Bouckært and Van de Walle 2001; Kelly, Mulgan, and Muers 2002) suggest that the relationship between service provision and trust is highly complex and unclear. These studies should also be taken within the social and economic context of each country concerned.

The Nordic approach of providing prepopulated tax forms (described earlier), for example, can save users valuable time, but it may also raise many concerns about security and privacy in countries less accustomed to such an integrated use of central registers. This also illustrates how increasing levels of trust in government can lead to other financial and public benefits in terms of administrative savings and increases in innovation, thereby establishing a "virtuous cycle" of good governance and legitimacy. A recent survey, for example, ranks Norway number three in terms of the population's perception of online safety. Forty percent of Norwegians feel that it is safe to use the Internet to provide the government with personal information (Taylor Nelson Sofres 2003).

The Mexican e-government initiative provides a good example of how e-government has been used as a tool to promote good governance—in particular, for increasing the transparency and accountability of government. The Mexican Social Security Institute (IMSS) set up a new portal in 2004 that publishes a list of prospective purchases, as well as the terms and conditions under which the purchases are to be made. As one of the largest purchasers in the Mexican government, IMSS's purchase and expenditures portal not only opens up the market to a substantial set of competitors, but also reduces corruption and saves taxpayers' money (OECD 2005d).

Mexico has also used e-government to improve access to public information for all citizens. The parliament passed a Freedom of Information Act in 2002 that led to the creation of the IFAI (Instituto Federal de Acceso a la Información Pública), a public institution in charge of giving citizens access to public information. IFAI and the Mexican Ministry of Public Administration have developed Sistema de Solicitudes de Información (SISI),[3] an online system that manages citizens' information requests on a wide array of public information: from ministers' mobile telephone expenditures and public purchases to budget accountings and organizations' investments. When SISI receives a viable request, the system chooses the most appropriate agency and government official to provide the information requested. Once the agency and the official are notified, they are legally bound to reply to that request through the SISI system within a period of ten days if the information is public and twenty days if the information is not. SISI has proved to be a useful tool: 43,000 information requests were received through SISI in 2003, and the number of requests grew by almost 3 percent in 2004. Ninety-three percent of requests to IFAI are now made online through SISI.

In its first five years of existence, Mexico's e-government initiative has increased the transparency of government processes. An OECD survey of the Mexican government in 2004 found that over 70 percent of Mexican e-government officials responding to the survey saw an increase in governmental transparency as the result of the SISI system while almost 40 percent saw an increase in trust in government (OECD 2005d).

The value achieved through e-government can grow exponentially when it moves beyond simply implementing e-services to reinforcing a culture of good governance and reform. The Internet exposure of public decisions and accounts, as well as over-bureaucratic, unclear, or duplicative forms, has in many cases triggered strong reactions from users and media, urging agencies to explain decisions, change existing practices, and simplify forms and back-office procedures. Internet exposure makes public servants more accountable in their decision making. In the area of administrative simplification, for example, agencies have sometimes used "shaming strategies" as a driver for further simplification among reluctant reformers (OECD 2003a).

The challenge remains to develop reliable indicators to measure the impact of e-government on good governance. Developing a better understanding of the relationship between e-government and citizen trust is a subject of particular political interest as politicians seek to increase citizen engagement, but public servants also realize that proactive efforts are necessary in order to be responsive to citizen demands. Measures of public value will help governments develop valuable e-government initiatives and reduce unintended effects and externalities.

Conclusion

This chapter examines three types of benefits and costs to government and citizens of electronic government: (1) direct financial benefits and costs; (2) direct nonfinancial benefits and costs; and (3) indirect benefits and costs. Current available data on the impact of e-government remains, for the most part, limited to financial costs and benefits just for government. Such data may be sufficient for some decisions on individual ICT investments. However, an exclusive focus on this category leaves out five other types of benefits and costs (see table 3.1). Electronic government may facilitate development of synergies among the many channels of transactions the government has with citizens (e.g., through data integration). There is also an increased realization that electronic government can be a tool for transformation, altering the relationship between government and the society that it serves. There are major potential impacts on citizen satisfaction with transactions with government, as well as increased accountability of and trust in government due to increased transparency (as chapter 6 highlights). In addition, to the extent that transactions with government affect citizen trust of online transactions overall, successful provision of online services will potentially nurture purely private-sector transactions as well. More generally, insofar as there is a link between government performance and economic growth and equity, the online provision of public services should be expected to also show benefits in these areas.

A broader set of indicators is therefore needed to evaluate potential e-government initiatives, capturing the full range of benefits and costs to both citizens and government. Explicit measurement and consideration of different types of benefits will also better equip governments to make difficult policy choices: for example, whether to increase financial benefits to government by shutting down some traditional service channels or to favor nonfinancial benefits to users by promoting choice and equity. The categories of indicators used at any given point will be dependent on the purpose of the evaluation, but without indicators drawing on a common methodology, definitions, and understanding of e-government, one cannot understand its full impact. Current initiatives by the OECD, the European Commission, and other international organizations and national governments seek to fill this need.[4] A more complete understanding of the impact of e-government will help governments with the development, design, and subsequent evaluation of future e-government initiatives.

Notes

1. The author would like to thank Paul Foley of De Montfort University and Sheetal Maithel of Harvard University's John F. Kennedy School of Government, who have both written analytical reports for the OECD E-Government Project that have contributed to this chapter. The opinions expressed and arguments employed in this chapter are the sole responsibility of the author and do not reflect those of the OECD or of the governments of its member countries.

2. http://www.whitehouse.gov/omb/inforeg/sbpr2004.pdf.

3. http://www.sisi.org.mx/.

4. http://www.oecd.org/gov/egov/; http://ec.europa.eu/information_society/soccul/egov/index_en.htm.

References

Bouckært, Geert. 2003. "Comparing Measures of Citizen Trust and User Satisfaction as Indicators of "Good Governance": Difficulties in Linking Trust and Satisfaction Indicators." *International Review of Administrative Sciences* 69, no. 3: 329–343.

Bouckært, Geert, and Steven Van de Walle. 2001. "Government Performance and Trust in Government." Paper presented at the European Group for Public Administration Annual Conference, Vaasa, Finland, September.

Crain, W. Mark. 2005. "The Impact of Regulatory Costs on Small Firms." U.S. Small Business Administration, Washington, DC.

Deloitte Research. 2003. "Citizen Advantage: Enhancing Economic Competitiveness through E-Government." Deloitte Development.

EC. 2000. *Benchmarking Enterprise Policy*. Brussels: European Commission.

Hart-Teeter Research. 2003. *The New E-Government Equation: Ease, Engagement, Privacy & Protection*. Washington, DC: Council for Excellence in Government.

Holzer, Marc, James Melitski, Seung-Yong Rho, and Richard Schwester. 2004. "Restoring Trust in Government: The Potential of Digital Citizen Participation." IBM Center for the Business of Government, Washington, DC.

IADBC eGovernment Observatory. 2005. "Background Research Paper: The Impact of E-government on Competitiveness, Growth and Jobs." European Communities.

Institute for Citizen-Centred Service. 1998. "Citizens First." Available at http://www.iccs-isac.org/eng/pubs/CF%2098%20Sum.pdf (accessed February 26, 2005).

Kampen, Jarl K., Kris Snijkers, and Geert Bouckært. 2005. "Public Priorities Concerning the Development of E-government in Flanders." *Social Science Computer Review* 23, no. 1: 136–139.

Kelly, Gavin, Geoff Mulgan, and Stephen Muers. 2002. *Creating Public Value: An Analytical Framework for Public Service Reform.* London: UK Government Strategy Unit.

Larsen, Elena, and Lee Rainie. 2002. *The Rise of the E-Citizen: How People Use Government Agencies' Web Sites.* Washington, DC: Pew Internet and American Life Project.

NOIE. 2003. *eGovernment Benefits Study.* Canberra, Australia: National Office for the Information Economy.

Nye, Joseph S. 1997. "Introduction: The Decline of Confidence in Government." In *Why People Don't Trust Government,* ed. Joseph S. Nye, Philip D. Zelikow, and David C. King, 1–18. Cambridge, MA: Harvard University Press.

OECD. 2001. *Businesses' Views on Red Tape.* Paris: Organisation for Economic Co-operation and Development.

OECD. 2003a. *From Red Tape to Smart Tape: Administrative Simplification in OECD Countries.* Paris: Organisation for Economic Co-operation and Development.

OECD. 2003b. *ICT and Economic Growth: Evidence from OECD Countries, Industries and Firms.* Paris: Organisation for Economic Co-operation and Development.

OECD. 2003c. *OECD e-Government Studies: Finland.* Paris: Organisation for Economic Co-operation and Development.

OECD. 2004a. *Information Technology Outlook.* Paris: Organisation for Economic Co-operation and Development.

OECD. 2005b. *E-Government for Better Government.* Paris: Organisation for Economic Co-operation and Development.

OECD. 2005c. *Modernising Government.* Paris: Organisation for Economic Co-operation and Development.

OECD. 2005d. *OECD E-Government Studies: Mexico.* Paris: Organisation for Economic Co-operation and Development.

OECD. 2005e. *OECD E-Government Studies: Norway.* Paris: Organisation for Economic Co-operation and Development.

Pew Research Center. 1998. "How Americans View Government." Available at http://people-press.org/reports/display.php3?ReportID=95.

Taylor Nelson Sofres. 2003. *Government Online Study 2003.* TNS Global.

WEF. 2004. *The Global Competitiveness Report; 2004–05.* Davos, Switzerland: World Economic Forum.

Case Illustration

"E-Government Is an Outcome": Michael Armstrong and the Transformation of Des Moines

Viktor Mayer-Schönberger and David Lazer

When Michael Armstrong became CIO of the City of Des Moines in 1997, he faced a tremendous challenge. He remembers: "[Information technology (IT)] was fragmented, outdated, and ineffective. Neither Internet access nor email was available. Most business processes were still manual. No standards or architecture were in place. The IT unit was part of the Finance Department, with low visibility and little strategic impact. Staff did not possess the skills necessary to move the organization forward."[1] Organizationally, the IT environment he found mirrored the stovepiped city organization in many ways.

Des Moines' energetic new city manager, Eric Anderson, who saw IT as supporting the overall transformation of the city government into a lean organization serving the citizens, had selected Armstrong to transform IT services for the city. Armstrong moved swiftly. "We managed IT as an enterprise function. Decision making was moved to the enterprise level and became more collaborative. Funding for IT was centralized. Most importantly, we moved relentlessly to consolidate and standardize," recounts Armstrong.

His efforts were aided significantly by an agreement with a cable franchise that gave the city possession of a high-speed fiber-optic network connecting all buildings, thus also enabling the rapid deployment of new workstations citywide. Armstrong's IT department ran and maintained the network, but he calculates that it saved them approximately $2.3 million a year. When they later added Voice-Over-IP to the network services, it reduced telecommunications cost by another $100,000 annually.

In early 1999, Armstrong reorganized his IT department, reducing staff immediately from thirty to eighteen. Through further layoffs—bringing the total to nineteen staff members let go—he was able to hire new people with the skills he needed to implement his strategy. The IT department was not the

only one undergoing dramatic change. As other department heads left the organization, the city manager was able to hire new staff comfortable collaborating and working with technology. Therefore, when Armstrong embarked on
his strategy of "disruption and recovery," of phasing in new IT systems that
would disrupt old bureaucratic practices and force departments to rethink
and restructure their activities based on efficiency and collaboration, new staff
in other departments were more receptive to change. It enabled him to deploy
ERP (Enterprise Resource Planning), electronic permitting and licensing, CRM
(Citizen Relationship Management), and public safety systems, each time
uprooting old and inefficient practices and replacing them with sounder and
more efficient ones. In a virtuous cycle, the transformation of the IT department and the function of IT facilitated the general transformation of Des
Moines' city government and vice versa.

The results are impressive: the city's IT department operates a network that
offers broadband connection to its seventy facilities with 99.99 percent availability, and supports data, voice, and video. It standardized on one (and only
one) provider from servers to desktops, from hardware to software to databases. All employees have e-mail and Internet access. IT has become a strategic
and core contributor to citywide management and decision making. Remark-
ably, this has been achieved while reducing cost. While other municipalities
struggle with the black hole of ever-increasing IT budgets, Armstrong has
reduced headcounts and budget. Des Moines has twenty-one staff members in
its IT department, compared with a national average of fifty-nine for similar-
sized cities. Its IT budget is 1.4 percent of the city's total budget, compared
with 2.24 percent for similar cities.[2] Its annual cost per city resident is
$16.50—almost half the national average of $31.54. Even factoring in the
overall reduction in headcount, the IT department was able to reduce annual
IT costs per city employee to $1,737, less than two-thirds the national average
of $2,899.

Des Moines' success has been embraced by its citizens, demonstrating that
increased efficiency does not lead to less service for citizens. When the city's
new service-focused website launched in 2002, Armstrong explains that usage
by citizens immediately increased by more than 50 percent and doubled annually in the years thereafter. The city has twice been rated first in the United
States in its population class in the Digital Cities Survey conducted by the

Center for Digital Government, and the city's website was a finalist in the 2004 Best of the Web competition, placing it among the top ten municipal sites nationwide.

Armstrong acknowledges that the broadband network and the transformation of the entire organization helped make possible his success. Additional key ingredients for success, he emphasizes, were the importance of the strong relationship between him as CIO and the city manager as CEO, his role as a "bridge" between business needs and technical concepts and the shared vision and goal of all involved. The City of Des Moines does not have an explicit narrow "electronic government strategy." E-government was never just about online public services, but defined more broadly and seen as part of overall strategic change. Des Moines' success, Armstrong maintains, was predicated on an organization that "made good use of the technological tools available to support and deliver services, and with their use could transform itself to consider things from the citizen's viewpoint." The result has been lauded as successful "electronic government" (in the broader sense), although Armstrong simply prefers to call it "good government."

Notes

1. This quote and others here are from an interview with Michael Armstrong on May 23, 2005.
2. 2003 data tables from International City/County Management Association, Center for Performance Management (http:www.icma.org).

4

Challenges to Organizational Change: Multi-Level Integrated Information Structures (MIIS)

Jane E. Fountain

Introduction

Governments are extraordinary information creators, users, and disseminators. I-government focuses attention on the flow and structuring of information within government (chapter 12). Government actors engage in knowledge work, specifically, in the creation, sharing, and communication of information. They design and redesign processes by which information flows according to legislative mandate, organizational practice, and public need. Recently, they have sought to rethink information flows in order to leverage benefits from information and communication technologies. When public-sector actors seek to change these information flows at any appreciable level of complexity, they inevitably engage in complex organizational and interorganizational change.

This chapter presents a multi-level integrated information system (MIIS) to describe and explain how information is structured at three interrelated levels. Each level follows a different internal logic. First, at a microlevel, individuals share and make sense of information in small groups through ongoing social relations within and across organizations. Second, at organizational and interorganizational levels, actors design and use processes and systems to codify and structure information in order to routinize repeated behaviors, transactions, and information processing sequences. Third, at an institutional level, highly codified and regularized information flows are produced through the enactment of property rights, laws, regulations, contracts, and other overarching formal rule systems. Interactions among these three levels suggest that when information flows change at one level, the other two levels typically are affected. The tri-level nature of change renders it complex to implement and difficult to predict the effects and path of organizational change. The MIIS framework synthesizes findings drawn from recent research streams in network analysis, neo-institutionalism, and public management. It complements an emerging body of empirical research on public-sector interorganizational networks by filling gaps in theory and by offering prescriptive advice to public managers.

Governments try to use new technologies to rethink information, to increase responsiveness to citizens by lowering search and other transactions costs, and to gain efficiencies through business process redesign in which redundancies are removed by restructuring process flows (Fountain and Osorio-Ursua 2001; King and Konsynski 1993a,b; Neo, King, and Applegate 1993; West 2005). Similarly, innovative firms in nearly every economic sector have sought to develop effective supply chain and business process management (Abernathy et al. 1999; Cash, Nohria, and Eccles 1994; Hammer and Champy 1993; Litan and Rivlin 2001; Shapiro and Varian 1999).

The types of organizational change enumerated here assume the ability of public managers to work across agency boundaries in a more integrated way than most governments have imagined (Cash et al. 1994; Fountain 2001; Hammer and Champy 1993). It is now eminently clear that the chief challenge for government is not the implementation of new technologies; it is organizational change required to develop more productive information flows. Yet the failure rate of efforts to restructure and integrate information flows remains high in the private and public sectors because information flows and structures are the result of complex social, economic, and political relationships built up over time. In many cases, the reason for presumed technology failure lies in inadequately conceptualized and managed organizational change efforts meant to build collaborative interorganizational capacity (Cohen and Prusak 2001; Davenport 1995; The Economist 2002). The knowledge base for analyzing, much less predicting, collaboration remains highly varied, fragmented, and empirically weak (Fountain 2001; Milward and Provan 2000; Oliver 1990).

Why is integration problematic? Approaching the problem through the lens of a rational choice perspective, an agency may view integration of information as a public good, which is paid for by agencies through the development of and a commitment to shared goals and procedures, consistent protocols, and the like. Rational agencies, therefore, will tend to underinvest in the public good. A rational agency would prefer that other agencies use resources for such learning and adjustment. Yet this model ignores the value to an agency of its engagement in joint knowledge creation. A free-riding agency may be disadvantaged because it will not gain value from the negotiations and learning processes in which decision makers develop shared goals, procedures, and standards around a new information regime. By contrast, integration might be viewed as a club good whereby members gain benefits only when they are part of the club, here meaning that they develop compatible standards and practices.

Viewing the problem of integration differently, through a Hobbesian lens, a rational agency might prefer that an overarching entity, an honest broker with authority, create an integrated system. Such an approach might ensure that all agencies and their interests will be treated fairly. But the honest broker may lack the in-depth, tacit knowledge and varied experiences that reside in each agency and that, if brought to bear on integration, would ensure realistic, useful results. Thus, it is difficult to ignore the need to develop joint participation and communication.

Rational choice perspectives offer insights into the structure of incentives that either inhibit or encourage collaboration. But neoclassical economics as an underlying theory of integration ignores noninstrumental sources of motivation for collaboration, possesses weak explanations for the emergence of informal norms, and treats preferences and important elements of the environment as given. These processes have been the province of sociology. To illuminate organizational change, researchers must be able to explain contextual and emergent variables that are inside the "black box" of most rational choice perspectives.

The next section of this chapter considers in turn recent streams of research focused on each of the three levels in the MIIS framework in order to examine underlying structures and processes of organizational change. The third section presents a brief case illustration of Grants.gov, a U.S. federal government project undertaken to improve information flows across agencies and organizations that manage federal grants. The case illustrates the three levels of the framework and some of the relationships among the three levels.

Individuals, Organizations, and Institutions: How Information Is Structured

Government information flows can be conceptualized across three levels of analysis. Interactions at the individual and small group level constitute ongoing social relations and form the locus of shared information and sense making. For example, civil servants regularly contact colleagues to make sense of new policies, to compare notes on implementation successes and failures, and to ask or give advice, support, and referrals. In the process of these interactions, they decide who to trust, with whom to communicate, and with whom to share knowledge.

Moving up a level of analysis, organizations and interorganizational arrangements, or networks, codify and routinize information through systems and processes. Routinized information is, in part, what is meant by organization. Individuals and small groups are constrained by these organizational processes. Innovators in governments have focused on rethinking and modifying these processes.

Proceeding to an overarching level, institutions further codify and structure information via formal norms and rules. Institutional mechanisms, largely outside the control of any particular agency or ministry, include property rights, laws, regulations, and fundamental governmental processes such as accountability, oversight, and budgeting. Thus, this MIIS influences behavior directly and indirectly. Organizational change often perturbs all three layers, producing unanticipated effects.

Individual and Group-Level Influences on Information

The basic actors in networks are individuals and small groups. In this chapter, I refer to networks of individuals as "social networks" and networks of organizations as "interorganizational networks." Some overlap exists between the two types of networks, but the distinction is important. In the conventional meaning of a collaborative social network, actors must successfully develop joint production processes without recourse to strong overarching authority. Public managers who are important actors in such networks typically play critical linking roles. An array of empirical social network research provides evidence for this observation. Applied case illustration research on public-sector networks corroborates the importance of brokering and linking roles.

Researchers have found that network brokers require strong interpersonal skills—specifically, the ability to work with other professionals whose perspectives differ from theirs. Other needed skills include the capacity to build interpersonal relationships and to communicate openly, flexibility, a propensity to envision new ways of operating, and the ability to take risks (Cohen and Mankin 2002; Hoban 1987; Hoel 1998; Huggins 2001).

The initial development of collaborative effort depends critically on the interpersonal skills of individuals. Huggins (2001) notes: "It is primarily the facilitators and brokers, rather than the firms participating in network initiatives, which initially hold the key in the crucial outset period to producing interaction that can subsequently lead to the formation of embryonic networks.... The most successful network initiatives are those that have facilitators or brokers who act as community or civic entrepreneurs" (447). In fact, some researchers have suggested that the selection of public managers with such skills is critical to the success of networked organizational projects. Other researchers focus on dyadic relations and have recommended that organizations foster formation of "collaborative pairs" by linking key individual brokers across organizations (Cohen and Mankin 2002). In networked arrangements, individual-level incompatibilities translate to structural weakness.

A challenge to restructuring information flows within organizations stems from what organization theorists have called position bias, or subunit goal optimization, the tendency of managers to attend to goals that relate directly to their position rather than to broader, organizational goals (March and Simon [1958] 1993). Heintze and Bretschneider (2000) found that public program managers involved in organizational restructuring were more likely to view information technologies and the organizational change project in which they participated as successful if the managers also reported that restructuring supported their positions.

But Ketokivi and Castañer (2004) studied 164 organizations in five countries, a subset of which engaged in participatory strategic planning processes. They found that participatory planning processes reduced the incidence and strength of position bias. By extension, it may be that the development of joint production rules across agencies also requires participation and communication in the process of strategic planning to enhance integrative potential. Bardach (2001) offers a conceptualization he has termed "managerial craftsmanship" and argues that the creative opportunity provided by joint projects is itself one of the attributes that facilitates collaboration. Desire for professional development and creative, important work can, therefore, be balanced against views of individual behavior based on narrow self-interest and subunit goal optimization.

The commitment and skill of key individuals, or champions, remain important throughout the duration of collaborative efforts. Their importance is noted in studies of networked firms in the biotech and pharmaceutical industries where individuals who act as "network managers, 'marriage counselors,' and honest brokers" sustain coherence when interests and intentions conflict (Powell 1998). Other researchers have observed the adverse impact on projects when a champion moves on (Kernaghan 2003).

Middle managers play key roles in interorganizational arrangements, often sustaining interactions with decision makers at other levels, in their own organization, and across organizational boundaries (Doz 1996). And "radical," or creative and far-reaching, innovations tend to be championed by managers and executives at the lower levels of a corporate hierarchy (Day 1994).

Having briefly noted the attributes and behaviors of individuals that are associated with collaboration and network sustainability, I turn to research results from social network analysis that point to attributes of collaborative networks themselves.

Ongoing Social Relations

In his seminal article (1985), Granovetter establishes the centrality of embeddedness which, he argues, is constituted through ongoing social relations. Granovetter (2005) summarizes the many effects of social networks on information, trust, and norms and states that "social networks affect the flow and the quality of information. Much information is subtle, nuanced and difficult to verify, so actors do not believe impersonal sources and instead rely on people they know" (33). Rewards and punishments are magnified in social networks because the source of the reward or punishment is likely to be known. Trust emerges in situations where individuals have incentives to exploit others in the context of a social network but choose not to do so. These structural features of networks imply the importance of interpersonal skills and the efforts of champions and network brokers to model trusting behavior and to use social rewards and sanctions, via group approval and disapproval, to strengthen an emergent network.

Applied researchers observe the importance of open and effective communication for the development of interorganizational arrangements. This finding resonates with one of the more frequently replicated results of social network analysis: Network density is proportional to the influence of norms in the network. That is, the more connections there are as a percentage of all possible connections among individuals in a network (in other words, the higher the network density), the more powerful is the influence of norms. Conceptions of appropriate behavior are clearer, reinforced more often, and sanctioned more quickly in case of deviance in high-density networks (Granovetter 2005, 34). Thus, frequent and open communication among actors in a network leads to higher network density and, thus, more influential network norms of behavior. Larger groups, which tend to have lower network density, would have to have champions and brokers willing to work harder to encourage communication or who have the ability to establish effective communication systems to overcome the disadvantages of network size in order to realize similar gains from trust and internalized group norms.

Trust

Rational choice theorists who have tried to model the emergence of cooperation in Prisoner's Dilemma games have found that an iterated Prisoner's Dilemma, in which actors engage in repeated interactions over time, increases the probability of cooperation among parties by increasing the expectation that others can be trusted not to defect (Axelrod 1984; Fudenberg and Maskin 1986; Ostrom 1990). Milward and Provan (2000) have applied these findings to frame solutions to collective action problems in networked governance.

Repeated interactions allow reciprocity, and thus trust, to emerge. Oliver (1990) found that "a considerable proportion of the literature on [interorganizational relationships] implicitly or explicitly assumes that relationship formation is based on reciprocity" (244). Students of collaboration have found that trust is a critical element of successful collaborative teams, that it varies directly with team flexibility and adaptability, and that it is correlated with the ability of actors to work together and with project outcomes (Bardach 2001; Biedell et al. 2001; Zaheer, McEvily, and Perrone 1998).

According to Huggins (2001), "although networks are a group endeavor, the 'on-the-ground practicalities' of 'networking' necessarily consists of behavior that is often dyadic in nature" (449). Similarly, Zaheer, McEvily, and Perrone (1998) distinguish between interorganizational and interpersonal trust. Interpersonal trust affects interorganizational trust that in turn has a significant influence on relational exchange.

Applied public management researchers observe that organizational actors require time to build relationships across boundaries and that allocation of time signals commitment (Hoel 1998; Huggins 2001; Johnson et al. 2003). It is not clear whether time in these studies is equivalent to repeated interaction. But the conceptual and behavioral clustering of variables such as "repeated interactions," "time," and "commitment" suggests that they are related to the robust findings that network density is positively related to the strength of norms and that repeated interactions are positively related to the development of trust.

Social Capital

Trust, norms, and networks are constituent elements of social capital, a construct that provides a solution to collective action problems (Bourdieu 1979; Coleman 1988; Putnam 1993). Following Coleman (1988, S98), social capital indicates "social structures" that "facilitate actions within that structure." By the same logic, individuals who develop collaborative joint production capacity have developed social capital.

Social capital indicates cohesion and is correlated with innovative capacity. Nahapiet and Ghoshal (1998) argue that "structural social capital"—formal ties between roles—promotes trust, which fosters cooperation, an antecedent to the production of intellectual capital, or innovation. They present a model of the relationship among social capital, intellectual capital, and the innovative capacity of organizations. Fountain (1998) also found a relationship between social capital and innovation in science and technology operating chiefly through the knowledge gains and novel combinations of ideas made possible by joining disparate networks.

Large, cross-agency networks across organizations do have to overcome coordination costs and possibilities of defection. Yet they possess advantages over high-density networks due to what Granovetter (1973, 1983) called the "strength of weak ties," which is the propensity of new information to flow through weak, rather than strong, ties between individuals. So a perspective on government that emphasizes information and innovation would emphasize not only trust and group coherence but also the need for innovation, new ideas, and critical thinking, all of which rely on weak and bridging ties. For example, the Bush administration launched twenty-five cross-agency e-government projects. The initial impetus for a cross-agency approach was consolidation and standardization of government processes via integration across the enterprise. Yet actors in the networks developed for each project have brought together ideas from several sources, thereby increasing opportunities for innovation during project development. In some of the projects, weak ties have led to innovative developments that were unanticipated in the original standardization strategy.

A focus on information in government will therefore have to attend to the effects of ongoing social relations on information flows. Interpersonal skills, trust, and small group cohesion are necessary but not sufficient for sustainable cross-agency collaboration. The complexities and scale of information flows in government require structures and processes embedded in organizations and institutions in addition to ongoing social relations at the level of individual and group-level interactions. As Nee and Ingram (1998) observe: "When structural sociologists reify ongoing social exchanges, they assume a 'harder' image of the fabric of social life than may be warranted. The imagery of network ties as a 'hard' structural arrangement, for example, can lead an analyst to overlook their 'softer,' more elusive and contradictory qualities" (22). In other words, social networks can rarely, if ever, fully replace regular organizational or interorganizational structures and processes as carriers of information.

Organizations and Interorganizational Networks

Organizations are information processing units, and the central means of understanding and analyzing organizations is by illuminating the structures and channels organizational actors develop to regularize information collection, storage, use, and flows (March and Simon [1958] 1993). Complex organizations develop to overcome the cognitive limitations of individuals (i.e., bounded rationality). They do this by routinizing large swathes of organizational life including communication, performance, reporting, and planning. Organizations typically develop routines, standard operating procedures, and performance programs that can then be matched against situations and deployed. As March and Simon ([1958] 1993) formulated: "Organizational actors deal with each other ... by creating and using systems of rules, procedures and interpretations that store understanding in easily retrievable form" (2). When we consider interorganizational networks in the context of a web of existing complex organizations, we assume that individuals in those networks are located within an organization.

Organizational actors generally try to change routines and operating procedures at the margins, rather than whole cloth, because of interdependencies across routines. Many unanticipated consequences of organizational change stem from second-order effects on routines, procedures, and communication channels. Disjunctive change, occasioned by new technologies, makes change at the margin less feasible because these technologies enable fundamental changes in information flows. Stock markets operate by computer. International standards and monitoring support global organizations. Periodic communications from an organizational leader are replaced by an organizational website, or e-mail, that communicates information in almost real time. Cisco, a global firm, uses the same web interface and corporate communications for every location as a means of unifying disparate offices, cultures, and country settings. The United Nations has experimented with knowledge management systems that link experts worldwide, for example, in clean water technologies or mosquito-borne diseases. Field workers can query one another and transfer expertise through a global system of communication that works in real time.

Social networks fill gaps in formal organizational channels. Yet formal organizational channels carry a heavy freight of information without which complex production requiring division of labor and specialization would be impossible. Similarly, interorganizational networks use routines to regularize information flows. Such networks differ from ongoing social networks. Interorganizational networks in government, in particular, rely on formal processes and structures due to their accountability and oversight requirements (Isett and Provan 2005; O'Toole 1997). When individuals in interorganizational networks develop shared goals, systems, and procedures, they regularize and codify information. The challenge for network actors is to build and operate such structures without the overarching, formal authority present in hierarchies. Formalization and codification of interorganizational structures and processes lends a degree of stability and relative permanence not present in social relations.

Among the key structures network actors must build are those for governance, communication, and task performance through division of labor and specialization. The sustainability of such networks depends strongly on task significance and clarity as well as adequacy of resources. Researchers have found that successful cross-agency networks develop and effectively manage a variety of governance and coordinating groups, including a steering committee, advisory groups composed of technical or special staff such as legal or financial experts, external stakeholder groups, and cross-departmental work teams. Singapore, long a leader in the development of networked public-private-nonprofit governance, relies extensively on cross-sectoral, quasi-governmental boards as coordinating and governance instruments for several information-based projects.

Applied public management researchers note the importance of effective communication structures for prospective network partners (Bardach 2001; Cohen and Mankin 2002; Johnson et al. 2003). Communication is not simply a means to build group coherence and identity, it is a vital tool of coordination, particularly when network actors are building something new and thus do not have established operating routines with clear means of coordination.

Actors are more likely to identify with and commit to significant tasks. Thus the task, goal, or mission of the network must be important enough to justify the risk and effort of building new processes and specific enough to communicate it clearly to those in different organizations. Researchers recommend that parties clearly articulate the joint goals and anticipated outcomes of a collaborative effort (Biedell et al. 2001; Chiat and Mickiewicz 1999; Hoel 1998; Johnson et al. 2003). Brown et al.

(1998) observed that project complexity had a negative effect on government agency collaboration based on a case illustration of a shared geographic information system. Project complexity is correlated with—or synonymous with—lack of clear goals, objectives, and criteria for performance.

Moving beyond goal agreement, researchers similarly argue that partners articulate and formalize roles, tasks, and responsibilities. Division of labor and decision-making authority must be clarified. Some researchers suggest that parties develop "formal agreements that clarify roles, responsibilities, expectations and relationships...as early as possible in the project" (Cohen and Mankin 2002, 121). Isett and Provan (2005) demonstrated that such agreements in government networks typically are formalized through contracts that remain in force even when repeated interactions over time might warrant less formality. This is not due to lack of trust, they argue, but to government oversight and accountability requirements. Their finding stands in contrast to research on interorganizational networks in markets where Gulati and Singh found that formalization in successful network partnerships tends to decrease over time (Gulati 1995; Gulati and Singh 1998).

Kernaghan (2003) states that "getting the 'pre-nuptial' agreement right is extremely important to getting the partnership arrangements right" because specification of roles, tasks, and responsibilities clarifies expectations and forces discussion of division of labor, dispute resolution mechanisms, and decision-making authority. Crawford (1994) found that clarification of organizational objectives mitigates negative effects on collaboration of power differentials among agencies. Similarly, interorganizational network partners require shared performance evaluation processes and measures (Cohen and Mankin 2002). Leach, Pelkey, and Sabatier (2002) found a positive effect of evaluation criteria on length of partnership in the case of interstate partnerships to improve watershed management. Brown, O'Toole, and Brudney (1998) found that formality including formalized procedures improved performance and customer service in a government project to promote shared development and use of geographical information systems.

The Treasury Board of Canada Secretariat—the Government of Canada's Management Board—has developed detailed and comprehensive guidelines for managing collaborative arrangements that call for documentation clearly detailing requirements for the interorganizational processes described here (Treasury Board 2003). The guidelines even include sample memoranda of understanding (MOUs) for establishing funding, staffing, and other flows across departments. In the U.S. federal government, cross-agency collaborative systems and processes are typically codified and formalized through the use of MOUs, which must be developed, reviewed, and approved by each governmental body. The commitment to develop MOUs is itself an act of integration and part of a strategic planning process. The act of specifying joint goals, processes, and systems implies commitment to a network and necessarily involves learning and joint problem solving rather than simply negotiation and bargaining.

Adequacy of resources, notably budget and staff, are critical to network sustainability (Brown, O'Toole, and Brudney 1998; Johnson et al. 2003; Kernaghan 2003; Moon 2002). During the initial stages of a network, staff and budget constraints may pose considerable challenges to core network actors as they try to regularize resource flows and develop equitable networked arrangements. For example, the U.S. Congress passed the E-Government Act of 2002 and authorized substantial funding for e-government initiatives. But much of the funding was not appropriated, and agencies were required to find and share funding within their budgets. Lack of funding and staff have hampered network development and the progress of the twenty-five cross-agency e-government projects by reducing the time that staff can spend on projects, reducing the ability of agencies to contract for technical development, and, more generally, making it difficult for agencies to maintain "existing" processes while simultaneously building new ones.

Crafting collaborative arrangements implies that interorganizational network partners can learn collectively. Doz (1996) examined a wide range of strategic alliances and found that the initial alliance conditions and interorganizational design either "facilitate or hamper the partners' learning about the environment of their alliance, how to work together to accomplish the alliance task, their respective skills, and each other's goals" (64). Thus, just as social capital tends to accrue as the carrying out of productive tasks leads to experience and learning, interorganizational network actors continue to learn iteratively as their base of knowledge and experience grows over repeated interactions.

Information in networked organizations is structured internally through routines and systems, as I have just described, and through the results of ongoing social relations, which formed the first part of this discussion of levels of analysis. An important source of information that constrains action remains to be examined. Institutions specify and formalize a large number of overarching and fundamental information structures including legislation, regulations, accountability systems, budgeting processes, and oversight mechanisms. It is to these that we now turn.

Institutional Arrangements and Information in Government

A critical function of government is development of institutions that confer legitimacy, credibility, and trust. Government institutions cannot "go out of business" for performance failures. A government agency may be dissolved; a constitution cannot readily be modified. Institutional stability, meaning resistance to change, implies that institutions represent broad societal agreements.

Nee and Ingram (1998) refer to institutions as a *"web of interrelated norms—formal and informal—governing social relationships"* (19). They argue that institutions influence behavior in ongoing social relations in two ways. First, institutions directly affect the formation of preferences because they are core constituent elements of context. Examples in this case include the U.S. Constitution and other enduring features of government that contribute to a citizen's identity and norms of behavior. Second, institutions constrain organizations that, in turn, shape individual and group behavior in social networks. Examples here include laws and regulations. For example, sunshine laws require government organizations to make information available to the public via channels and documents that citizens can understand and access. Formal contracts usually specify performance criteria, dispute resolution mechanisms, and some of the ways in which actors will be expected to interact, including written disclosures, notices of intent, verbal representations, and the like. In short, contracts describe and prescribe information flows.

At a macrolevel, institutions define national and global structures of incentives, and thus influence cultural and national levels of trust and norms that influence processes of exchange. A robust set of findings in a broad stream of research provides evidence for the correlation between government institutions that support interfirm networks in an economy and the presence of such networks (Lane and Bachmann 1997; Fountain 1998; Piore and Sabel 1984; Rooks et al. 2000; Saxenian 1994).

Four types of institutional structures that characterize most industrialized democracies require discussion: the vertical structure of bureaucracy, which is the fundamental form of the executive branch of government, and three central governance processes that flow from it—accountability, legislation, and budgeting.

The Vertical Structure of Bureaucracy
Max Weber, one of the twentieth century's most influential sociologists as well as a public intellectual, sought to delimit the power of government leaders by specifying

the "modern" bureaucratic organization as one with clear jurisdiction and authority relations ordered through superior-subordinate relationships. Weber argued that bureaucracy was the only form of organization capable of coordination and control in industrializing societies. This form of organization is deeply institutionalized in most industrialized political economies. Evidence of it is found in the dominance of relatively autonomous government agencies, which are accountable to legislatures and parliaments, and the linear, vertical logic of accountability, budgeting, and legislation.

The past twenty-five years of management and organization theory and practice has been largely devoted to breaking down the dominance of this model in theory and practice, to conceptualize and allow information flows that vary greatly from it. Markets provide one alternative; networks another. Yet in agency autonomy, budgeting, legislation, and accountability, the basic structure of the bureaucratic form persists and is strongly reinforced by interdependencies among these systems and by precedent.

In the schematic depiction in figure 4.1, the traditional hierarchical model is sketched with boxes representing autonomous departments. Cross-agency collaboration is sketched using slightly overlapping ovals. To move from one model to the other, an agency must decide to achieve at least some of its goals through cooperation, in a positive-sum calculation, rather than conceptualizing decisions as zero-sum calculations in which one department's gain forms another's loss. But a more

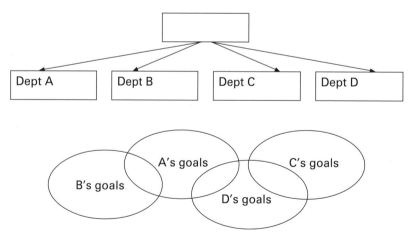

Figure 4.1
The nondecomposability of department goals.

important implication is the need for accountability, budgeting, and legislation systems that are better aligned with the second sketch in which some jurisdiction, resources, and operations overlap.

The main structural barrier to collaboration is the departmental model. While central oversight agencies can use control measures to promote interdepartmental collaboration, such an approach counters current trends toward decentralization, particularly in traditionally centralized ministerial governments. For example, the Government of Canada has recently devolved greater authority to departments. Thus central agencies have proceeded cautiously, providing advice and incentives rather than forcing integration. Similarly, the U.S. Office of Management and Budget (OMB) has moderated its relationship with twenty-five cross-agency projects from one of controller to one of facilitator and knowledge broker in an effort to catalyze, rather than to order, horizontal collaboration. If oversight units could order cooperation, they would do so. But the information and incentive structures to support cross-agency initiatives are too complex to yield to simple fiat.

Accountability Processes
Accountability flows directly from the vertical structure of bureaucracy. In U.S. federal government, an agency director is directly accountable to Congress for the actions of his or her agency. A recent, vivid example of agency accountability followed the response of the Federal Emergency Management Agency (FEMA) to Hurricane Katrina and the accountability of its former director, Michael D. Brown, a presidential appointee. Brown was forced to resign due to the poor performance of his agency in demonstrating accountability and its consequences for leaders. In parliamentary systems, ministers are the principal link between the parliament and the public service. The minister is legally responsible for the policies, programs, and administration of his or her department and is required to resign in the event of serious departmental error.

Behn (2001) follows a long line of public administration researchers in his observation that

behind the traditional concept of organizational accountability is the implicit assumption that one organization is responsible for one policy—or that at least every policy is the responsibility of just one organization. It is another beauty of bureaucracy and hierarchical accountability. The law assigns the clear and full responsibility for implementing each policy...to one organization....And for each component of the organization, one individual is clearly in charge. Thus one individual is clearly accountable. (65)

Networked arrangements blur lines of authority and accountability. Thus public servants are challenged to maintain vertical accountability while supporting horizontal initiatives for which lines of accountability are unclear. The risk in networked arrangements is not the same as the risk involved in contracting out. With respect to the latter, a contract clearly delineates the requirements imposed on the contractor and the penalties for failure to perform. Cross-agency arrangements rarely clarify division of labor, authority, and responsibility in such stark terms. Moreover, the emerging stages of cross-agency collaboration entail experimentation, trial and error, and provisional systems as a network of actors negotiates and learns.

For nearly twenty years, public managers in several countries have accrued practical experience with the development of sustainable cross-agency operations, particularly in human, social, and environmental policy domains. Although practice has developed, theory, government systems, and policies to support networked agency practice have lagged behind practice. The problem is not one of developing individual incentives for cooperation but of reformulating governance principles and practices—that is, institutions—in light of increased coordination across agency boundaries (Allen et al. 2005; Fountain 2001; Lenihan et al. 2003; Millar and Rubinstein 2002; Wilkins 2002).

Legislative Processes

In recent years, legislators have increasingly mandated multiple entities to cooperate to achieve public ends. In these cases, legislation is not problematic—unless other challenges prevent mandated cooperation. Much legislation mandates without providing needed resources or even authority for the mandate. In other cases, much existing legislation reinforces departmental autonomy. Kernaghan (2003) reports in the results of a study of integrated service delivery projects in Canada that "legislative and regulatory barriers are of the show-stopper variety and require political consent for their removal…It is clear, for example, that privacy acts restrict the sharing of some kinds of data" (17–18). The point here is not to ignore privacy issues, but to point to structural barriers to interagency collaboration. Dawes and Prefontaine (2003) point to the relationship between law and legitimacy; new models of collaborative service delivery, they contend, "need to establish a new kind of institutional legitimacy. Most often, legitimacy begins with a basis in law or regulation" (42). Yet in many cases of collaboration, informal negotiations and planning proceed long before formal authority and arrangements change to accommodate new practices.

Budget Processes

Shared resources are a significant source of cohesion for cross-agency networks, in part because they change the nature of the relationship from multiple exchanges to a shared system (Hoel 1998). Brown, O'Toole, and Brudney (1998), in their study of the role of partnership in a government information technology (IT) project, found that the amount of resources shared by the group is one of the determinants of partnership effectiveness. Bardach and Lesser (1996) argue that the U.S. federal funding system confines interorganizational collaboration by placing undue restrictions on the use of funds. Yet they do not articulate how to remove restrictions and maintain accountability. In most industrialized democracies, the budget process appropriates funds to individual departments for department-specific programs. The budget process reinforces the vertical structure of government. The challenges of obtaining joint funding are political and structural because shared funding streams blur lines of accountability (Allen et al. 2005; Kernaghan 2003).

Institutions function in the background when organizational actors carry out regularized routines. But during periods of organizational change, particularly when changes in information flows are involved, public management innovations collide with deeply entrenched institutions. When government actors innovate and change information flows, they may find that their actions create a lack of alignment with formal rules in their environment. Eventually, they may have to address these tensions or may be reprimanded or find their activities prohibited by formal rules. The tensions produced by this mismatch pose challenges to key participants. But when such tensions can be resolved, possibilities for new institutional forms may be developed, gain legitimacy, and, subsequently, become new constraints for decision makers (Giddens 1976, 1984). Institutions can and do change, but the logics by which they change differ from those of fairly fluid ongoing social networks or from routinized organizational processes.

Framework for a Multi-Level Integrated Information System

A focus on information in government invites researchers and practitioners to consider the distinctions, as well as the similarities, discussed so far in this chapter among informal norms of collaboration, organizational systems that might help coordinate cooperation, and, not least, institutional structures that provide the overarching context and rules within which collaboration might develop. Organizational change efforts, as I have argued previously in the chapter, require strategies to manage all three levels in the government environment. Actors involved in organizational change sometimes neglect one level while focusing on others. For example, some managers rely almost exclusively on interpersonal skills to establish collaboration and may neglect developing the interorganizational structures of communication and coordination that will be necessary to regularize information flows. In other cases, a champion might focus on the need to modify legislation needed for an interorganizational project to move forward and may, in the process, neglect the emerging social relationships that will sustain commitment and trust. In still other cases, astute operational managers might fail to communicate adequately and to build appropriately participative systems. Not all actors have to participate all the time. The point is that collaborative networks require that actors perceive their interests and goals being furthered equitably in the joint process. Thus, a MIIS offers considerable promise to illuminate the challenges of organizational change when actors seek to rethink information.

Nee and Ingram (1998) adapted a framework developed by Williamson (1994) to model the interactivity among small group interactions, organizations, and institutions. Their objective, an important one for our purposes, was to specify differences between informal norms, typically the chief constraints in ongoing social relations, and formal norms, encoded in institutions. In brief, the purpose here is to account for constraints on information flows posed by institutions, organizational routines, and ongoing social relations.

The MIIS framework adapts and extends the Nee and Ingram model in three ways. First, it assumes that individuals and small groups not only interact face-to-face but develop and sustain informal norms through a variety of mediated interactions, including e-mail, listservs, blogs, web conferencing, and other shared information and communication spaces and channels. There is no claim here that these modes supersede face-to-face interactions, particularly with respect to the early development of trust. Yet their ubiquity and importance can hardly be ignored. They are flagged but not elaborated.

Second, Nee and Ingram (1998) follow other economic sociologists in assuming that networks of firms are the primary actors and that these networks are embedded in markets regulated by states. Our focus on interorganizational networks within government allows us to consider in a different context relationships among government actors and institutionalized governance structures offering a finer-grained view of "the state" than is typically drawn. Third, the empirical referent in Nee and Ingram is the interorganizational arrangement. The role of the single organization in the original model is extended to include and explain interorganizational arrangements as these emerge from informal social networks of public servants.

The arrows connecting the boxes that depict the three levels in the following figure represent interrelationships across the three levels. Individuals develop informal norms through social interaction. These informal norms affect the level of compliance and opposition to formalized organizational routines and rules. Informal norms and emergent innovation may come to be formalized themselves and adopted at the interorganizational and organizational levels. Flowing in the opposite direction, organizational and interorganizational rules constrain behavior in informal networks.

Moving up to sketch some of the relationships between organization and institution in government, public agencies can rarely influence legislation. But working with external stakeholders, typically interest groups, they can influence Congress and sometimes wrest control of decisions that Congress would prefer not to make (Carpenter 2001). But such influence is rare. In general, agencies submit budget requests and may have input into legislation that affects their programs. Institutions, on the other hand, work powerfully with respect to agencies and agency networks. Budgets and legislation can eliminate or create programs at the stroke of a pen. And the generosity of budgets and the requirements of legislation make the difference between programs that hobble and those well able to carry out their mandates.

Thus research at all three levels is needed to encompass the complexities of social, operational, structural, and political elements of organizational change.

The next section illustrates the MIIS framework (figure 4.2) by means of a brief case illustration of an interagency network, Grants.gov, developed to streamline the complex process of managing federal grants. The development of Grants.gov exemplifies the interplay of behavior and process at multiple levels of analysis and the interplay of differing internal logics that operate at each respective level.

Grants.gov: Challenges of Information Integration

In February 2002, the Grants.gov project was launched, part of the Presidential Management Initiative, a modernization effort including twenty-five cross-agency initiatives.[1] Years of discussion and development efforts meant to standardize grants administration across agencies preceded Grants.gov. Thus, a network of grants professionals in the federal government had been established and had built communication channels and a set of informal norms around a shared, important task.

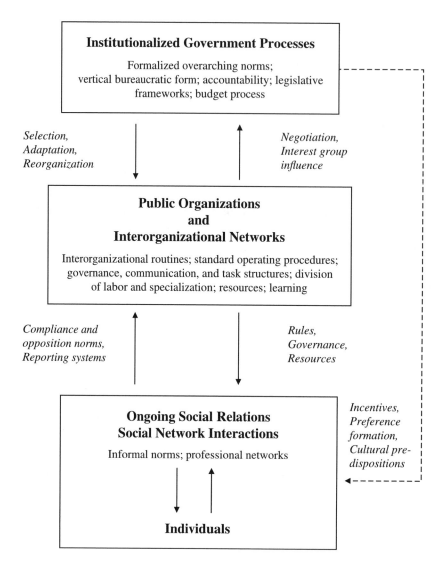

Figure 4.2
A multi-level integrated information system (MIIS).
Source: Adapted from Nee and Ingram 1998, 31.

The goal of the first phase of Grants.gov was to build and deploy one cross-agency, web-based interface to consolidate search and application for federal grants. The first project phase did not seek to standardize grants processes across agencies but to build a standard, web-based interface to which all agencies would connect. It has been assumed that the virtual integration would create a path to deeper integration across agencies that might be pursued in future phases. Thus the project participants understand the need to build commitment incrementally and over time as network actors learn more deeply about one another's processes and the challenges of integrating them. The initial product—a centralized, web-based "storefront"—was launched by then Secretary of the Department of Health and Human Services Tommy Thompson in November 2003. From its inception, the cross-agency network has benefited from high-level political support from the White House, the OMB, and the secretariat of the Department of Health and Human Services (HHS).

Approximately $360 billion in federal grants are offered annually by twenty-six federal agencies through approximately eight hundred programs and comprising more than 210,000 individual awards. Grants are disbursed to state, local, and tribal governments, educational institutions, and nonprofits. The grants process is relatively mature, having developed during the past twenty-five to thirty years. Thus grants processes, although challenging to integrate, are clearly specified and well understood. But strong autonomous cultures for grants processing and idiosyncratic agency data requirements have also evolved over time.

As agencies began to automate their grant processes, it became clear that hundreds of stovepiped, computerized grants systems would result. Ironically, customer service strategies and decentralized approaches to innovation and computing led to hypercustomization, further fracturing grants processes across the government. The net result for the public was cacophony, not greater responsiveness. In the culture of decentralized agency computing during the 1990s, attempts to use emerging technologies to integrate grants processes had been attempted several times, particularly during the Reinventing Government reforms of the Clinton administration, but without success. Thus, although the goal of integration was rhetorically attractive, the context and incentives that would allow actors to collaborate were not in place.

An integrated grants administration system would benefit internal agency operations through simplification of myriad complex processes. For the public, lowering search and application costs would reduce barriers to entry for those organizations without the resources to find programs and maneuver through arcane application processes. The cross-agency initiative is part of a larger effort to disintermediate the relationship between corporate and individual citizens and their government by simplifying information.

Mark Forman, former director of the OMB Office of E-Government and Information Technology, led a participatory meeting in February 2002 that included constituents, users, and agency team members. They decided upon shared phase one objectives: First, they agreed to develop a single web interface "storefront" to enable potential applicants to find appropriate grants and to apply for them. Second, they agreed to standardize grants application information and processes, develop unique identifiers for applicants that would be used by all agencies, and link their agency to the unified web interface. Thus the network participants clarified and agreed upon a shared goal, related objectives, performance measures, and an ambitious timetable and milestones for completing the "storefront." This was done in a participatory meeting to signal open communication, joint problem solving, and an equitable voice for agencies. Forman used his position and credibility as the nation's first chief information officer (CIO) to begin to establish a rigorous, collaborative culture for the project with systematic project management systems.

The largest federal grantor, HHS was designated by OMB, in concert with public managers, as the managing partner agency for Grants.gov. Other partner agencies include the Departments of Transportation, Education, Housing and Urban Development, Justice, Labor, Agriculture, Commerce, Defense; the National Science Foundation; and FEMA. The initial program manager, Charles Havekost, is a career civil servant with considerable professional experience managing IT projects, including a brief period in a private-sector dot.com startup. Havekost became the CIO of HHS during the first phase of Grants.gov. Rebecca Spitzgo, the former deputy program manager, succeeded Havekost. As one of the champions of the project, Havekost, and later Spitzgo, established and sustained relationships with counterparts from other agencies by building a strong network among managers and executives.

Project goals, participating agencies, and oversight in an OMB program office were agreed upon during the first weeks of Grants.gov, but key resources—funding, staff, and space—were the responsibility of the program manager. It was decided that agencies would jointly fund the collaborative projects. Lack of funding forced Havekost and Spitzgo to spend considerable time during the first year of the project developing interagency budgetary MOUs and tracking budgetary transfers between agencies. Agency participants set project staffing at fifteen people and the budget at

$20 million over the first two years. Managers jointly developed a funding algorithm, dividing partner agencies into three groups—large, medium, and small—according to the proportion of grants processed annually. The shared funding approach became a model for other cross-agency projects. The development of an interorganizational system for funding is indicative of the need for routinization of key management elements in networks.

Havekost and Spitzgo had to convince agencies to contribute staff to the project. They focused on the professional development benefits and the advantage to departments of having "eyes and ears" on the project. By the end of 2002, Grants.gov was staffed at prescribed levels with career civil servants, largely on six-month details to the project. The team structure promoted cross-fertilization of ideas from different agencies. But the use of six-month details required staffing to be addressed continually. Program team members persuaded HHS senior management to approve designated space for the project. This was not an easy process, but the shared space, and regular informal team gatherings, contributed strongly to an esprit de corps, a sense of shared identity and commitment, among project members. Thus resource decisions aligned with social network building and cohesion.

One of the key issues involved in working across agencies is governance. While senior government management may agree in principle to collaborate, in practice middle managers from separate agencies carry out the work of integration and often have goals that are not aligned with those of the cross-agency project. To address this challenge, Havekost created a governance structure including an executive board and a steering committee. Senior agency representatives with authority to speak for their respective agencies were appointed. The simple structures proved valuable for conflict resolution and political support. The shared governance structure also has been adopted as a "best practice" by other cross-agency projects and lends support to the importance of interorganizational systems to support networks of actors.

According to Havekost, there was little disagreement among agency representatives over the concept of the program; that is, almost all agreed that the project was a good idea. That the program was *possible* was harder to agree upon. The program team focused on four main tasks in order to build momentum.

First, the team demonstrated to agency partners that their objective had already been accomplished in another form by a related project. Federal Business Opportunities—the FedBizOpps.gov project—is similar to Grants.gov in concept and functionality. Second, the team actively engaged the agencies' clients and constituents, which persuaded grants applicants that the program team was committed to building a truly interagency process. It also signaled to agencies that their external stakeholders were aware of the project and would exercise their voices if the progress was delayed by an individual agency. The project team looked for creative ways to work around lack of cooperation and noncompliance of some partner agencies by introducing flexibilities and multiple variations into the shared system.

Third, early on the project team forced agreement on an issue that had proved a stumbling block in prior efforts to streamline federal grants processes. In July 2002, well ahead of the stated October deadline, partner agencies agreed on the standard data to be collected by grant applicants. The adoption of standard data collection was operationally important and psychologically significant. The early accomplishment reportedly built a strong reputation for the project and the seriousness of intent of its participants. It also reinforced the reputation of Havekost as an entrepreneur who could deliver results.

At the institutional level, it has been interesting to observe adjustments in the relationship of newly integrated agency activities and Congress. The development of a shared approach to budgeting for cross-agency projects offers a pointed example. Many of the cross-agency e-government projects have developed innovative, shared funding mechanisms that rely on formulas worked out by the agencies participating in an initiative. Large agencies would fund a greater proportion of project expenses than smaller agencies, for example, or agencies that process larger numbers of grants would fund more of Grants.gov than agencies with smaller grant programs. These funding mechanisms, while emergent, were until recently becoming formalized and diffused to similar joint projects throughout the federal government. It is not yet known whether they characterize a new form of funding or the proliferation of an ad hoc solution to a seemingly intractable structural problem (Fountain 2006).

In response to these innovations in budgeting, Congress has passed a provision within a much broader appropriations bill—Section 841 of the Transportation, Treasury, Housing and Urban Development, the Judiciary, the District of Columbia, and Independent Agencies Appropriations Act of 2006—that prohibits the use of these shared funding mechanisms without prior congressional approval (Miller 2005; Skrzycki 2006; U.S. Congress 2005). This development provides a surprising and vivid example of the power of institutions to constrain the behavior of networked actors. The strong reaction of Congress to the emergence of an integrative approach to budgeting offers a striking example of lack of alignment between the institution of the legislature and the collaborative projects that have been under development with White House approval since the beginning of the Bush administration.

In summary, the Grants.gov project has built an interagency interface to integrate the process of finding and applying for federal grants. Project participants agreed on the importance of the goal, although they doubted its feasibility. They developed governance and funding structures that have become models for other cross-agency projects. The entrepreneurship and skill of the project leader proved critical to building trust and project management systems that would work within the institutional environment. A shared perception of equity in terms of agency contributions has been a vital element of success. The interorganizational network built new systems and was able to continue its work until it ran aground on institutional budget processes that Congress, at this time, has not allowed to change. It is expected that in the negotiated process between the Senate Appropriations Committee, OMB managers and cross-agency program leaders, a new consensus, and possibly the beginnings of a modified institution will emerge.

Conclusion

In a traditional view of government, public servants are agency-centric actors who face a set of perverse incentives as they make decisions regarding the possible benefits of new information uses, sharing, and flows for their programs and agencies. In most adversarial democracies, public executives learn to try to accumulate larger budgets and more staff in order to increase the power and autonomy of their agency. They also learn to negotiate skillfully for appropriations for their program and agency. In fact, in adversarial democracy, such conflicts among programs and agencies are assumed to force public servants to sharpen their arguments and rationales for programs, to produce results in order to sustain resources. This view of adversarial democracy dates at least as far back as J. S. Mill and the theories of neoclassical economics. But the adversarial model of democracy does not align well with new possibilities for structuring information in government.

For this reason, public executives face perverse incentives. If public managers implement new information flows and uses that are horizontal in nature, they may not gain greater agency resources in terms of dedicated agency budget: They are likely to have their budget decreased. If they implement new ways of using information that reduce redundancies across agencies and programs, again, they are likely to lose resources rather than gain them. If they develop interagency and enterprise-wide systems with their colleagues in the bureaucracy, they will lose autonomy rather than gain it. If the goal to be achieved is better governance, then the decisions are clearly in the direction of collaboration across boundaries. But when the proximate goal is to increase, or maintain, agency budget and authority, the criteria for decision making are vastly different and tend toward the agency-centric. So the traditional incentives by which public executives have worked are "perverse" incentives for networked governance.

The case of Grants.gov illustrates the multi-level integrating information system within which organizational change takes place. The MIIS framework explains events that are otherwise categorized as "unanticipated consequences" or second-order effects of change. Informal interactions, carried out by individuals on behalf of their organizations, when handled with respect and some measure of interpersonal skill, can create trust across boundaries and the beginnings of a shared sense of purpose. At a more formal level, interorganizational relationships require strong governance, coordination, communication, and control systems that must nevertheless be implemented in a collaborative way to sustain the participation of actors. Projects require governance bodies as much for the legitimacy and authority they confer on fledgling projects as for their substantive decision making. Cross-agency collaborations in government tend to develop within institutional environments designed to work in highly vertical, command-and-control organizational settings. Entrepreneurs and innovators in government learn to work within, and, when opportunities arise, to modify these institutional arrangements.

Notes

The author acknowledges the research assistance of Amanda Coe, Michelle Sagan Gonçalves Robin McKinnon, Ines Mergel, and Eun-Yun Park. Amanda Coe contributed to the literature review that forms a part of this chapter. Robin McKinnon carried out the primary research and initial draft of the Grants.gov case illustration. This material is based upon work supported by the National Science Foundation under Grant No. 0131923 and 0630209. Any opinions, findings, and conclusions or recommendations expressed in this material are those of the author and do not necessarily reflect the views of the National Science Foundation.

1. Case illustration data were gathered through archival research and face-to-face, tape-recorded interviews with the program managers, assistant manager, project staff, OMB officials, and stakeholders. At its inception, the project was known as "E-Grants" and changed officially to "Grants.gov" in 2003. The name Grants.gov will be used throughout. See http:// www.grants.gov for the project website.

References

Abernathy, Frederick H., John T. Dunlop, Janice H. Hammond, and David Weil. 1999. *A Stitch in Time: Lean Retailing and the Transformation of Manufacturing.* New York: Oxford.

Allen, Barbara, Luc Juillet, Gilles Paquet, and Jeffrey Roy. 2005. "E-Government as Collaborative Governance: Structural, Accountability and Cultural Reform." In *Practicing E-Government: A Global Perspective,* ed. Mehdi Khosrow-Pour, 1–15. New York: Idea Group.

Axelrod, Robert. 1984. *The Evolution of Cooperation.* New York: Basic Books.

Bardach, Eugene. 2001. "Developmental Dynamics: Interagency Collaboration as an Emergent Phenomenon." *Journal of Public Administration Research and Theory* 11, no. 2: 149–164.

Bardach, Eugene, and Cara Lesser. 1996. "Accountability in Human Services Collaboratives—For What? And To Whom?" *Journal of Public Administration Research and Theory* 6, no. 2: 197–224.

Behn, Robert D. 2001. *Rethinking Democratic Accountability.* Washington, DC: Brookings Institution Press.

Biedell, Jeff, David Evans, Daniela Ionova-Swider, Jonathan Littlefield, John Mulligan, and Je Ryong Oh. 2001. "Facilitating Cross-Agency Collaboration." Unpublished paper, Robert H. Smith School of Business, University of Maryland.

Bourdieu, Pierre. 1979. "Les Trois États du Capital Culturel." *Actes de la Recherche en Sciences Sociales* 30: 3–5.

Brown, Mary Maureen, Laurence J. O'Toole, and Jeffrey L. Brudney. 1998. "Implementing Information Technology in Government: An Empirical Assessment of the Role of Local Partnerships." *Journal of Public Administration, Research and Theory* 8, no. 4: 499–525.

Carpenter, Daniel P. 2001. *The Forging of Bureaucratic Autonomy: Reputations, Networks, and Policy Innovation in Executive Agencies, 1862–1928.* Princeton, NJ: Princeton University Press.

Cash, James I., Nitin Nohria, and Robert Eccles, eds. 1994. *Building the Information-Age Organization: Structure, Control, and Information Technologies.* Boston: Irwin.

Chiat, William S., and Michele Mickiewicz. 1999. "Collaboration for Success: Facilitating Large Group Interventions." *Annual Quality Congress* 53: 142–148.

Cohen, Don, and Laurence Prusak. 2001. *In Good Company: How Social Capital Makes Organizations Work.* Boston: Harvard Business School Press.

Cohen, Susan G., and Don Mankin. 2002. "Complex Collaborations in the New Global Economy." *Organizational Dynamics* 31, no. 2: 117–133.

Coleman, James S. 1988. "Social Capital in the Creation of Human Capital." *American Journal of Sociology* 94 (suppl.): S95–121.

Crawford, Adam. 1994. "Social Values and Managerial Goals: Police and Probation Officers' Experiences and Views of Inter-Agency Collaboration." *Policing and Society* 4: 323–339.

Davenport, Thomas H. 1995. "The Fad that Forgot People." *Fast Company* 1 (November): 70.

Dawes, Sharon S., and Lise Prefontaine. 2003. "Understanding New Models of Collaboration for Delivering Government Service." *Communications of the ACM* 46, no. 1: 40–42.

Day, Diana. 1994. "Raising Radicals: Different Processes for Championing Innovative Corporate Ventures." *Organization Science* 5, no. 2: 148–172.

Doz, Yves L. 1996. "The Evolution of Cooperation in Strategic Alliances: Initial Conditions or Learning Processes?" *Strategic Management Journal* 17, Special Issue: 55–83.

The Economist. 2002. "Getting IT." *The Economist* 365, no. 8295: 16.

Fountain, Jane. 1998. "Social Capital: A Key Enabler of Innovation in Science and Technology." *Science and Public Policy* 25, no. 2: 103–115.

Fountain, Jane. 2001. *Building the Virtual State: Information Technology and Institutional Change*. Washington, DC: Brookings Institution Press.

Fountain, Jane E. 2006. "Central Issues in the Political Development of the Virtual State." In *The Network Society: From Knowledge to Policy*, ed. Manuel Castells and Gustavo Cardoso, 149–181. Washington, DC: Center for Transatlantic Relations, Johns Hopkins University, School of Advanced International Studies and Brookings Institution Press.

Fountain, Jane, and Carlos Osorio-Urzua. 2001. "Public Sector: Early Stage of a Deep Transformation." In *The Economic Payoff of the Internet Revolution*, ed. Robert Litan and Alice Rivlin, 235–268. Washington, DC: Brookings Institution Press.

Fudenberg, Drew, and Eric S. Maskin. 1986. "A Folk-Theorem in Repeated Games with Discounting and with Incomplete Information." *Econometrica* 54: 533–554.

Giddens, Anthony. 1976. *New Rules of Sociological Method*. New York: Basic Books.

Giddens, Anthony. 1984. *The Constitution of Society: Outline of the Theory of Structuration*. Berkeley: University of California Press.

Granovetter, Mark. 1973. "The Strength of Weak Ties." *American Journal of Sociology* 78, no. 6: 1360–1380.

Granovetter, Mark. 1983. "The Strength of Weak Ties: A Network Theory Revisited." *Sociological Theory* 1: 201–233.

Granovetter, Mark. 1985. "Economic Action and Social Structure: The Problem of Embeddedness." *American Journal of Sociology* 91, no. 3: 481–510.

Granovetter, Mark. 2005. "The Impact of Social Structure on Economic Outcomes." *Journal of Economic Perspectives* 19, no. 1: 33–50.

Gulati, Ranjay. 1995. "Does Familiarity Breed Trust? The Implications of Repeated Ties for Contractual Choice in Alliances." *Academy of Management Journal* 38: 85–112.

Gulati, Ranjay, and Harbir Singh. 1998. "The Architecture of Cooperation: Managing Coordination Costs and Appropriation Concerns in Strategic Alliances." *Administrative Science Quarterly* 43, no. 4: 781–814.

Hammer, Michael, and James Champy. 1993. *Reengineering the Corporation*. New York: HarperCollins.

Heintze, Teresa, and Stuart Bretschneider. 2000. "IT and Restructuring in Public Organizations: Does Adoption of IT Affect Organizational Structures, Communications and Decision-Making?" *Journal of Public Administration Research and Theory* 10, no. 4: 801–830.

Hoban, Thomas J. 1987. "Barriers to Interagency Cooperation." *Journal of Applied Sociology* 4: 13–29.

Hoel, James L. 1998. *Cross-System Collaboration: Tools That Work*. Washington, DC: Child Welfare League of America.

Huggins, Robert. 2001. "Inter-Firm Network Policies and Firm Performance: Evaluating the Impact of Initiatives in the United Kingdom." *Research Policy* 30, no. 3: 443–458.

Isett, Kimberly Roussin, and Keith G. Provan. 2005. "The Evolution of Dyadic Interorganizational Relationships in a Network of Publicly Funded Nonprofit Agencies." *Journal of Public Administration Research and Theory* 15, no. 1: 149–165.

Johnson, Lawrence J., Debbie Zorn, Brian Kai Yung Tam, Maggie Lamontagne, and Susan A. Johnson. 2003. "Stakeholders' Views of Factors That Impact Successful Interagency Collaboration." *Exceptional Children* 69, no. 2: 195–209.

Kernaghan, Kenneth. 2003. *Integrated Service Delivery: Beyond the Barriers*. Report prepared for the Chief Information Officer, Government of Canada.

Ketokivi, Mikko, and Xavier Castañer. 2004. "Strategic Planning as an Integrative Device." *Administrative Science Quarterly* 49: 337–365.

King, John L., and Ben Konsynski. 1993a. "Singapore Leadership: A Tale of One City." Harvard Business School Case 191-025, Harvard Business School, Cambridge, MA.

King, John L., and Ben Konsynski. 1993b. "Singapore TradeNet (A): A Tale of One City." Harvard Business School Case 191-009, Harvard Business School, Cambridge, MA.

Lane, Christel, and Reinhard Bachmann. 1997. "Co-Operation in Inter-Firm Relations in Britain and Germany: The Role of Social Institutions." *The British Journal of Sociology* 48, no. 2: 226–254.

Leach, William D., Neil W. Pelkey, and Paul A. Sabatier. 2002. "Stakeholder Partnerships as Collaborative Policymaking: Evaluation Criteria Applied to Watershed Management in California and Washington." *Journal of Policy Analysis and Management* 21, no. 4: 645–667.

Lenihan, Donald G., John Godfrey, Tony Valeri, and John Williams. 2003. "What Is Shared Accountability?" *Policy, Politics & Governance*, vol. 5. Ottawa, Ontario: KTA Centre for Collaborative Government.

Litan, Robert E., and Alice M. Rivlin, eds. 2001. *The Economic Payoff from the Internet Revolution*. Washington, DC: Internet Policy Institute and Brookings Institution Press.

March, James, and Herbert Simon. [1958] 1993. *Organizations*, 2nd ed. New York: Wiley.

Millar, Craig, and Daniel Rubenstein. 2002. "Government Response to the Fourth Report of the Standing Committee on Fisheries and Oceans 'Report on the Oceans Act.'" Fisheries and Oceans Canada, Government of Canada, March.

Miller, Jason. 2005. "OMB Delivers Report to Better Sell E-Government." *Government Computer News*, January 18. Available at http://www.gcn.com/vol1_no1/daily-updates/37953-1.html. (accessed January 18, 2005).

Milward, H. Brinton, and Keith G. Provan. 2000. "Governing the Hollow State." *Journal of Public Administration Research and Theory* 10, no. 2: 359–379.

Moon, M. Jae. 2002. "The Evolution of E-Government among Municipalities: Rhetoric or Reality?" *Public Administration Review* 62, no. 4: 424–433.

Nahapiet, Janine, and Sumantra Ghoshal. 1998. "Social Capital, Intellectual Capital, and the Organizational Advantage." *The Academy of Management Review* 23, no. 2: 242–266.

Nee, Victor, and Paul Ingram. 1998. "Embeddedness and Beyond: Institutions, Exchange, and Social Structure." In *The New Institutionalism in Sociology*, ed. Mary C. Brinton and Victor Nee, 19–45. New York: Russell Sage Foundation.

Neo, Boon-Siong, John L. King, and Lynda Applegate. 1993. "Singapore TradeNet (B): The Tale Continues." Harvard Business School Case 193-136, Harvard Business School, Cambridge, MA.

Oliver, Christine. 1990. "Determinants of Interorganizational Relations: Integration and Future Directions." *Academy of Management Review* 15: 241–265.

Ostrom, Elinor. 1990. *Governing the Commons: The Evolution of Institutions for Collective Action*. New York: Cambridge University Press.

O'Toole, Laurence J. 1997. "Treating Network Seriously: Practical and Research-Based Agendas in Public Administration." *Public Administration Review* 57, no. 1: 45–52.

Piore, Michael J., and Charles Sabel. 1984. *The Second Industrial Divide: Possibilities for Prosperity*. New York: Basic Books.

Powell, Walter W. 1998. "Learning from Collaboration: Knowledge and Networks in the Biotechnology and Pharmaceutical Industries." *California Management Review* 40, no. 3: 228–240.

Putnam, Robert D. 1993. *Making Democracy Work: Civic Traditions in Modern Italy*, Princeton, NJ: Princeton University Press.

Treasury Board. *Managing Collaborative Arrangements: A Guide for Regional Managers.* Treasury Board of Canada Secretariat, Ottawa, 2003. Available at http://www.tbs-sct.gc.ca/rc-cr/guide_rm/index_e.asp (accessed January 20, 2006).

Rooks, Gerrit, Werner Raub, Robert Selten, and Fritz Tazelaar. 2000. "How Inter-Firm Co-Operation Depends on Social Embeddedness: A Vignette Study." *Acta Sociologica* 43: 123–137.

Saxenian, Annalee. 1994. *Regional Advantage*. Cambridge, MA: Harvard University Press.

Shapiro, Carl, and Hall R. Varian. 1999. *Information Rules: A Strategic Guide to the Network Economy*. Boston: Harvard Business School Press.

Skrzycki, Cindy. 2006. "Document Portal Sticks on Funding," *Washington Post*, January 10, p. D01. Available at http://www.washingtonpost.com/wp-dyn/content/article/2006/01/09/AR2006010901702.html (accessed January 18, 2006).

U.S. Congress. 2005. Transportation, Treasury, Housing and Urban Development, the Judiciary, the District of Columbia, and Independent Agencies Appropriations Act of 2006. Public Law No. 109-115. 119 Stat. 2396.

West, Darrell. 2005. *Digital Government: Technology and Public Sector Performance.* Princeton, NJ: Princeton University Press.

Wilkins, Peter. 2002. "Accountability and Joined Up Government." *Australian Journal of Public Administration* 61, no. 1: 114–119.

Williamson, Oliver E. 1994. "Transaction Cost Economics and Organization Theory." In *The Handbook of Economic Sociology*, ed. N. J. Smelser and R. Swedberg, 77–107. Princeton, NJ: Princeton University Press.

Zaheer, Akbar, Bill McEvily, and Vincenzo Perrone. 1998. "Does Trust Matter? Exploring the Effects of Interorganizational and Interpersonal Trust on Performance." *Organization Science* 9, no. 2: 141–159.

Case Illustration

From Computerization to Convergence: The Case of E-Government in Singapore

Ines Mergel

To understand e-government in Singapore, one must understand Singapore—or at least its recent history. The trajectory of Singapore over the last half century has been impressive: from colonial, third world backwater to a wealthy, cosmopolitan hub in the world economy. One foundation of Singapore's remarkable success has been its investments in a knowledge economy interconnected by a physical and virtual (ICT) grid. With little in the way of natural resources, the only advantage Singapore has is location, physically and sociologically—in the middle of Asia, a multiethnic city, a former colonial trading post that bridges Europe and Asia. However, in order to become a hub in the world economic network, Singapore itself had to become tightly networked. This strategy has been manifested in its investments in network infrastructure, in education, and in public-private partnerships. Today Singapore has one of the highest PC, Internet, and wireless penetrations in the world.

E-government is a natural extension of Singapore's overall strategy. The e-government development in Singapore is characterized by a succession of different integrated national programs, each designed to build on the success of the previous, and in step with the general strategy of creating a networked knowledge society. E-services are not only provided for citizens (www.ecitizen.gov.sg, or the eCitizen portal) and businesses (www.business.gov.sg), but also to government agencies, through intranet and messaging infrastructure government websites (www.gov.sg).

E-Government: Institutional Arrangements

Singapore, a city-state with a highly centralized governing structure (patterned on the British system of parliamentary government), lacks any autonomous local governments. Responsibility for e-government is vested in the Ministry of Finance (MOF), which is responsible for all central information and communication technologies (ICT) infrastructure, services, and policies within the public service. Critically, the MOF also requires all government agencies to work with the same external vendor—National Computer Systems (NCS), a subsidiary of Singtel (the incumbent telecom operator).

Within the overall e-government initiative, the Infocomm Development Authority (iDA) of Singapore serves as the chief technology officer and chief information officer. iDA provides technical advice and recommendations to MOF; defines and recommends ICT policies, standards, and procedures to MOF; performs service-wide ICT master planning; and manages central ICT infrastructures and initiatives.

MOF, iDA, and NCS thus provide the foundation of Singapore e-government. iDA works together with all ministries and agencies involved to deliver service packages that incorporate requirements as to the steps that the public has to undergo to complete a specific government-related activity (such as filing taxes, paying road fees). iDA then proposes an implementation plan to the MOF, which makes final decisions. NCS then implements the technology. In short, e-government responsibilities are placed in the power center of a powerful state, and supported by a large-scale technical infrastructure, with all work conducted by the same vendor, creating a uniquely powerful centralizing force in the development of e-government in Singapore.

E-Government Strategy

The self-conscious objective of e-government is to reduce transaction costs for the government and the private sector; not included are initiatives to increase inclusiveness of processes of governance (i.e., e-democracy). The centerpiece of e-government is *e-citizen*: a one-stop shopping portal from which citizens can access all government services online (http://www.ecitizen.gov.sg). It is organized by needs within different areas of a citizen's life cycle (Culture, Recreation and Sports, Defense and Security, Education, Learning and Employment, Family and Community Development, Health and Environment, Housing, Transport and Travel). "My e-citizen" is a website that can be customized for each citizen with e-services and payment notifications by short message service

(SMS) or e-mail, such as road tax renewal, library book reminders, season parking reminders, etc.

Initial efforts at e-government were not fully successful. The government was able to provide services online in a notably integrated fashion. However, moving citizens to the efficient virtual offices of government away from brick and mortar proved to be a more difficult challenge. The government responded through the development and launch in 2003 of "Singpass" (Singapore Personal Access). Singpass is a unique identifier offering access to a wide array of online government services; and, perhaps more important in terms of providing impetus for adoption, it facilitates a wide array of private-sector transactions, from banking transactions to ordering drinks in bars. Singpass has rapidly gained users since it was instituted. As of December 2005, roughly one-third of Singapore's inhabitants had a Singpass, where the number of transactions averages about 1.2 million per month.

Case Illustration

Dubai's Electronic Government

Viktor Mayer-Schönberger and David Lazer

Dubai, part of the United Arab Emirates, is a small but, with well over a million inhabitants, relatively populous emirate located in the Persian Gulf. Unlike its neighbors, it has diversified its economy, deriving less than 6 percent of its GDP directly from oil. Its port and airport function as important regional and global hubs. Recently, tourism and real estate development has contributed to the emirate's significant economic growth. Not unlike that of Singapore, Dubai's continued success depends on the emirate's ability to remain a haven of stability, comfort, and economic opportunity as well as its capacity to develop and innovate faster than its regional and global competitors.

Given its hierarchical governing structures, with strong leadership on top, and its relatively small size, a centralized, command-and-control implementation of its e-government strategy similar to Singapore's would have been an obvious choice. Yet Dubai chose a different path. Instead of centralizing power, Dubai Electronic Government (DEG), the public agency responsible for advancing e-government in the emirate, saw its role as one of fostering coordination and cooperation. For example, DEG offers public agencies often used and branded building blocks for their e-government initiatives—electronic payment ("pay"), for example—but refrains from mandating adoption of particular standards and technologies. It also collects expertise on e-government implementation in the form of "best practices" that are then shared with public agencies.

The only "stick" that DEG wields is making transparent the development of e-government projects through extensive measuring based on a customized framework of criteria, capturing everything from the planning process to the implementation and subsequent use of particular functionalities. This information is made available to all public agencies, thus putting pressure on agencies to perform well in these benchmarks.

Since DEG began offering this information, compliance of e-government activities in the various government agencies with DEG guidelines has increased substantially. By 2005, 81 percent of Dubai's public services had been offered online, with DEG reporting quarterly savings of at least 37m Dirhan ($10 million).

II

The Blurring of the Informational Boundary between State and Society

5

Weak Democracy, Strong Information: The Role of Information Technology in the Rulemaking Process

Cary Coglianese

Government regulation has a significant impact on society and the economy, affecting the operation of such vital institutions as banks, airlines, utilities, telecommunications systems, chemical plants, and transportation networks. In most developed countries, regulators make thousands of critical policy decisions each year that have major effects on economic growth, investment security, consumer prices, and public health and safety (Kerwin 2003). Given their ubiquity and significance, regulatory decisions require the most accurate information and best expert judgment obtainable. To regulate sensibly and without creating undue burdens on industry or undesirable side effects, decision makers need a thorough and accurate understanding of how regulated industries operate and what causes underlie regulatory problems (Coglianese, Zeckhauser, and Parson 2004). For this reason, legislatures often delegate regulatory policy decisions to specialized agencies that possess in-house expertise and a capacity to collect and analyze a large volume of information.

Although expert delegation helps solve the informational problem associated with making regulatory policy, it in turn creates a problem with respect to democratic legitimacy. Regulatory decisions involve more than just complex technical challenges calling for specialized information and expertise; they frequently also entail critical value choices. For example, in setting air pollution control standards, regulators must certainly understand how different chemicals affect human health as well as the costs associated with various types of pollution-control technology. But they must also decide how much risk from air pollution society should bear (Coglianese and Marchant 2004). Similar value choices are embedded in many other areas of regulation. In establishing standards for drug safety and approving new drugs, for example, regulators must often make a trade-off between maximizing the safety of new drugs and the speed with which they can be brought to market. No amount of technical expertise endows unelected regulatory officials with special insight into how to make these kinds of value judgments (Dahl 1989).

Scholars and other observers have long questioned the democratic legitimacy of policymaking by bureaucratic officials. Traditionally, this question has been answered through the establishment of procedures to govern how agencies make new regulations. By providing a modicum of transparency and an opportunity for public comment, rulemaking procedures can materially affect the quality and effectiveness of regulatory decision making—and ultimately its legitimacy. These procedures determine the degree to which those with a stake in the outcome can affect the content of new regulations.

More recently, some scholars and policymakers have suggested another answer to the legitimacy question, one rooted in modern information technology. Indeed, they have proclaimed that information technology will transform or even "revolutionize" rulemaking from its current state of relative obscurity to one in which government is completely transparent and ordinary citizens participate regularly (Brandon and Carlitz 2002; Johnson 1998; Noveck 2004). Several so-called e-rulemaking projects in the United States specifically aim to tap into the purported transformational potential of the Internet, recognizing the "critically important role citizens play in the rulemaking process" and with the aim of "improving the public's ability to find, view, understand, and comment on regulatory actions" (Nelson 2004).

It is indisputable that information technology can make it easier and cheaper to connect governmental regulators with those whom they regulate and with ordinary citizens. Yet despite the technological optimism of many proponents of participatory democracy—or "strong democracy," as it is sometimes called (Barber 1984)—nothing in the federal government's current e-rulemaking agenda is likely to deliver more than marginal changes in the degree to which citizens will participate in rulemaking. In this chapter, I explain why current e-rulemaking efforts cannot be reasonably he expected to meet the aspirations of strong democracy's adherents to replace bureaucratic decision making with citizen deliberation (Barber 1984, 262).

E-rulemaking can advance, however, another form of democratic legitimacy, one that emphasizes the pluralistic involvement of those most directly affected by and knowledgeable about new government regulations. Legitimacy in this sense depends upon minimizing the potential biases that arise in closed policymaking environments while maximizing the amount of detailed information and the quality of adversarial arguments essential to improve policy decision making (Dahl 1961). In lieu of "strong democracy," information technology can thus promote a form of "weak democracy" that provides a "strong" base of information for regulators. Information technology can facilitate the kind of input and oversight necessary to check the potential errors that can arise from biased or insulated expert decision making.

This chapter begins with an overview of the governmental rulemaking process and current efforts to apply information technology to that process. I then turn specifically to concerns about the democratic legitimacy of rulemaking and explain the procedural strategies for addressing these concerns, including the reasons behind many observers' optimism regarding information technology's potential to promote strong democracy. Next, I offer the contrary view that information technology, especially as currently deployed, will not significantly advance the goal of strong democracy in rulemaking. Finally, I conclude by suggesting that the incapacity of e-rulemaking to advance strong democracy ought not to undercut innovative efforts to apply information technology to rulemaking. E-rulemaking initiatives should proceed insofar as they are targeted to advance the combination of weak democracy and strong information that can pragmatically enhance regulatory decision making.

Rulemaking and E-Rulemaking

To correct market failures and advance other values expressed in legislation, regulatory agencies in the United States, such as the Food and Drug Administration (FDA), the Department of Transportation (DOT), the Environmental Protection Agency (EPA), and the Equal Employment Opportunity Commission (EEOC), adopt thousands of rules each year. The Office of Management and Budget (OMB) estimates that U.S. health, safety, and environmental regulations yield up to $1 trillion in benefits to society each year (OMB 2001), while these same federal regulations impose annual costs to the economy of up to $230 billion. Other federal regulations, such as those in the areas of transportation, energy, telecommunications and international trade, may impose additional costs of up to $230 billion per year (OMB 2001).

When governmental agencies issue new regulations, they typically do so through a procedure called "notice and comment" or "informal" rulemaking. As outlined in the Administrative Procedure Act (APA), informal rulemaking calls for a regulatory agency to (1) publish a notice of proposed rulemaking (NPRM) in the *Federal Register*, a daily governmental publication that contains regulatory notices and other announcements from the executive branch; (2) specify a time period for public comment on the proposed rule and provide an address where public comments may

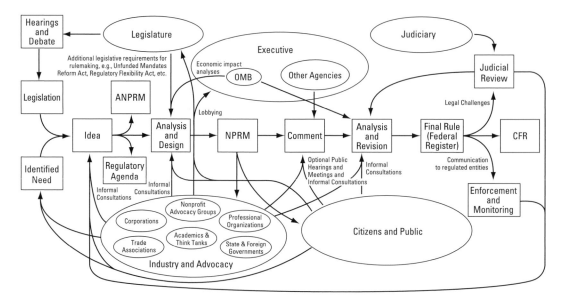

Figure 5.1
The rulemaking process.

be sent; and (3) consider these public comments in making any revisions to the proposed rule and when publishing the final rule in the *Federal Register*. In the main body of the *Federal Register* announcement—a section referred to as the *preamble*—the agency provides a written justification for the rule in its final form.

Although these three steps constitute the core of the rulemaking process, in reality regulatory agencies go through a much more involved and multilayered process. Figure 5.1 maps that process, illustrating the procedural complexity that has grown up around so-called informal rulemaking. In the first instance, this greater complexity is a function of the fact that the APA procedures cover only one segment of the rulemaking chronology. Much, if not most, of the work of a regulatory agency actually takes place prior to the development of the NPRM. As they develop their proposals, regulators frequently consult with industry representatives, other interested parties, and executive branch or legislative staff (Coglianese, Zeckhauser, and Parson 2004). Sometimes agencies issue an advance notice of proposed rulemaking (ANPRM) prior to the NPRM, providing detailed information about a forthcoming rule and encouraging those affected to provide early comments that can inform the development of the proposed rule.

Furthermore, the rulemaking process does not necessarily end with the publication of the final rule in the *Federal Register*. The government later publishes the rule's binding text in the *Code of Federal Regulations*, the official publication that organizes regulations by subject matter. Once the head of an agency has signed the final rule, objecting parties can file legal petitions forcing the agency to defend its decision in court. According to the APA, courts can reject agency rules if they conflict with statutory authority, violate the U.S. Constitution, suffer from procedural flaws, or are otherwise "arbitrary and capricious." To settle a lawsuit or respond to an adverse court ruling, agencies sometimes need to revise their rules even after they are published in the *Federal Register*.

In addition, both the president and the Congress have imposed requirements on the rulemaking process that extend beyond those stated in the APA. Some of these procedural requirements apply to only the most economically significant new rules. For example, since 1981 the White House has required agencies to conduct economic impact analyses of "major" or "significant" new regulations, which analyses are then subject to review by the OMB (Lazer 2001). Congress has effectively codified these presidential requirements in the Unfunded Mandates Reform Act of 1995, which independently requires agencies to analyze the costs and benefits of any proposed regulation entailing annual economic costs of more than $100 million. As a result of these requirements, the OMB's Office of Information and Regulatory Affairs now plays a key role in reviewing, and sometimes requesting revisions of, significant proposed and final rules.

Other rulemaking procedures govern the availability and disclosure of government-held information. For example, the Freedom of Information Act requires that, with some exceptions, all information supporting an agency's rulemaking be made publicly available. In addition, court decisions and statutory provisions have led agencies to develop "dockets" for each rulemaking proceeding. These dockets contain all the supporting documents associated with each rulemaking, including copies of all the public comments submitted on the rule as well as summaries of communications between agency staff and anyone from outside of government (so-called ex parte communications). For a long time, agency dockets have consisted of large rooms full of file cabinets, sometimes with documents later archived on microfiche.

As one might imagine, information collection and management makes up most of the administrative effort associated with rulemaking, as regulatory agencies collect, process, and analyze large volumes of information in order to complete a single rulemaking (Coglianese 2004). To address the information management challenges inherent in rulemaking while gathering ever more information, agencies have started to employ digital technologies in the rulemaking process. In the early 1990s, the Clinton administration began encouraging federal agencies to increase their use of information technology. Around the same time, the Office of the Federal Register made the *Federal Register* and the *Code of Federal Regulations* available on the Internet, while Congress adopted legislation that aimed to increase the online availability of regulatory agency information.

Regulatory agencies now apply information technology in a variety of ways, including using the Internet to enhance transparency and facilitate public participation in rulemaking. Agencies post key studies and other rulemaking documents on their websites. Some agencies allow the public to submit comments via e-mail. Early on, electronically submitted comments played a role, for example, in the Federal Aviation Administration's rulemaking on small-scale rockets and the Department of Agriculture's rulemaking on the labeling of organic foods. Other early adopters of electronic commenting included the Nuclear Regulatory Commission and the Federal Communications Commission (FCC). A few agencies have used information technology to analyze public comments submitted on proposed rules.

In 1998, the DOT became the first regulatory agency to make available an online, department-wide regulatory docket (dms.dot.gov), providing full electronic access to all studies, comments, and other documents contained in the agency's rulemaking records. The DOT system also allows the public to submit electronic comments on all rules proposed by the department. A few years later, the EPA also adopted an agency-wide system called EDOCKET. Several other agencies have subsequently begun implementing similar docket management systems.

In a major effort to expand information technology capabilities across the federal government, the George W. Bush administration launched an e-government initiative as part of its President's Management Agenda. The administration's e-government initiative, coordinated through the OMB, consists of approximately two dozen projects, one of which is e-rulemaking. The eRulemaking Initiative, spearheaded by the EPA, has been designed to deploy in three stages.

The first stage, completed in January 2003, involved the creation of a search-and-comment portal located at www.regulations.gov. The Regulations.Gov portal relies on the Office of Federal Register's listings of notices of proposed rules and enables users to search all proposed rules that are open for public comment. It enables members of the public to comment on any proposed rule issued by any governmental agency from a single location on the Internet. Comments submitted electronically at Regulations.Gov are then automatically distributed to the appropriate agencies.

The second stage of the Bush administration's e-rulemaking project, currently in progress, further expands public access by creating a new government-wide docket management system, the Federal Docket Management System (FDMS). At present, more than a dozen agencies are connected, and eventually FDMS is supposed to make available to any interested party all documents related to every new regulation across the government.

The third stage, still under development, will install on the desktops of regulatory agency staff a standard suite of knowledge management tools. These tools will be specifically designed to assist with data collection, analysis, decision making, and rule writing.

Even after the Bush administration leaves office, e-rulemaking will likely continue. The passage of the E-Government Act of 2002 promotes the use of information technologies throughout government, and in particular directs regulatory agencies to accept electronically submitted comments and to establish comprehensive electronic dockets for all rulemakings. The act also creates a new Office of Electronic Government within OMB, requires that this office produce guidelines for all agency websites, and generally calls upon agencies to adopt innovative uses of information technologies.

The entrenchment of e-rulemaking in administrative systems does, though, raise the question of what difference information technology will make in the quality of public policy decision making and in the democratic legitimacy of regulatory policymaking. Specifically, will e-rulemaking enable the regulatory process to involve many more ordinary citizens in meaningful deliberation over regulatory policy? Researchers and policymakers have begun to consider whether information technology can help fulfill the aspirations of democratic theory.

Rulemaking and the Problem of Democratic Legitimacy

For much of the last century, if not longer, scholars have wrestled with the democratic legitimacy of agency decision making (Coglianese 2001). Agency-issued rules have a major impact on society and constitute binding law, legally on par with statutes passed by Congress, yet these rules are issued by agency officials who are neither elected by the public nor otherwise directly accountable to them (Freedman 1978; Lowi 1969). The powers exercised by regulatory agencies are delegated powers, given over to bureaucrats by laws adopted by the more directly accountable branches of government. Furthermore, even though the heads of these agencies are political appointees, these appointees often in turn delegate to career civil servants the responsibility for, and discretion over, the drafting, analysis, the design of policy and regulations.

Delegation of rulemaking authority thus significantly stretches the chain of governmental accountability. Rather than a government of and by the people, regulatory decision making moves the country in the direction of a government of and by unelected bureaucrats. For this reason, some scholars oppose any delegation of policymaking authority to regulatory agencies. Schoenbrod (1993), for example, argues that rulemaking authority should remain vested completely in the democratically elected legislature. Despite the theoretical appeal of such a strict approach, eliminating delegation to agencies would be impracticable, placing an onerous burden of policy decision making on the legislative agenda, and taxing Congress beyond the limits of its institutional capacities (Meidinger 1992). Furthermore, the likely response of any legislature to such a burden would be to delegate internally to committees and subcommittees, which would then need substantially larger staffs and would no doubt assume even more power than they already have (Krehbiel 1991; Stewart 1987), in effect simply relocating and replicating the problem of delegation to nonelected actors situated inside the legislature.

Recognizing the pragmatic necessity for at least some delegation to bureaucrats, others have suggested that democratic legitimacy be enhanced by tightening the connections between regulatory agencies and the electorally accountable branches of government. These connections could be effectuated through institutional *control* or institutional *oversight*. In the first instance, the legislature would *control* regulatory agencies' authority by providing more specific instructions through statutes (Lowi 1969). Rather than delegating broad discretion to agencies to regulate in virtually any manner (e.g., "protect the public from the harm of automobile accidents"), statutes creating regulatory authority can specify more concretely what the legislature expects the agency to do (e.g., "adopt standards for air bag devices that will protect occupants in head-on collisions at or above 30 miles per hour"). Of course, maximally specific legislation would essentially eliminate all agency discretion, which would have the same effect as bypassing delegation altogether, with the attendant untenable burden on Congress. Short of backing into that extreme position, enhancing institutional control by specific legislation only serves to constrain an agency's policymaking discretion, not to eliminate it, and hence does not solve entirely the underlying problem of democratic legitimacy.

A second way to build closer connections between regulatory agencies and the electorally accountable branches of government is through institutional *oversight* (McCubbins and Schwartz 1984). Legislators hold hearings at which they summon the leaders of regulatory agencies to produce information and answer questions. Legislators can also always exploit the appropriations process to influence agencies' discretionary decisions. In addition, U.S. regulatory agencies must submit to Congress copies of the most significant rules they adopt, and Congress may vote to disapprove these rules and send them back to the relevant agencies. In addition, the establishment of a regulatory review process in the OMB helps ensure that regulatory agencies are more closely tied to the electorally accountable executive branch of government (Kagan 2001; Lazer 2001).

By enhancing both institutional oversight and control in these ways, it is possible to strengthen the connections between regulatory agencies and their democratically elected principals (Epstein and O'Halloran 1999). However, these strategies advance democratic ties to the public only indirectly. As shown in figure 5.2, the

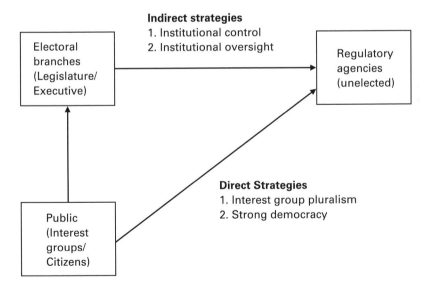

Figure 5.2
Strategies for legitimizing rulemaking.

linkage between the public to a given regulatory agency is only indirect, since the public elects the legislature or president and then the legislature or president in turn seeks to influence the policy decisions of the agency.

An alternative, but complementary, strategy of legitimization would open the rulemaking process to direct public involvement. As indicated in figure 5.2, two strategies for such involvement exist: (1) interest group pluralism and (2) strong democracy. The first of these, *interest group pluralism*, seeks to involve directly a subset of the general public consisting of organized groups and experts with a high level of interest in and knowledge about a particular rulemaking. In one of the most widely influential articles in administrative law, Richard Stewart (1975) argued that interest group pluralism explains a variety of procedural features of U.S. rulemaking. The notice and comment process, the imposition of open meeting requirements, and freedom of information laws mandating the disclosure of governmental actions to affected parties are all examples of interest group pluralism in operation. This notion of democratic involvement also lies behind a variety of judicial reforms, such as the expansion of standing, which have allowed groups organized around regulatory benefits to seek redress in the courts.

Although interest group pluralism provides opportunities for direct participation in the rulemaking process, and therefore overcomes certain limitations inherent in the indirect strategies of institutional control and oversight, democratic purists still find it wanting. At the root of the problem, in their view, is the fact that although everyone has an equal opportunity to participate, equal opportunity does not translate into equal participation by or equal representation of all those affected by regulatory policy. In practice, most of the participants in rulemaking proceedings are businesses and industry trade associations. For this reason, critics charge that pluralism effectively privileges a select and biased set of interest groups, namely those that possess the resources necessary to organize and participate in policy-making (Schattschneider 1960).

Pluralism's critics often put forth *strong democracy* as a more robust means to ensure the legitimacy of regulatory policymaking. Strong democracy empowers not just organized interest groups in regulatory decisions, but also the ordinary citizens who will be affected by those decisions. The involvement of citizens in the policy-making process counteracts the biases inevitably expressed through the pluralistic universe of interest groups. Moreover, proponents of strong democracy maintain that citizen involvement is vital to the health of democracy itself because it is through direct participation and deliberation that citizens come to a better understanding of not just their own individual interests but the collective welfare of their society.

In short, strong democracy promotes civic virtue. By engaging citizens directly in dialogue over both the proper ends and means of government, strong democracy encourages "the active consent of participating citizens who have imaginatively reconstructed their own values as public norms through the process of identifying and empathizing with the values of others" (Barber 1984, 137). Strong democracy is, as Barber (1984) has written, "the politics of amateurs, where every man is compelled to encounter every other man without the intermediary of expertise" (152). According to this view, only by involving citizens directly in deliberation over their own collective fate will regulatory policy decisions gain genuine democratic legitimacy.

Advances in information and communications technology appear to hold great promise for enhancing citizen deliberation and ultimately the legitimacy of rulemaking. After all, businesses and other organized interest groups, as well as the political branches of government to whom agencies are indirectly accountable, already participate extensively in the rulemaking process, and have done so in the absence of new information technology. Ordinary citizens have been largely absent from the rulemaking process. According to one study from the 1990s, less than 6 percent of the comments filed in EPA rulemakings were submitted by individual citizens (Coglianese 1996). It is precisely these citizens who strong democrats believe can be reached and recruited by new information and communication technologies. Barber (1984) has written that "the interactive possibilities of video, computers, and information retrieval systems open up a new mode of human communications that...can be used to strengthen civic education...and tie individuals and institutions into networks that will make real participatory discussion and debate possible across great distances" (274).

Such enthusiasm, or "techno-optimism," regarding the potential for the Internet and other information technologies to broaden citizen participation is widespread among both democratic theorists and e-government scholars who, as Stanley and Weare (2004) explain, "tout the ability of technology to make government more efficient and responsive and to strengthen citizen participation by making political information more compelling, lowering the costs of participation, and creating new opportunities for involvement" (504). Shane (2005) argues that the federal government's e-rulemaking initiative "seems to hold out the potential to enlarge significantly a genuine public sphere in which individual citizens participate directly to help make government decisions that are binding on the entire polity" (148). It is clear that, for many observers, e-rulemaking affords a most promising means for achieving the aspirations of strong democracy (Johnson 1998; Schlosberg, Zavestocki, and Shulman 2005).

Will E-Rulemaking Lead to Strong Democracy?

The participatory allure of e-rulemaking has been heightened by a number of instances in which a relatively large number of individual citizens have used the Internet to submit comments on proposed regulations (Cuéllar 2005). For example, a U.S. Department of Agriculture rulemaking on organic foods garnered more than a quarter of a million comments (Shulman 2003). Other recent rulemakings have elicited similarly large numbers of comments filed by members of the public, including an FCC rulemaking on the concentration of ownership of media outlets (de Figueiredo 2006), an EPA rulemaking on mercury emissions (Schlosberg, Zavestocki, and Shulman 2005), and the Forest Service's rulemaking proceedings to ban roads in wilderness areas (Borenstein 2005).

Do cases like these show that advances in information technology will strengthen rulemaking's legitimacy as envisioned by adherents of strong democracy? The sheer number of comments filed in rulemakings such as those cited earlier would certainly appear to provide support for the "revolutionary" potential of information technology to transform rulemaking from a largely invisible backwater of government to a process that involves a broad segment of the citizenry. Yet despite the large absolute number of comments filed in a few highly controversial rulemakings, it is far from clear that information technology will, as a general matter, transform rulemaking into anything close to the ideals of strong democracy.

For one thing, the rulemakings that do generate comments in the hundreds of thousands constitute only a minute fraction (even a fraction of a fraction) of the several thousands of rules issued each year. Most rulemakings continue to elicit little attention from the public (GAO 2003). A comprehensive study of five years' worth of comments filed with the FCC demonstrates that the volume of comments submitted on the media ownership rule was over twenty times the normal rate for other FCC rules (de Figueiredo 2006).

Furthermore, for the exceedingly rare rule that may generate a half million or even a million comments, this volume of participation would still represent less than 5 percent of the total voting-age population in the United States, a country of approximately 200 million adults and 150 million registered voters (Coglianese 2005). Participation by citizens in presidential elections—the most salient avenue for public participation in government—has declined steadily since the 1960s, with only slightly more than half of citizens of voting age participating in presidential elections (Patterson 2002). If general rates of voting in the United States are lower than those in other developed countries, we should certainly be surprised if the mere existence of information technology were to lead to a consequential increase in the rate of participation in rulemaking.

Information technology may well bring down the costs associated with accessing information and submitting comments to agencies, but many rules will continue to have significant consequences for citizens without eliciting much public attention. Other barriers to citizen participation will remain, perhaps most saliently, the specialized knowledge requisite to meaningful participation—not only familiarity with the organization and operation of government but with the technical issues underlying a given rulemaking. After all, if the issues underlying rulemaking were sufficiently technical or difficult as to lead Congress to delegate to an expert agency to begin with, then by definition these issues will be difficult for ordinary citizens to understand. Moreover, even with greater accessibility to rulemaking information via the Internet, most citizens are unlikely to have or to take the time to learn about the technical issues surrounding rulemaking.

Furthermore, a fairly high degree of sophistication is necessary for citizens merely to navigate the dockets of information that agencies have made available on the Internet. In fall 2004, I conducted a brief study to see how readily a group of motivated and sophisticated citizens could access information about a specific rulemaking. Twenty-two graduate students of government at Harvard University were asked to search for four specific rulemaking dockets at the DOT and the EPA websites. Subjects were given information about the four rulemakings and were asked to find a specific numbered document in the docket for each rulemaking. The study was designed to simulate the experience of a typical user who, upon learning of a proposed rule through the media, would search online for more information about the rule from the agency's online docket. The object of the study was to measure the ease with which users can find information on the Internet, and to assess whether e-rulemaking will in fact "mak[e] it easier for citizens to participate in the regulatory process" (Daniels 2002).

Strikingly, even these sophisticated students, adept at using the Internet, had difficulty identifying the correct dockets within the time allotted. The overall average number of correct dockets identified by each subject was 1.9, or only half the target number. Only 26 percent of the subjects were able to correctly identify at least three of the four dockets. Overall, these results reveal that the theoretical *availability* to rulemaking information through online docket systems does not mean that citizens will actually be able to *retrieve* that information.

Why were these students—who were, after all, presumably better educated than the average citizen—not more successful, even when given a clear description of the rule and the precise name of the agency that proposed the rule? A debriefing session revealed a number of the challenges they had faced in information retrieval. First, they encountered difficulty distinguishing among multiple rules on the same subject. For example, one of the target EPA rules aimed at reducing mercury pollution, but as it turned out the EPA was simultaneously addressing mercury exposure through a number of other rules. Students who typed the word "mercury" in the search engine retrieved seventeen different dockets and faced great difficulty in identifying the specific rule they were looking for.

Second, sometimes multiple dockets address exactly the same rulemaking. It is not unusual for an agency to open a docket in connection with an early investigation of a subject of a potential new rulemaking, and then another one later when filing an NPRM. As it turned out, one of the DOT rules was associated with two dockets, even though only one was listed in the agency's NPRM filed in the *Federal Register*. Nor was there any clearly identifiable online link between these two dockets.

Finally, even when subjects were able to find websites with information about particular rulemakings, these sites provided no direct links to the corresponding rulemaking dockets. For example, to find the mercury emissions docket from the EPA's homepage, the user needed to click through four levels of the agency's website and open a protected document file containing the NPRM before locating the docket number from within the NPRM. At that point, the user needed to go back to the EPA's homepage to link to the agency's EDOCKET and then search for the docket number within the EDOCKET system. Needless to say, substantial time and motivation are necessary to navigate through these various levels and pathways.

Even with further improvements in the underlying technology, users who are not already sophisticated and knowledgeable about particular rulemakings will continue to face similar barriers to gathering information about rulemakings. To imagine that information technology by itself will foster the kind of sustained and consistent involvement by citizens in rulemaking that strong democracy adherents envision is a bit like imagining that giving automobile owners the ability to download technical manuals and order car parts online would turn a great number of them into do-it-yourself mechanics. A small subset of people, such as engineers and car buffs, would be better able to fix their own cars, but most of us would be none the wiser. For similar reasons, even with technologies more advanced than those the government is currently implementing, the accessibility of regulatory information on the Internet provides no guarantee that a significantly greater number of citizens will actually be able to process that information effectively.

Expectations about what e-rulemaking can achieve should be further tempered by a consideration of the nature and quality of the comments that are submitted electronically by ordinary citizens. While a few agencies have received tens of thousands of comments (or more) on a few especially salient rulemakings, the vast majority of these comments have been unsophisticated and either formulaic or completely devoid of information (Cuéllar 2005). Increasingly, electronic form letters are being sent to agencies not directly from citizens themselves, but indirectly via the websites of advocacy groups that feature buttons allowing visitors instantly to send messages to Washington. According to a recent study of rulemaking comments, "mass-mailed form comments originating from various environmental and other interest groups make up the vast majority of comments submitted on rules" (Schlosberg, Zavestocki and Shulman 2005, 25). That same study reported that out of 500,000 comments submitted on a recent controversial EPA rule, only about 4,000 were deemed by the agency to contain any original idea. For these reasons, more participation does not necessarily mean more *meaningful* participation. Some may even question whether clicking a button on an interest group website constitutes participation in rulemaking at all. Certainly this is not the kind of deliberative civic engagement envisioned by proponents of strong democracy.

On the other hand, even if such electronic form letters do not result in much citizen deliberation, perhaps they provide agencies with a much better indication of citizen preferences. Yet if that turns out to be the case, information technology would achieve something quite remote from strong democracy's ideal of developing collective public decision making, rather than just aggregating individual preferences (Barber 1984, 290). Moreover, even accepting preference aggregation as a worthwhile function of electronic commenting, the fraction of the public that files comments will probably never be representative of the public as a whole (the latter being the constituency whom the agency presumably seeks to serve). If regulatory agencies sought to capture the preferences of the overall public and incorporate them into their regulatory decisions, they could do so more effectively by commissioning public opinion surveys that asked questions of a random sample of citizens. A few hundred survey responses would be, if randomly generated, a more accurate and credible measure of the overall views of the public than tens or hundreds of thousands of self-initiated comments (Lee 2002).

In the end, information technology appears unlikely to bring regulatory policymaking into closer alignment with the principles of strong democracy (Dahl 1998, 106). Electronic efforts to improve the *accessibility* of rulemaking information cannot be counted on to generate dramatic increases either in the *usability* or the actual, meaningful *use* of this information by ordinary citizens. It appears that current e-rulemaking efforts will at best facilitate an increase in relatively superficial participation by a select, probably unrepresentative, portion of the public.

Technology and Regulatory Pluralism

The barriers to the achievement of strong democracy, especially in the context of technical rulemaking, appear much steeper than can be surmounted by new applications of information technologies. As long as most citizens have little more than the most rudimentary knowledge of how government works and of the technical issues underlying most rulemakings, e-rulemaking will not effectuate any but the most trivial change in ordinary citizens' engagement with regulatory policymaking. Even Barber (2003) has recently conceded that the prospects for using technology to promote strong democracy are "more ambivalent than early democratic enthusiasts had hoped" (xiv).

If information technology fails to engage a broad segment of the public in meaningful deliberation about regulatory policy issues, is e-rulemaking a waste of time and resources? Given the motivational and informational barriers that will continue to keep most citizens from participating in rulemaking, should efforts to introduce new technology into the rulemaking process be abandoned? These questions should be answered in the affirmative only if e-rulemaking's sole or main purpose is to advance strong democracy. Yet, despite the claims of some of its proponents, this is not the only basis on which e-rulemaking can be justified. A much more pragmatic goal of, and more realistic justification for, e-rulemaking is to expand and solidify the information base underlying regulatory decision making.

Earlier I pointed out that interest group pluralism has been viewed as a way to enhance the democratic legitimacy of rulemaking, even though its critics have correctly faulted its tendency to privilege certain interests over others in the policy process. Despite its deficiencies, pluralism retains what Shapiro (2005) refers to as pragmatic value. Specifically, it provides a way to generate better information and improve the quality of regulatory decision making, while serving as an antidote to insulated or secretive decision making by a few unelected regulatory officials.

Pluralism offers the beneficial effects that come from airing dissenting views (Seidenfeld 2001; Sunstein 2003). When multiple affected interests participate in a rulemaking, the regulator benefits from the competition in the marketplace of ideas created by pluralism, even when that competition falls short of being fully representative (Lazer 2001). Since agencies are required to supply reasons for their decisions and respond to significant comments submitted on proposed rules, they have an incentive to pay attention to the full range of views that emerge from pluralistic competition.

Regulators are undoubtedly better informed when they receive input from outside experts and interested parties. These outsiders bring distinct perspectives on regulatory problems based both on their differences in interests and differences in the scale or level at which they interact with a regulatory issue (Pike et al. 2005). The local sanitation engineer for the City of Milwaukee, for instance, will probably have useful insights about how new EPA drinking water standards should be implemented that might not be apparent to the American Water Works Association representatives in Washington, DC. E-rulemaking makes it more feasible for that local sanitation engineer, as well as other experts and affected interests across the country, to become aware of and submit comments on relevant regulations. An open and networked regulatory process can thus expand the potential information that comes to regulators' attention.

Hence, while the goals of strong democracy are unlikely to be advanced by the tool of e-rulemaking, it is reasonable to expect that the goals of pluralism can be so advanced. That is, information technology is not likely to "transform" or "revolutionize" rulemaking to allow ordinary citizens to deliberate in any meaningful way, but it can allow a *broader* set of well-organized and sophisticated actors to mobilize their resources, monitor government decision making, and share potentially valuable information and insights with decision makers.

For any given regulatory action, there may only be a relatively limited number of organizations and actors that are both affected by and significantly knowledgeable about the relevant issues. Until now, it has been hard to ensure that all of these organizations and actors have known about or been able to comment on all the rulemakings to which they could valuably contribute. Because it will lower the cost of participation to those individuals and organizations, e-rulemaking can increase the number of knowledgeable actors who participate in the rulemaking process, while also allowing each of them in turn to participate in a larger overall number of rulemakings because of the reduced costs of accessing and transmitting information.

For many smaller organizations, as well as individual engineers, economists, scientists, and other experts, the barriers to their participation have been precisely those that information technology is best equipped to break down, such as the need for physical proximity to Washington, DC, or the ability to hire messengers to retrieve documents from a docket housed at an agency's headquarters. These informed individuals and organizations possess the knowledge to understand and participate meaningfully in rulemaking, but in the past, when written comments on rules had to be delivered by hand or mailed to the agency docket offices, it was much more costly to contribute. Previously, even the *Federal Register* and the *Code of Federal Regulations* were accessible only at certain public or law libraries, making it much harder for experts around the country to keep abreast of regulatory developments.

E-rulemaking's contribution may be to recalibrate pluralism so that fewer organized interests and knowledgeable experts are excluded from the process simply because they did not know that a rulemaking was taking place or could not gather government information about a proposed rule in time to offer comments on it. In other words, even though information technology cannot eliminate the core barriers that stand in the way of broad citizen participation, technology may lower precisely the right kind of barriers to participation by experts, the logistical or physical ones. The remaining barriers—ones of knowledge and motivation—might not necessarily be so bad, at least from an informational perspective. Such barriers can serve as screens or filters providing a "quality control" function for regulatory decision makers. Those individuals who are able to clear the knowledge-based hurdles and then go on to submit original comments (as opposed to form letters) are more likely to make contributions that have informational value.

In evaluating the contributions of information technology to regulatory policymaking, then, observers should pay heed if efforts such as Regulations.Gov or online dockets result in even a relatively small increase in the number of truly helpful comments, or a slightly more diverse set of arguments from knowledgeable actors than would otherwise have been received. Such seemingly modest gains could very well represent a much more meaningful measure of the success of e-rulemaking than the generation of a million e-mail form letters submitted by ordinary citizens.

Conclusion

Although both scholars and public officials have characterized e-rulemaking's potential contribution to the democratic legitimacy of rulemaking in terms of fostering strong democracy, the reality is that even with the Internet significant barriers to ordinary citizens' engagement in rulemaking will remain. Most citizens are disengaged from politics and public policy to such a degree and for reasons that no amount of computer programs or technological innovations are likely to change. Rather than inspiring members of the public to participate in the arcane or technical discussions surrounding regulatory policymaking, modern information technology is and will continue to be more widely used by citizens for other purposes, such as communicating with friends and family or accessing entertainment.

Even among the relatively few citizens who might have an interest in regulatory policy, knowledge will remain a significant barrier to their meaningful participation. As illustrated by a study of graduate students using online dockets, the technical complexity of many rulemakings necessarily inhibits broad and meaningful citizen access to and participation in rulemaking. If highly educated graduate students cannot easily navigate today's online regulatory dockets, surely most ordinary citizens will face similar if not greater difficulties participating in rulemakings even with the advent of more advanced technologies.

While hopes for information technology transforming rulemaking into a strongly democratic process may be unrealistic, this does not mean that e-rulemaking is unimportant or misguided. Rather, it means strong democracy is the wrong goal for e-rulemaking. Given the complexity of rulemaking, its democratic legitimacy will probably always be "weak," in the sense that such legitimacy will continue to depend mainly on indirect institutional ties with elected branches of government and on direct involvement by organized interests rather than by ordinary citizens. Nevertheless, even if it is only possible to achieve "weak democracy" in the rulemaking process, information technology can be useful in promoting "strong information." E-rulemaking holds much greater promise for expanding the pluralist process so that a larger group of experts and interested organizations can help inform regulatory decision-makers. If e-rulemaking accomplishes this goal, its impact will be more incremental than revolutionary, but over time it will enable government to make better regulatory decisions.

Note

The author gratefully acknowledges helpful comments on this chapter by David Lazer, Viktor Mayer-Schönberger, Rick Otis, and Joanna L. Rutter. My work on e-rulemaking has been supported by the National Science Foundation (NSF) under award number EIA-0226053 and portions of the first part of this chapter draw on a report to the NSF under that grant.

References

Barber, Benjamin R. 1984. *Strong Democracy: Participatory Politics for a New Age*. Berkeley: University of California Press.

Barber, Benjamin R. 2003. *Strong Democracy: Participatory Politics for a New Age*. Berkeley: University of California Press.

Borenstein, Seth. 2005. "Bush Officials Lift Development Ban on Millions of Acres." *Philadelphia Inquirer*, May 6, A15.

Brandon, Barbara H., and Robert D. Carlitz. 2002. "Online Rulemaking and Other Tools for Strengthening Our Civic Infrastructure." *Administrative Law Review* 54: 1421–1478.

Coglianese, Cary. 1996. "Litigating within Relationships: Disputes and Disturbance in the Regulatory Process." *Law & Society Review* 30: 735–765.

Coglianese, Cary. 2001. "Administrative Law." In *International Encyclopedia of Social and Behavioral Sciences*, vol. 1, ed. Paul B. Baltes and Neil J. Smelser, 85–88. Amsterdam: Elsevier.

Coglianese, Cary. 2004. "E-Rulemaking: Information Technology and the Regulatory Process." *Administrative Law Review* 56: 353–402.

Coglianese, Cary. 2005. "The Internet and Citizen Participation in Rulemaking." *I/S: Journal of Law and Policy for the Information Society* 1: 33–57.

Coglianese, Cary, and Gary Marchant. 2004. "Shifting Sands: The Limits of Science in Setting Risk Standards." *University of Pennsylvania Law Review* 152: 1255–1360.

Coglianese, Cary, Richard Zeckhauser, and Edward Parson. 2004. "Seeking Truth for Power: Informational Strategy and Regulatory Policy Making." *Minnesota Law Review* 89: 277–341.

Cuéllar, Mariano-Florentino. 2005. "Rethinking Regulatory Democracy." *Administrative Law Review* 57: 411–500.

Dahl, Robert A. 1961. *Who Governs? Democracy and Power in an American City*. New Haven, CT: Yale University Press.

Dahl, Robert A. 1989. *Democracy and Its Critics*. New Haven, CT: Yale University Press.

Dahl, Robert A. 1998. *On Democracy*. New Haven, CT: Yale University Press.

Daniels, Mitchell E. 2002. Memorandum on Redundant Information Systems Relating to Online Rulemaking Initiative, May 3. Available at http://www.ksg.harvard.edu/cbg/Conferences/rpp_rulemaking/OMB_Opens_Reg_Process.pdf.

de Figueiredo, John M. 2006. "E-Rulemaking: Bringing Data to Theory." *Duke Law Journal* 55: 969–994.

Epstein, David, and Sharyn O'Halloran. 1999. *Delegating Powers: A Transaction Cost Politics Approach to Policy Making under Separate Powers*. Cambridge: Cambridge University Press.

Freedman, James O. 1978. *Crisis and Legitimacy: The Administrative Process and American Government*. Cambridge: Cambridge University Press.

General Accounting Office (GAO). 2003. "Electronic Rulemaking: Efforts to Facilitate Public Participation Can Be Improved." GAO-03-901, September 17.

Johnson, Stephen. 1998. "The Internet Changes Everything: Revolutionizing Public Participation and Access to Government Information through the Internet." *Administrative Law Review* 50: 277–338.

Kagan, Elena. 2001. "Presidential Administration." *Harvard Law Review* 114: 2245–2385.

Kerwin, Cornelius. 2003. *Rulemaking: How Government Agencies Write Law and Make Policy*, 3d ed. Washington, DC: CQ Press.

Krehbiel, Keith. 1991. *Information and Legislative Organization*. Ann Arbor: University of Michigan Press.

Lazer, David. 2001. "Regulatory Review: Presidential Control through Selective Communication and Institutionalized Conflict." Regulatory Policy Program Working Paper No. RPP-2001-03.

Lee, Taeku. 2002. *Mobilizing Public Opinion: Black Insurgency and Racial Attitudes in the Civil Rights Era*. Chicago: University of Chicago Press.

Lowi, Theodore J. 1969. *The End of Liberalism: Ideology, Policy, and the Crisis of Public Authority*. New York: Norton.

McCubbins, Matthew, and Schwartz, Thomas. 1984. "Congressional Oversight Overlooked: Police Patrols versus Fire Alarms." *American Journal of Political Science* 28: 165–179.

Meidinger, Errol. 1992. "Administrative Regulation and Democracy." Baldy Center for Law and Social Policy Working Paper No. OP92.01.

Nelson, Kimberly. 2004. EPA Chief Information Officer Statement before the House Committee on Government Reform, March 24.

Noveck, Beth. 2004. "The Electronic Revolution in Rulemaking." *Emory Law Journal* 53: 433–522.

Office of Management and Budget (OMB). 2001. "Making Sense of Regulation: 2001 Report to Congress on the Costs and Benefits of Regulations and Unfunded Mandates on State, Local and Tribal Entities." Available at http://www.whitehouse.gov/omb/inforeg/costbenefitreport.pdf.

Patterson, Thomas E. 2002. *The Vanishing Voter: Public Involvement in an Age of Uncertainty*. New York: Alfred A. Knopf.

Pike, William, Brent Yarnal, Alan M. MacEachren, Mark Gahegan, and Chaoqing Yu. 2005. "Retooling Collaboration: A Vision for Environmental Change Research." *Environment* 47, no. 2: 8–21.

Schattschneider, E. E. 1960. *The Semi-Sovereign People*. New York, Holt, Rinehart and Winston.

Schlosberg, David, Stephen Zavestocki, and Stuart Shulman. 2005. "'To Submit a Form or Not to Submit a Form, That is the (Real) Question': Deliberation and Mass Participation in U.S. Regulatory Rulemaking." Paper presented at the annual meeting of the Western Political Science Association, Oakland, CA, March 17–18.

Schoenbrod, David. 1993. *Power Without Responsibility: How Congress Abuses the People Through Delegation*. New Haven, CT: Yale University Press.

Seidenfeld, Mark. 2001. "The Psychology of Accountability and Political Review of Agency Rules." *Duke Law Journal* 51: 1059–1096.

Shane, Peter M. 2005. "Turning GOLD into EPG: Lessons from Low-Tech Democratic Experimentalism for Electronic Rulemaking and Other Ventures in Cyberdemocracy." *I/S: Journal of Law and Policy for the Information Society* 1: 147–170.

Shapiro, Sidney. 2005. "Pragmatic Administrative Law." *Issues in Legal Scholarship*. Available at http://www.bepress.com/cgi/viewcontent.cgi?article=1057&context=ils.

Shulman, Stuart W. 2003. "An Experiment in Digital Government at the United States National Organics Program." *Agriculture and Human Values* 20: 253–265.

Stanley, J. Woody, and Christopher Weare. 2004. "The Effects of Internet Use on Political Participation: Evidence from an Agency Online Discussion Forum." *Administration and Society* 36: 503–527.

Stewart, Richard B. 1975. "The Reformation of American Administrative Law." *Harvard Law Review* 88: 1667–1813.

Stewart, Richard B. 1987. "Beyond Delegation Doctrine." *American University Law Review* 36: 323–344.

Sunstein, Cass R. 2003. *Why Societies Need Dissent*. Cambridge, MA: Harvard University Press.

Case Illustration

The EPA EDOCKET System

Gopal Raman

The U.S. Environmental Protection Agency (EPA) launched its electronic public docket and online comment system, also known as EDOCKET, in May 2002. The system provided access to the EPA's dockets and allowed the public to search and comment on the EPA's programs and proposed rules electronically.

The idea for an electronic docket was initiated in 1996 after a survey of the EPA's docket users revealed that customers wanted electronic access to docket materials and the ability to search across all EPA docket information. In 1998, the Department of Transportation (DOT) became the first federal agency to allow users to have online access to its docket management system, which served as a model for the EPA's own EDOCKET system launched four years later.

The EDOCKET system allowed users to search the EPA's major public dockets online, view the index listing of the contents for dockets included in the system, and download and print those materials that are available online. The system also allowed users to comment online when a particular docket is open for public comments and to view comments left by others for that docket. The key idea was to streamline the EPA's rulemaking process by simplifying disbursement of information and collection of public comments for use by the EPA's regulatory officials.

The EDOCKET system proved to be extremely popular and averaged over 500,000 hits per month. In 2003, the EPA's EDOCKET system won the E-government Trailblazer Award and was widely recognized as the government-wide model for e-rulemaking. The EPA also estimated cost savings of about $400,000 per annum by diverting traffic to its online EDOCKET system.

In October 2002, the EPA was appointed the managing partner to oversee the eRulemaking Initiative under the President's Management Agenda and was tasked with expanding the EDOCKET solution into an integrated federal rulemaking and docket management system. As part of bringing all federal entities with rulemaking responsibilities to the Federal Document Management System (FDMS) at http://www.regulations.gov by the end of 2006, the EPA's EDOCKET System migrated to FDMS on November 25, 2005.

6

Freedom of Information and Electronic Government

Herbert Burkert

Knowledge is participation.
—Robert B. Parker, *Bad Business*

In eighteenth-century Sweden, freedom of information legislation was installed to make freedom of the press principles meaningful in a changing political environment. I show in this chapter how today freedom of information legislation is necessary to overcome the limitations of electronic government concepts that focus too narrowly on the efficiency of administrative transactions. An integral element of an information government perspective, freedom of information is a critical mechanism to keep democratic participation meaningful in a citizen-centered information government. It has to be recognized, however, that e-government approaches so limited by e-commerce and e-consumer philosophy are themselves expressions of a broader change that also affects our thinking on freedom of information. The dialectical nature of these changes not only will open opportunities for reconceptualizing electronic government through the lens of information government, but also may lead to a new and broader understanding of freedom of information itself.

The Development of Freedom of Information

Electronic government represents but another attempt to reorganize information flows between citizens and governments in view of technological changes. These reorganization processes have to acknowledge the normative environment in which these information flows occur. Two types of legislation have marked the era of information-related law in the second half of the last century: freedom of information legislation (also called access to government information legislation), which provides a right of access to administrative documents (with exceptions) without the need to show special interest or standing, and privacy legislation (also called data protection legislation), which protects personal information—again with exceptions for overriding public and private interests. Privacy legislation is usually perceived as an information technology–related response—although its underlying concepts are older than electronic information processing. Freedom of information legislation, on the other hand, as the historically older type of information legislation, has been associated with the development of democratic principles.

A closer look at the history of freedom of information law, and particularly its historical beginnings in Sweden, however, reveals a strong linkage to progress in information technology as well. The first Swedish freedom of information law of 1766 was an element of the first freedom of the press law of that time. Freedom of the press had become a political issue in eighteenth-century Sweden when the parliamentary faction, then newly voted into power after thirty years of opposition, realized the potential of the printing press to promote its political cause. While until then even parliamentary procedures—and thus the mere record of activities in Parliament—had been kept secret, through access for and freedom of the press, they could now promote their political ideas on change. Access and the freedom of the press principles became the instrument to demonstrate that the new faction in power really meant change, and that its implementation of change could be monitored through the press. This motivation for freedom of information laws would reappear in other countries when they set out to follow the Swedish example.[1]

Reference to the Swedish experience and the magic year of 1766 has become commonplace in international democracy reform debates, although in the nineteenth and the first half of the twentieth century the history of the Swedish access principle with its ever-increasing secrecy exemptions was far from glorious (as discussed later). Still, the reference to history served its purpose in the international promulgation of the access idea. Whenever and wherever the access idea resurfaced, it could use this history as legitimation, where the "ancient practices" of the eighteenth century shielded it against arguments that such notions were too progressive.

The freedom of information principle could do both, proclaiming modernizing change—by enabling access to government records where there was no access before—and demanding the conservative preservation of good practice—arguing that this was not a break with the past, but the continuation of a long tradition. The long-term success of this double strategy is shown in a 2004 survey by David Banisar (2004), which counts more than fifty countries that have implemented freedom of information legislation of some sort.

Sweden, too, started the modern age of access legislation by debating what modern information technology in administrations would mean for the access principle. As with privacy protection, legislation information technology was at first perceived as a threat to the notion of access.[2] Access rights had focused on the administrative document, but with the new technology the concept of a document would become volatile—a temporary assortment of data put together at the will of a software program (see, e.g., Seipel 1981, 18). Explicit changes in the legislation as well as adaptive interpretation by the courts were necessary to eventually ensure that electronic documents, too, were covered by freedom of information laws. Canada's Federal Access to Information Act of 1985 went a step further and made it clear that a requester could ask the administration to generate a document that had not existed before in that form:

> For the purposes of this Act, any record requested under this Act that does not exist but can, subject to such limitations as may be prescribed by regulation, be produced from a machine readable record under the control of a government institution using computer hardware and software and technical expertise normally used by the government institution shall be deemed to be a record under the control of the government institution.[3]

Almost twenty years later, the widespread use of the Internet again brought about new opportunities. Even before the Internet, many access to information regulations (oftentimes also called freedom of information laws) had already included active information duties for public administrations. In order to facilitate access requests by citizens, agencies had to publish descriptions of their internal structure and purposes of operation as well as inventories of their information holdings. The Internet provided an ideal platform for further information exchanges, given network and information economics. Now, in addition to processing requests on a case-by-case basis as already required by law, government agencies could now make available online the most frequently requested documents, thus radically reducing processing costs for the most common requests. In addition, the Internet has the charming quality that users bear the charges for searching, downloading, printing, and eventually storage costs, and in most cases still feel better served than before because they see themselves as autonomous and empowered and think they receive information much faster than before. In order to ensure the accrual of these efficiency benefits to administrations from these developments, implementation was not left to benevolent heads of administrations, but instead was quickly mandated through administrative law.[4]

In order to not lose legitimacy, e-government initiatives have to offer transparency at least on the level of what freedom of information legislation guarantees for paper environments. In countries lacking paper-based freedom of information legislation, electronic government activities will push freedom of information higher on the agenda because of the obviously greatly reduced burden on the government in providing citizens access in a technically more sophisticated environment.

Any such change toward greater transparency has to be secured by law, for at least three reasons. First, the benevolent government administrator needs to be able to point to legislation to reduce individual risks of benevolence. Reference to law transfers this responsibility to the legislature. To shift responsibility back to the bureaucracy requires bringing a case before the courts, alleging individual misinterpretation or excess of discretion in applying the law. Courts rarely question bureaucratic (mis)interpretation, and even when they do, they rarely find a specific individual responsible. Instead they usually invoke collective bureaucratic responsibility for creating and maintaining an environment, in which such acts of misinterpretation are possible. Hence, reference to access legislation disencumbers individual decisions on transparency by collectivizing responsibility.

Second, administrations demanding resources have to be able to point to legislation they have to administer; access laws put them in a better budgetary bargaining position.

Third, citizens (as well as the private sector submitting information that might eventually be passed on to third parties on the basis of such legislation) can develop secured expectations on information handling by public authorities, and, if they fail, may seek redress from the courts.

However, the sheer existence of freedom of information legislation does not ensure adequate integration of its normative requirements into e-government activities, if the essential conflict between current service-oriented electronic government models and freedom of information regulations is not clarified and addressed properly.

The Essential Conflict between Freedom Information and Current E-Government Concepts

According to a typical definition of electronic government, electronic government is meant to ensure "better delivery of government services to citizens, improved interactions with business and industry, citizen empowerment through access to information, or more efficient government management ... less corruption, increased transparency, greater convenience, revenue growth, and/or cost reductions."[5]

Quite obviously, this definition acknowledges the state of the art in freedom of information legislation and emphasizes transparency as an element of citizens' empowerment. The underlying general message, however, is efficiency. This must come as no surprise. In conceptualizing e-government, public administrations have borrowed language, visions, and concepts from e-commerce and e-business designs. In e-business/e-consumer models, however, information does not flow for transparency's sake; it flows for a purpose: the commercial transaction between consumer and seller. E-government concepts that have internalized this orientation will similarly focus on the facilitation of transactions in order to realize the added value of the new technological possibilities. This transaction orientation favors a reductionist understanding of information. Administrations will be inclined to provide only such information or at least primarily focus on such information that is needed for transactional purposes.

However, citizens' transactions are not the same as consumer-client transactions. A fundamental qualitative difference remains. The latter—even if only in theory—are based on choice; they might involve negotiation around offers and demands. In the interaction with administrations, on the other hand, citizens usually have less choice (although new management concepts at least seek to create the impression of choices). Citizens typically interact with administrations in what might be called political transactions. In such transactions, citizens claim rights/liberties, exercise rights/liberties, and/or resign rights/liberties according to a framework, which in turn is legitimized by citizens themselves having established it through the democratic process.

Transparency obligations in such a context address not only individual transactions between citizens and administrations. Transparency aims at the entire political process, including the political activities of the government in power, routine activities of bureaucrats for which the government is accountable, but also a general understanding of the structures and procedures of a democratic system in which governments operate and citizens act. Knowledge gained through transparency encourages alternatives and helps put alternatives into action. In the process, citizens might possibly realize that the space of action left to them by constitutional arrangement is too small. While participation builds on understanding and understanding builds on transparency, transparency might thus quite likely lead to the understanding that broader participation is both possible and necessary. However, participatory structures in democracies are the outcome of negotiated power compromises. Attempts at changing participatory patterns are an attempt to thaw frozen compromises, to set free political energy with unpredictable results. Consequently they provoke strong attempts at insulation and immunization from those threatened by change. Much of the resistance to transparency in democratic systems can be read as an attempt to quell change at the early informational stage. These reactions point to a deeper reason for guaranteeing access to information principles through laws. Such laws—by eventually involving courts and having involved government and legislature—help ensure that the drive for information and participation is kept within the proper democratic system of checks and balances.

Access rights add to the functionality of the system of balances. Their very existence creates an unforeseeable element of informational checks to be exercised by anyone, at any time, on almost any subject the administrations are dealing with. These potential checks have structural consequences. Parliament's information requests addressed to the administration have to consider tactical and strategic implications deriving from a partial overlap of interests between the ruling parties in Parliament and "their" government. Information requests from the press have to be seen in the complex relationship between the press and the government that has its own specific rules. Information from the government may have its own political goals, and not all information that reaches the press is published immediately or is unfiltered since the press too may have its own tactical and strategic goals. In contrast, access based on access laws—at least potentially—introduces an uncontrollable instrument of checks because it is breaking through all these formal and informal arrangements of information exchanges between the established participants of the informational checks and balances.

Finally, information gained through access laws is not subject to editing. While legal exemptions to access may lead to information being partially withheld, or even deleted, or not provided at all, such deletions and omissions are explicit. The remaining information is provided as it is. This aspect of freedom of information legislation has often been criticized. It has been argued that providing citizens with unedited and uncommented information is a disservice since it may lead to misinterpretation or leave the requester completely helpless as to how to put information into context. This line of argument has been used in defending, for instance, the federal Austrian "access law,"[6] which provides citizens with a right to obtain information about the contents of government documents (or about other activities of the government) but not access to documents themselves. With such a limitation, however, this "access law" may even fall outside freedom of information legislation as defined previously. If context information is deemed necessary, freedom of information laws do not bar administrations from providing such additional context information if they wish to do so to clarify. Providing information about information instead of information as is invites editing and severely limits the informational control capacity of freedom of information laws.

Freedom of information consequently goes beyond transactional information and aims at transparency of the framework in which all citizen-government interactions take place, and it introduces an additional instrument of informational checks into the existing system of checks and balances. Freedom of information rights are not targeted at particular transactions; they remain as a floating possibility of control. Because of this core function of control, even in traditional "paper" contexts freedom of information requesters do not have to prove a special purpose or show specific standing. Informational access as an individual right of unforeseeable control over bureaucratic activities turns into an essential structural component of the democratic system of checks and balances in sync with technological change. As new channels for effectiveness may evolve that will strengthen this control mechanism even further,[7] access rights as structural component can no longer be reduced to an element merely to be considered in the design of transactions. Instead, freedom of information concepts provide the *normative* informational framework in which transactional concepts of what is called e-government have to be designed to meet information government expectations.

Only then and only as societal control structures, access principles may aim toward efficiency in their own operations. This efficiency, however, is not the transaction-oriented efficiency of private electronic commerce exchanges. Rather, it is an efficiency that addresses informational power balances in a civil society. The benefit entering the cost-benefit analysis is not simply economic value creation but social and political sustainability.

Implementing freedom of information rules in such a broader information government context will not only be a challenge for current electronic government systems too narrowly construed around transactional models, but also to freedom of information legislation itself. Implanting access rights into broader designs will test the seriousness and efficiency of freedom of information legislation as well. Many of the more than fifty freedom of information laws around the world will face new scrutiny. I have already referred to the problematic Austrian federal law (at least it does not call itself a freedom of information law). Other laws, too, will be assessed based on the access they provide to information: For example, do they provide a sufficiently broad definition of accessible documents? How broadly are exemptions framed? Is there a time limit imposed on administrations for answering information requests? How strongly is it enforced? Are administrative decisions on information requests subject to an independent review by courts? In short, what is needed is a benchmarking of the various claims made by access laws. What is necessary is to look into the mid- and long-term sustainability of the freedom of information concept as such.

Requirements for Freedom of Information Laws in E-Government Environments

So far I have stated the following as essential elements of freedom of information legislation:

• a right of access to government information, with access as the default principle (although exemptions may apply),

• the exercise of which requires no special standing by the requester (or special proof of interest),

• and is comprehensive and technologically adaptive in terms of the information objects it is aiming at.

Unfortunately the large majority of the more than fifty freedom of information laws do not fulfill even these minimal requirements.[8]

Several attempts to benchmark freedom of information legislation have already been made in the process of internationalizing the concept. Perhaps the most prominent attempt is the encouragement the Committee of Ministers of the Council of Europe addressed to European member states in 1981 to follow the (at that time) few cases of national freedom of information legislation. The committee suggested the following requirements:

• "Everyone within the jurisdiction of a member state shall have the right to obtain, on request, information held by the public authorities other than legislative bodies and judicial authorities. . . .
• Effective and appropriate means shall be provided to ensure access to information. . . .
• Access to information shall not be refused on the ground that the requesting person has not a specific interest in the matter. . . .
• Access to information shall be provided on the basis of equality. . . .
• The foregoing principles shall apply subject only to such limitations and restrictions as are necessary in a democratic society for the protection of legitimate public interests (such as national security, public safety, public order, the economic well-being of the country, the prevention of crime, or for preventing the disclosure of information received in confidence), and for the protection of privacy and other legitimate private interests, having, however, due re-

gard to the specific interest of an individual in information held by the public authorities which concerns him personally....
• Any request for information shall be decided upon within a reasonable time....
• A public authority refusing access to information shall give the reasons on which the refusal is based, according to law or practice....
• Any refusal of information shall be subject to review on request."[9]

More than twenty years later, not even a single European Union member state has established national laws that would pass this test.

However, although the state of freedom of information legislation still remains unsatisfactory in many nations, the more than fifty nations with access laws taken together offer a rich source of legislative material, experiences, trials and error, and best practices from which even more suitable and detailed requirements for access laws can be derived and against which access laws have to be measured. This body of legislative experience indicates that freedom of information laws have to eventually incorporate all of the following features, and have them exercised in everyday practice in order to achieve the individual and structural control expectations we mentioned:[10]

• Access for the general public has to be the rule, subject to clearly defined and restrictively interpreted "limitations and restrictions as are necessary in a democratic society for the protection of legitimate public interests..., and for the protection of privacy and other legitimate private interests, having, however, due regard to the specific interest of an individual in information held by the public authorities which concerns him personally"[11]—with the possibility that compelling public interests would override private and public secrecy interests.

• A clearly defined interaction with privacy protection regulations and privacy authorities resolving conflicts in a manner that takes into account public interest and public responsibilities must exist.

• Reasonable and clearly prescribed time limits for answering information requests must exist, and speedy and well-monitored review procedures must be in place.

• Active information duties for information holders to provide easily accessible and usable inventories and guidance for the use of such resources must exist, along with requirements to provide as much information as possible proactively (information deemed of general public interest).

• The technical definition of the informational objects accessible has to be broad and access procedures for information requesters have to be facilitated by technology as much as possible.

• Access to the remainder of the information objects has to be provided even if parts of these are found to be exempt from access.

• The information requester has to be able to decide on the format in which the information is to be supplied.

• Access costs have to be based on proper operational administration costs reflecting the framework character of transparency.

• Refusal of access has to be properly justified and is subject to judicial review that takes into account the time-dependent character of information.

• Centralized oversight mechanisms must be in place that regularly monitor the practice of administrations in handling information requests and provide reports to the public.

Let me be clear: the bar is high. Although the number of countries that have passed what they term freedom of information laws is increasing, there is still no single country that would meet all these criteria. Yet only if all those criteria are met there exist efficiency of freedom of information under the broader meaning of efficiency introduced previously.

Fundamental Challenges to the Freedom of Information Concept?

But even if all freedom of information laws were to meet all criteria, they cannot avoid facing additional challenges that affect the ability of freedom of information concepts to act as an appropriate normative framework for information government.

When one remembers the Swedish history of freedom of information, it seems obvious that such challenges may come from a changing appreciation of security in society. This in turn would lead to new secrecy rules reducing accessibility and structural transparency. These new secrecy rules would hardly be tested as rigorously for efficiency as transparency had been (assuming that secrecy per se is efficient). The Swedish case, again, is illustrative. Since about the middle of the nineteenth century, Swedish access laws have required that legislation containing exemptions from the access principle be included in a special law. This act—the Secrecy Act[12]—consequently contains an exhaustive list of all exemptions to freedom of information, and thus—at the very least—functions as a highly visible indicator of a society's appreciation of transparency and its balancing interests. So far, at least anecdotal evidence—from Watergate to the aftermath of 9/11—suggests that societies undergo pendulum swings in their appreciation of secrecy and transparency.[13]

Other challenges exist, however, perhaps less visible or less visible as fundamental challenges, and where there is little expectation of pendulum swings, as these challenges affect the very foundation on which the freedom of information concept rests.

Two such challenges include

• the still essentially individualistic character of freedom of information rights despite of the importance of structural transparency, and

• vital shifts in the basic understanding of what constitutes the private and the public sector.

The first challenge seems to be amendable: freedom of information rights are set out to provide a counterbalance to administrative information power. This power is not only based on the time advantages and informational prerogatives of the administration (like the capability to enforce the provision of information) but also rests on its organizational potential to collect, process, store, and distribute large amounts of information in high complexity over a long period of time. As I have stated, the individual access right can be seen as developing toward a structural component and supplement of the system of checks and balances. But this structural component—and the individual right—can only counterbalance the organizational advantages of administrations if these rights and structures are embedded in an organizational environment as well. The social environment, in which freedom of information concepts operate, therefore, must encourage self-organization and organization on the same technological level as the administrations. Borrowing from the e-jargon, e-access must be embedded in an e-society capable of e-self-organization. More specifically, freedom of information legislation must enable information requesters to feed information into these organizational backups. Thus, freedom of information regulations have to ensure that requesters receive information free from legal obligations, like copyright, and in a format and structure that enables them to technically and organizationally pool information from individual requests in order to create collectively organized knowledge bases.[14] Freedom of information legislation must allow for, if not encourage, the creation of such knowledge bases by removing proprietary as well as cost restrictions including government copyright, third-party restrictions on reuse or redistribution, and prohibitive fee requirements.

Restrictions on reuse are spreading, particularly in European freedom of information legislation.[15] Such restrictions not only keep access within its individualistic confinements without providing the opportunity to develop its structural potential, but also are symptomatic of the other fundamental challenge we have identified: against the background of administrative reform, of using more information technology in public administrations and of developing comprehensive transaction-centered electronic government concepts, we are observing a persistent shift from public (information) government to private (information) governance.[16]

Information holdings wander off into the private sector together with former administrative functions they were meant to serve. For example, privatizing meteorological services as it is happening in some countries means putting meteorological information into private hands. Private-sector operators will price such information holdings based on market considerations rather than public needs, unless a cautious legislator has secured availability when such needs arise. Unfortunately, freedom of information laws conceptually focus on information holdings of the public sector, affecting private-sector information only if and where such information has to be shared with the public sector. This shift continuously reduces the amount of meaningful information accessible through freedom of information requests.

Even where information is still held by the public sector, there is increasing pressure to make commercial use of such information—by establishing access and reuse fees close to market prices, by entering private-sector/public-sector cooperation agreements to exploit these resources commercially, or by auctioning off exclusive exploitation rights. Where public administrations are still explicitly barred from such exploitation approaches, public-sector functions might remain with the administration while their information resources wander off to newly constructed private-sector entities with which private-sector cooperation agreements are concluded, or hybrid organizations are created that also put the application of access laws into question. Since freedom of information laws traditionally exclude access to information that is available otherwise even if only via the commercial information market, the amount of information that can be accessed by freedom of information rights is thus reduced even further.[17]

Transactional electronic government approaches, if they stay too close to their conceptual origins in e-business and e-commerce concepts might well tempt to take marketing even further. Information platforms may evolve in close cooperation between the public and the private sector, which will make it very difficult for information requesters to know whether they are approaching the information holder as citizens with a right of access or as customers with the possibility of a contract. Only complex and costly court procedures might eventually provide transparency for the application of transparency rules in these situations.

While many nations still struggle to fully implement traditional access laws, the very basis of such endeavors is already put into question by more "advanced" nations, creating ever more complex environments in which the contours of what is public and what is private become more and more obscured. Yet even if these trends prevail without any significant legislative reaction, we predict that there are dialectic counterforces to be reckoned with, and these counterforces, too, will become visible.

Freedom of Information, E-Government, and the Dialectics of the Public and the Private

Freedom of information laws are an indicator of the attention legal systems pay to information. This attention is not restricted to information in the public sector. Many privacy protection laws, for example, apply directly to the private sector or parts of it. The same is true, too, for many transparency and access to information regulations: the functioning of markets requires the availability of information and guarantees of information quality. Informational obligations generally turn into compensation mechanisms for other asymmetries in the access to resources of power. Such asymmetries are not restricted to the public sector. The concept of the "informed consumer" (although occasionally used defensively so as to avoid other intervention) has proved to be a powerful symbol for enacting consumer information legislation (see, e.g., Philipp 1989).

Most of these compensatory mechanisms count on the public sector as a kind of trustee and redistributor of such information. For example, in many countries pharmaceutical information has to be registered with public authorities from where it would become accessible to others under certain specified conditions. However, to the degree the state is withdrawing from such functions, direct information exchanges have to be implemented and organized to maintain the compensatory performance. Hence, more private-sector information obligations are likely to develop, to a lesser extent negotiated by public-sector institutions but directly arranged among private-sector participants. As a consequence, familiar e-business/

e-commerce mechanisms may be forced to operate under stronger informational requirements for participating organizations.[18]

There is, of course, still one fundamental difference: in the democratic context the model of the informed citizen is—as I have shown—but a prelude to participation in democratic decision making on the fate of the commonwealth. The informed consumer or business partner, on the other hand, is but a prelude to individual acts of consumption or market transactions. Nevertheless, societies are recognizing transparency as a tool to address power asymmetries. This knowledge from interactions in the public sphere is difficult to unlearn for private interactions. We may assume—and the concept of universal service already provides ample evidence for this assumption—that when essential services move into the private sector, or if with regard to such services the demarcation line between what constitutes the public sector and what constitutes the private sector becomes blurred, the remedies for addressing power conflicts can no longer be contained within the public sector. The remedies will start to wander with the asymmetries they are supposed to mend.

In informational terms, this might imply that it will become less probable that freedom of information concepts be restricted to apply only to public-sector information. Provided that adequate enforcement mechanisms will be secured, electronic government and e-commerce might indeed merge in an attempt to generalize efficiency criteria, but so will the normative environment—information government—by setting sector-independent information obligations as restraints.

Conclusions

This chapter has focused on the role of freedom of information legislation in the context of e-government. It has traced the evolution of access legislation, analyzing the duality of its roots as a modernizing and preserving force, its legitimizing power (and what constraints that implies), as well as the necessity of access rules being codified in statutes, if not in constitutional documents. I have examined the essential conflict between access legislation, founded on the primacy of transparency over efficiency, and traditional e-government concepts, which are influenced by e-commerce designs and reflect a purely transactional view of the relationship between citizens and government. Overcoming this conflict requires the reductionist character of current e-government concepts to give way to an inclusive one, in which transparency is permitted to play its fundamental role. Such a holistic view, labeled "information government" throughout this book, will necessitate a standard of freedom of information legislation that I lay out in this chapter.

Yet even access legislation fulfilling the standard set out in this chapter faces fundamental challenges. One is the recurring pendulum swing of societal desires for public secrecy. The two more fundamental ones, however, are less obvious. First, freedom of information legislation is of little value without a functioning ecosystem in which it is used. This requires the existence of viable civil society organizations requesting and disseminating public information obtained through access procedures. Second, recent trends obscure the border between private and public sectors. As public information is relocated to the private sector, access legislation may lose much of its bite.

The dialectic of the private/public dichotomy, however, may offer freedom of information principles an unexpected renewal: as the transactional nature of our lives increases, so will the desire of citizens as consumers to obtain the information relevant for their transactional decisions. Over time, these consumer preferences may force the private sector to become transparent and freedom of information legislation to cover at least part of the private sector.

Notes

1. For more details on the Swedish history of the freedom of information legislation, see Bergner 1968, Barudio 1981, Metcalf 1987, and Lamble 2002.

2. Sweden was also the first country to implement a national data protection law Datalag (SFS 1973, 289).

3. Art. 4(3) of the federal Canadian Access to Information Act (R.S. 1985, c.A-1).

4. See, for example, §552a(2)(D) of the Freedom of Information Act 5 U.S.C. §552, as amended by Public Law No. 104-231, 110 Stat. 3048.

5. This is the WordlBank definition available at http://www1.worldbank.org/publicsector/egov/definition.htm.

6. Bundesgesetz vom 15.Mai 1987 über die Auskunftspflicht der Verwaltung des Bundes und eine Änderung des Bundesministeriengesetzes 1986 (Auskunftspflichtgestz), last amended in 1998. The German-language title of the law already clarifies that it does not deal with "access" (Informationszugang) but with information in the sense of, for example, a help desk providing information (Auskunft).

7. For the United States, see, for example, Bimber 2003.

8. The survey by Banisar (2004, 12) describes, for example, correctly describes the Austrian situation as follows: "The 1987 Auskunftspflichtgesetz ... obliges federal authorities to answer

questions regarding their areas of responsibility within eight weeks. . . . However, the law does not oblige government bodies to provide access to the documents, only that they provide answers to requests for information."

9. Recommendation No. R(81)19 of the Committee of Ministers to Member States on the Access to Information Held by Public Authorities Adopted by the Committee of Ministers on November 25, 1981, adopted at the 340th meeting of the Ministers' Deputies. Available at http://www.coe.int/T/e/legal_affairs/Legal_co-operation/Administrative_law_and_justice/ Texts_&_Documents/Recommendation(81)19.asp.

10. See Burkert 1999. Similar attempts to summarize the requirements for freedom of information legislation can be found, for example, in Article 19 Group 2001.

11. Quoted from the Committee of Ministers Recommendation (see n. 9).

12. Very soon after the initial enactment, the access principle in Sweden started to be modified by ever increasing secrecy exemptions. By 1937 an attempt had been made to get a better overview of all these exemptions by bundling many of them in a secrecy act. In 1949 the access principle was reaffirmed in a restatement of the Freedom of the Press Act (SFS 1949, 105). But secrecy exemptions again started to grow, and in 1980 another attempt was made to make the secrecy exemptions transparent by collecting them in another secrecy act (SFS 1980, 100). This act has seen many further revisions and extensions since then.

13. For example, OpentheGovernment.org's 2005 report shows roughly a doubling of the number of official documents that have been classified (and thus access is restricted) annually in the United States, from 8.6 million in 2001 to 15.6 million in 2004, while at the same time the number of (older) documents being declassified decreased from 100 million in 2001 to 28 million in 2004; see http://www.openthegovernment.org/otg/SRC2005.pdf.

14. U.S. examples of such a support infrastructure are the National Security Archive at George Washington University (http://www.gwu.edu/~nsarchiv/nsa/the_archive.html) and the activities of the Electronic Frontier Foundation (http://www.eff.org).

15. See, for example, France: Art. 10 of the French access law (Loi n°78-753 du 17 juillet 1978 portant diverses mesures d'amélioration des relations entre l'administration et le public et diverses dispositions d'ordre administratif, social et fiscal; version consolidée au 24 décembre 2002). Available online at http://www.legifrance.gouv.fr/texteconsolide/PPEAV.htm. Or see Belgium: Art. 11 of the Belgian access law (Loi du 12 novembre 1997 relative à la publicité de l'administration dans les provinces et les communes). Available online at http:// www.juridat.be/cgi_loi/legislation.pl.

16. For the situation in the United States (at the state level), see, for instance, Feiser 2000.

17. Generally on the effects of what has become known as the commercialization of public-sector information (Burkert 2004).

18. An early example is the E-Commerce Directive of the European Union: Directive 2000/ 31/EC of the European Parliament and of the Council of June 8, 2000, on certain legal aspects of information society services—in particular, electronic commerce—in the Internal Market (directive on electronic commerce). *Official Journal of the European Union* L 178 (July 17, 2000): 1.

References

Article 19 Group. 2001. "Global Trends on the Right to Information: A Survey of South Asia." Available at http://www.article19.org/docimages/1116.htm, 38ff.

Banisar, David. 2004. "Freedom of Information and Access to Government Records around the World." Available at http://www.freedominfo.org/survey.htm.

Barudio, Günter. 1981. *Das Zeitalter des Absolutismus und der Aufklärung 1648–1779*. Frankfurt am Main: Fischer.

Bergner, Helmut. 1968. Das schwedische Grundrecht auf Einsicht in öffentliche Akten. Diss., University of Heidelberg.

Bimber, Bruce. 2003. *Information and American Democracy: Technology in the Evolution of Political Power*. Cambridge, New York, Melbourne: Cambridge University Press.

Burkert, Herbert. 1999. "Regelungstechnische Standards für ein Informationszugangsgesetz im internationalen Vergleich." *medialex*: 213–220.

Burkert, Herbert. 2004. "The Mechanics of Public Sector Information." In *Public Sector Information in the Digital Age: Between Markets, Public Management and Citizens' Rights*, ed. Georg Aichholzer and Herbert Burkert, 3–22. Cheltenham, Northampton: Edward Elgar.

Feiser, Craig D. 2000. "Protecting the Public's Right to Know: The Debate over Privatization and Access to Government Information under State Law." *Florida State University Law Review* 27: 825–864.

Lamble, Stephen. 2002. "Freedom of Information, a Finnish Clergyman's Gift to Democracy." *Freedom of Information Review*, no. 97 (February): 2–8. Available at http://members.optusnet.com.au/~slamble/freedom_of_information.htm.

Metcalf, Michael F. 1987. "Parliamentary Sovereignity and Royal Reaction, 1719–1809." In *The Riksdag: A History of the Swedish Parliament*, ed. Michael F. Metcalf, 109–164. Stockholm: The Swedish Riksdag and the Bank of Sweden Tercentenary Foundation.

Philipp, Renate. 1989. *Staatliche Verbraucherinformationen im Umwelt und Gesundheitsrecht*. Köln, Berlin, Bonn, Munich: Heymanns.

Seipel, Peter. 1981. *Teldoc and Open Records*. Svenska föreningen för ADB och juridikrapport 18, Stockholm.

Case Illustration

Protecting Privacy by Requesting Access: Marc Rotenberg and EPIC

Viktor Mayer-Schönberger and David Lazer

The Washington-based Electronic Privacy Information Center (EPIC) was founded in 1994 by Marc Rotenberg. A nonprofit organization, EPIC aims to focus public attention on emerging civil liberties issues, especially the protection of individual privacy in the information age. Rotenberg was no newcomer to privacy and open government matters. Before founding EPIC, he had worked on these issues for Senator Patrick Leahy (D-VT) and directed the Washington office of Computer Professionals for Social Responsibility (CPSR).

Since its inception, EPIC has used the Freedom of Information Act (FOIA) to gain access to government information pertaining to public policies on personal privacy. "People are sometimes surprised," Rotenberg explains, "that a 'privacy organization' would be such an aggressive and effective user of open government laws. But part of the key to our success is the recognition that there is little conflict between the efforts to protect the privacy of individuals and the need to ensure the accountability of government."[1]

A key element of EPIC's strategy is to maintain its focus on its core area of expertise—electronic privacy. EPIC is thus able to carefully craft its access requests, target appropriate agencies, and interpret the results. This combination of focus and expertise has enabled EPIC to turn itself into a trusted source of information about previously opaque government policies, thus influencing policy debates. A case in point was EPIC's work regarding the Pentagon's Total Information Awareness (TIA) project, an effort to massively expand government data mining of public- and private-sector data about individuals. EPIC was involved in extensive litigation with the Department of Defense (DoD) about access to key documents summarizing communication between

DoD and potential vendors about the scope of the program. The TIA project was eventually scrapped, in part due to the efforts of EPIC in making these materials available (they are available online at http://www.epic.org/privacy/profiling/tia/).

In many ways, EPIC is a modern information intermediary, utilizing FOIA and similar access legislation to facilitate informed public debate. EPIC was the first organization to make available online documents it obtained under FOIA, through its website (www.epic.org). Not all its activities, however, are confined to the Internet. For example, EPIC turned heavily redacted documents on the Clipper case into holiday greeting cards and offers one-page summaries of its FOIA requests (EPIC FOIA Notes) as well as longer reports. Initiatives like these, Rotenberg maintains, facilitate informed public debate. EPIC also works closely with a number of related organizations nationally and internationally to coordinate activities and to provide a platform for relevant information.

Recently, in a time of growing desire among the United States and many other governments to increase surveillance of the public, EPIC has seen its role directly challenged by government agencies, which have even questioned EPIC's status as a nonprofit organization (something that Rotenberg says had not happened ever before in EPIC's life). Despite its limited resources, EPIC has continued to be quite successful in uncovering important pieces of information through its information access activities. Rotenberg reasons that this is a result of EPIC's strategy to select the cases it pursues with great care and, if necessary, sue in court: "We don't always succeed in court, but by picking our cases carefully more often than not we have prevailed in FOIA battles with the government. And most importantly the public is better informed about the activities of its government."

Note

1. This quotation and others are from an e-mail exchange with Marc Rotenberg dated November 17 and November 30, 2005.

7

Socio-Technologies of Assembly: Sense Making and Demonstration in Rebuilding Lower Manhattan

Monique Girard and David Stark

The Practical Challenge

As they recovered from the immediate shock and devastation of the September 11 attack, the citizens of New York and their elected representatives were confronted with the daunting challenge of deciding the future of the World Trade Center (WTC) site. So much had been destroyed: Thousands had perished. Tens of thousands had been displaced from their jobs. Tens of millions of square feet of office space had been destroyed or damaged. Critical infrastructure hubs in transportation, telecommunications, and electricity had been devastated; large corporations had been forced to relocate; small retail, hotel, and restaurant businesses had been crippled; students, employees, and local residents had been displaced and traumatized. The meaning and identity of Lower Manhattan as a financial district was now uncertain, and a city whose dynamism was in large part as a global crossroads was now a place of insecurity. It was clear that redevelopment of the site would be one of the most significant undertakings in the city's history.

As they rose to meet these material and emotional challenges, New Yorkers were confronted by social and political challenges no less daunting. There were so many stakeholders with so many disparate claims: The families of victims had claims for compensation and moral claims about the status of "hallowed ground." The Port Authority, as the owner of the land, faced claims from its bondholders. The leaseholders of the properties, with claims from their creditors, placed claims on their insurers. Companies filed claims for compensation. And all of these business entities pressed their interests on various governmental units and agencies whose multiple and overlapping jurisdictions compounded the complexity of the decision-making process. Meanwhile, residents, schools, and religious and cultural institutions in the adjacent neighborhoods claimed a role in the redevelopment process, acknowledging the legitimacy of the claims of the victims' families but questioning proposals for a sixteen-acre memorial ("we don't want to live next to a cemetery"). Others pointed to studies showing that the economic and psychological impact of the attack was greater in neighborhoods distant from Ground Zero and argued that funds for redevelopment should be spent citywide. Some housing developers pointed to high vacancy rates among existing office buildings in Lower Manhattan and argued for new residential construction. Low-income groups argued that it should be affordable housing. Others argued for another kind of diversity that would bring universities, museums, and an opera house to the site. Environmentalists argued that the site should be a model of sustainable "green" development. Taxpayer groups argued that the properties should be developed with an eye to improved fiscal revenues. Architects pressed for impressive buildings, arguing that not only New Yorkers but all people touched by the event needed monuments as imaginative as the immensity of the tragedy. In turn, urban planners denounced the architects for proposals in which design leads the program instead of the program leading the design.

On one principle the various stakeholders agreed: redevelopment of the WTC needed to be an open and participatory process. The answer to the attack on our democracy could only be more democracy. Exemplary, in this respect, is the following passage from the mission statement of the Civic Alliance (2002), a confederation of scores of civic associations:

On October 1, 2001 more than 75 civic leaders gathered in an overcrowded conference room to begin a process so daunting we hardly knew where to start. The yet-to-be-named Civic Alliance to Rebuild Downtown New York had many different ideas on how to rebuild, but were united behind one goal—to transcend business-as-usual in support of an open, inclusive rebuilding process that would stand as a monument to democracy.

If all the participants agreed that the process must be democratic, there was little common understanding of what "an open, inclusive rebuilding process" might be. Multiple notions of democracy, multiple principles of representation, and multiple notions of public good exist. The citizens of New York, their elected and appointed officials, and their civic associations (many of which emerged after September 11) did not wait to come to an agreement about the rules and procedures for a democratic process. Faced with a situation unprecedented in its urgency and its challenges, each began to act congruent with its notions of democracy, representation, and participation. It is amid and through this extraordinary heterogeneity that New Yorkers engaged in a collective exploration.

Because the process of reconstruction would be as important as the product, rebuilding the physical space of Lower Manhattan launched a reshaping of the space of the public sphere. In the wake of September 11, small-scale public forums proliferated and were soon followed by more systematic efforts on the part of governmental agencies and leading civic groups to solicit input from the public about the design of an appropriate memorial and the future of the World Trade Center site. These public forums used very different technologies of deliberation: from ideas recorded on butcher block paper, to polling via personal touchtone keypads, to threaded online discussions, to websites and digital demonstrations. They offer a remarkable opportunity to examine technologies of citizen participation in governance when the reshaping of the public sphere occurs in an era when the forms of representation (in multiple senses of the term) are themselves coevolving with new digital technologies.

The Analytical Challenge

At midcentury, organizational analysts at Columbia University led by Robert Merton and Paul Lazarsfeld launched two ambitious research programs. On one track, Merton and his graduate students Peter Blau, Alvin Gouldner, and James Coleman examined the origins and functioning of bureaucracy using a rich repertoire of methods including small group analysis, ethnography, and survey research (Merton 1952). On the second, parallel track, Merton and Lazarsfeld established the Bureau of Radio Research to examine the dynamics of mass communication (Lazersfeld and Field 1946). Methodological pioneers, they developed the focus group method and used projection booths to study the demographics of audience reception well before their colleagues in comparative literature discovered "reception theory."

Whereas our Columbia University predecessors charted the rise of bureaucratic organizations and the emergence of mass communication, we have a new opportunity, at the turn of the century, to *chart the emergence of collaborative, nonhierarchical forms in an era of interactive media* (Beunza and Stark 2004; Dorf and Sabel 1998; Friedland 2001; Girard and Stark 2002; Sack 2005; Schuler 2004). But the analogy holds only to a point: if Merton and Lazarsfeld could pursue their twinned projects in parallel, ours must be conjoined in an era when questions of organizational design are closely related to design of the digital interface. We take up that challenge in this research project as we seek to develop concepts to study the changing topography of public space in a highly visible test of the potential of new technologies of deliberation and demonstration.

Search as Inquiry

If the era of Merton and Lazarsfeld was characterized by mass production in the field of the economy and mass media in the field of communication, mass movements typified the field of demonstration in the public sphere. While mass production, mass media, and mass movements remain important forms, the social forms that define our epoch, we believe, are more likely to be collaborative production, collaborative (interactive) media, and movements of collaborative search. Large social movements—for peace, justice, equality—are necessarily still on the political landscape. But today the space of public debate is as much a place of movement, of churn and heterogeneous turnings, as of *movements*. Fragmented and partial from the older point of view, this multivocality borders on the cacophonous. But this heterogeneity can be its strength. As knowledge is socially distributed in less hierarchical forms, the old boundaries between lay and expert, for example, begin to dissipate (Callon, Lascoumes, and Barthe 2001; Rabeharisoa and Callon 2002). When the tools of representation (as mediated images) become interactive, the task of representation (as who can speak for whom) can be reimagined. In an era when policy decisions involve complex technical questions, demonstrations are more likely to marshal charts, figures, models, and simulations than to mobilize popular movements in the street (Barry 2001). Alongside protest, public space is a zone of inquiry.

The field of information technology is rightly preoccupied with the problem of search. How can users find the information they are looking for? How can organizations locate knowledge that is distributed across departments and projects? How can citizens access relevant information across government agencies and civic associations? New technologies of search engines and knowledge management offer promising solutions, frequently combining semantic categories with new, network-based algorithms. However, we see the problem facing citizens and civic associations in New York as involving a distinctive type of search—a search when you don't know what you're looking for but will recognize it when you find it.

Unlike those searches that yield the coordinates of a known target or retrieve a phone number, product code, or document locator for a pre-identified entity or category, and unlike official inquiries (e.g., the Kennedy assassination, the Los Angeles riots, the Challenger disaster) that investigate a given calamity that occurred in the past, this form of search as inquiry is open ended. In New York this inquiry was collective, it was distributed nonhierarchically across many hundreds of organizations, meetings, and sites, and it involved a combination of deliberately directed action and spontaneously emergent self-organization. In these characteristics of distributed intelligence in open-ended inquiry, it resembles the practices of scientific research. In examining a collective sense making, we start from the key insight of John Dewey's philosophy of pragmatism that we can come to know the question only in the process of making active steps toward solutions (Dewey [1927] 1991, [1939] 1993, 1998; Dorf and Sabel 1998). Search, when you don't know what you're looking for.

Dewey is our necessary point of departure not only because he thought systematically about inquiry[1] but also because he explicitly linked these ideas to the study of democratic practices and communication technologies. For Dewey, individuals in daily life must negotiate the constant churn of unanticipated consequences, changed circumstances, and shifting social and physical contexts. This daily work of sense making often requires an adjustment, revision, or even transformation of received interpretive tools before new challenges can be recognized and addressed. The sustained inquiry that transforms uncertainty into manageable order cultivates a common human capacity for intelligent judgment that requires, in order to be fully realized, the give-and-take of free and open social discussion, debate, and deliberation.

Dewey despaired that the American public had lost its ability to participate meaningfully in democratic politics; and he attributed this loss primarily to the modern technologies of communication and circulation that undermined local affiliation and the daily exchanges of face-to-face community. Although increased mobility and mass media supported the dissemination of ideas and information across a dispersed population, it transformed the public into a passive receptacle of already formed ideas and opinions. Nonetheless, Dewey maintained that "democracy is belief in the ability of human experience to generate the aims and methods by which further experience will grow in ordered richness" (Dewey [1939] 1993, 244); Dewey's vision of democratic participation required that individuals actively take part in making sense of their experience. This, in turn, required a collaborative sense making possible only through the give and take of face-to-face dialogue directed toward understanding "things as they are" and how they might be reconfigured. In their calls for the process being as important a monument as the outcome, the civic activists in New York echoed Dewey's conviction that "democracy is the faith that the process of experience is more important than any special result attained, so that special results achieved are of ultimate value only as they are used to enrich and order the ongoing process" ([1939] 1993, 244). The question relevant to this volume, of course, is whether and how new interactive technologies might facilitate this process where the technologies of mass communication had failed.

Project Ecologies and Digital Ecologies

In examining nonbureaucratic forms, one of the key insights of the sociology of collaborative production is that the actual unit of organization is frequently less a formal organization than a project. Although producers are employed *by organizations*, they work increasingly *in projects*. Across a wide range of industries—film, construction, new media, automobiles, aeronautics, architecture, publishing, biotechnology, and many others—specialists from diverse fields (many of whom had not worked together before and, not uncommonly, who are employed by different organizations) collaborate in a project of limited duration (Grabher 2002a, 2002b; Sydow, Lindkwvist, and DeFillippi 2005).

The rebuilding of Lower Manhattan is such a construction project, not only because the sixteen acres of Ground Zero has literally been a site of recovery, then cleanup, and now construction, but also because the social construction of the rebuilding process has been a vast project similar, though not in scale, to project organization in the economy. The Lower Manhattan project is of limited duration involving many specializations and nonspecializations. Or, perhaps more accurately, we should think of a *project ecology*, involving hundreds, perhaps thousands, of smaller projects. With the exception of several dozens of government employees, almost no one is involved in these projects on a full-time basis. Citizens, professionals, and nonprofessionals assemble temporarily, sometimes forming named groupings (e.g., civic associations that spring up, lasting weeks, months, or less frequently years). But many of these microprojects could be a single meeting.

Although, as we will see, some of these assemblies can involve thousands of participants, the typical citizen assembly is not some grand popular parliament. Most are modest—the residents, employers, and workers of a mixed residential-commercial block in Chinatown, for example, or a team of citizen-architects, hastily assembled over a weekend like a pickup softball game. Many assemblies are face-to-face; some are almost exclusively online. Our research indicates, however, that many public assemblies involve a mix of physical and virtual forms. From a face-to-face meeting, announced by photocopied posters affixed to the bulletin boards of local schools, groceries, and beauty shops, someone produces minutes that are disseminated by e-mail and posted on a website linked to other websites. Assemblies are recombinant technologies of masking tape and digital servers. Accordingly, in place of studying new digital technologies per se, or engaging in yet another comparison of online and offline forms,[2] like the concept of project ecologies, we attend to *digital ecologies*.

Socio-Technologies of Assembly

In place of "the public," we think about public spaces of collective sense making. Public space is not a sphere, and it is not homogeneous. But this is not simply because some have more resources or more room. Public space is not a flat land on which the unequal territories of already known interests or constituencies are already drawn. Instead, it is a heterogeneous space, populated by very different kinds of actors who come into being and through their interactions create the many dimensions of the space itself (Mische and White 1998).

Therefore, in place of "the public," we think about variation in the forms of pubic assembly. Emphatically, however, assemblies are not populated simply by persons. Borrowing from Dewey directly and indirectly through his influence on science and technology studies, we develop a notion of publics as distinctive combinations of social networks, protocols, and technologies (Dewey [1927] 1991; Latour and Weibel 2005). There is no public, no public assembly, without protocols and technologies—even if these are as simple as chairs around a table and everyday conventions of conversational turn taking. Other assemblies are more complex. The key technologies of a public hearing, for example, are a microphone and a stopwatch, with protocols designating who among the socially constructed agents can speak (e.g., can a recognized speaker address the assembly as a "representative" or only as an individual citizen?) and for how long (e.g., "We are adopting a strict three-minute rule"), as well as rules about who cannot speak (e.g., the authorities present at the dais are authorized only to listen and must refrain from interjecting or responding).

Attention to variation in the socio-technologies of assembly bears directly on our conception of sense making as socially distributed search. For many, the statement that "cognition is socially distributed" would likely be interpreted as referring to a process whereby cognition is distributed across a network of persons. These commonsense assumptions are reinforced by the strong tendency of sociological network analysts to focus almost exclusively on ties among people. But recent scholarship on distributed cognition (e.g., Hutchins 1995) suggests that we need to bring not only people but also cultural and material artifacts into our network analysis. Doing so expands and enriches our conception of "the social." Cognition is socially distributed across persons and tools.[3] As Roy Pea (1993) writes in a study of distributed intelligence in the field of education (drawing on Vygotsky, on Simon, and especially on Gibson's [1979] notion of "affordances"): [M]ind rarely works alone. The intelligence revealed through these practices are distributed—across minds, persons, and the symbolic and physical environments, both natural and artificial" (47). To study collective sense making in the case of issues of public concern, we must be attentive to the instrumentation and infrastructure of deliberation. Different arrangements will provide different affordances—with differing opportunities and constraints. Socio-technologies of assembly are not simply settings, they are setups.

Assemblies will differ in the affordances they offer for different kinds of discursive practices.[4] Much of the literature on the public sphere has focused on a specific type of discourse—deliberation—to the expense of neglecting forms of participation that do not share its premises of rational and contained talk.[5] In an insightful essay, Sanders (1997) argues for other modes of giving input that do not have the exclusionary biases of deliberation: "[F]or example 'testimony'...might be a model that allows for the expression of different perspectives rather than seeking what's common. The contrast between the pursuit of commonality, and the simpler aim to include and represent a fuller range of critical voices, is at the core of the difference between deliberation and testimony (371).

In the following sections, we point to several socio-technologies of assembly in the Lower Manhattan project. As moments of collaborative inquiry, we start with "sensing" (e.g., gathering, collecting, sampling), turn to "sense making" (articulating, contrasting, discussing, re-cognizing), and conclude with "demonstrating" (showing, confronting, constituting).

Sensing

On the morning of September 11, 2001, Astronaut Frank Culbertson and his two Russian colleagues in the International Space Station had just completed their physical exams when they learned of the attack on the World Trade Center. As Culbertson (2001) wrote in a letter transmitted electronically later that day:

I glanced at the World Map on the computer to see where over the world we were and noticed that we were coming southeast out of Canada and would be passing over New England in a few minutes. I zipped around the station until I found a window that would give me a view of NYC and grabbed the nearest camera. It happened to be a video camera ... The smoke seemed to have an odd bloom to it at the base of the column that was streaming south of the city. After reading one of the news articles we just received, I believe we were looking at NY around the time of, or shortly after, the collapse of the second tower.

Culbertson's video images of the plume of smoke streaming from the collapsed towers were later followed by photographs from IKONOS, the first high-resolution Earth-imaging commercial satellite, as well as infrared images from the European Space Agency's low-flying SPOT satellite and NASA's Terra satellite.[6] Anyone in the world with an Internet connection could use these satellite prostheses to "see" the Ground Zero site from hundreds of miles in space. Cameras for government or corporate surveillance thus helped create a kind of reverse panopticon: in place of Bentham's architectural Panopticon where all prisoners were under surveillance from a central tower (Foucault 1979), in the WTC case all eyes were trained on the ruins of two central towers. The destruction of the commonplace had created a common ground (figure 7.1).

Civil engineer Guy Nordenson was much closer to the WTC than were the Space Station astronauts. His office is on Broadway only a block away from the site. From his home on that day, he began calling colleagues: engineers, emergency response specialists, and others in the earthquake engineering community. Aware that the city's emergency response headquarters had been destroyed with the WTC7 tower, Nordenson and his colleagues spontaneously began to assess the extent of damage to buildings in Lower Manhattan. To do so, they mobilized volunteer engineers through the Structural Engineers Association of New York (SEAoNY), and they started with resources close at hand. Earlier in the year, for a study for the Federal Emergency Management Agency (FEMA) to model the effects a medium-sized earthquake might have on Manhattan, Nordenson's team had created a database that described the structure of every building in Manhattan. With that database in hand, the SEAoNY volunteers carried out a series of physical and virtual inspections using Global Positioning System (GPS) technology, laser technology (known as LIDAR) with the capability of penetrating through the smoke to produce accurate elevation data, and thermal imagery for mapping hot spots in the rubble. Geographical Information Systems (GIS) provided the tools for integrating, analyzing, and displaying these spatial data. Within days, rather than weeks or months, they produced detailed mappings of the varying degrees of damage to buildings in Lower Manhattan.

In order to make sense of the disaster and begin the process of sense making about rebuilding (Beunza and Stark 2005), New Yorkers needed sensors. Without

Figure 7.1
Common ground.

waiting for centralized guidance, various specialists made their sensing tools available for public perception. As we saw, the first reconnaissance missions focused on the urgent tasks of determining the scope and boundaries of destruction. But almost immediately, reconnaissance also became a process of rediscovering the site. If the aerial photographs and thermal imaging provided a mediated access making visible the invisible, many people surged to the site to see for themselves. Despite the worldwide downturn in tourism after September 11, visitors started coming to New York in record numbers. Ironically, within months after its opening, the viewing platform designed by four prominent New York architects attracted more out-of-town visitors than the 1.8 million visitors that the WTC formerly drew to its observation deck each year (Lisle 2004).

To help them see, our Columbia University colleague, artist/architect Laura Kurgan, created a map, "Around Ground Zero: A map for walking in Lower Manhattan after September 11." Kurgan and her students watched visitors (even native

New Yorkers) wandering lost around the site, asking policemen where they were allowed to walk, or crowding around small xeroxed copies of FEMA maps posted for construction workers. They concluded that conventional street maps were of no help in providing orientation in the chaotic setting. Researched and produced by volunteers, Kurgan's map provided information about accessible streets and views, off-bound zones, suggested walking paths, memorial sites, and an inventory of damaged buildings. Writing for New York New Visions, a civic association of architects and planners formed after 9/11, whose Temporary Memorial Committee sponsored the map, Kurgan (2002) noted:

The map serves at once as a practical guide to the site and as a memorial document. Its aim is to help people make sense of what they are seeing, or, if that is asking too much, at least to measure their disorientation in the face of the unimaginable. The site around what was the World Trade Center is manifestly disorienting, for obvious reasons, and it should be in a sense, but the map addresses the unnecessary disorientation and allows visitors to take stock of what has happened.[7]

Inspired by artists who had produced a map of war-torn Sarajevo in 1996, the 18-by-24-inch foldable map was updated three times, first in December 2001, and more than 100,000 copies were distributed by volunteers at the site. As part of a pro bono project, New York new media firm Razorfish launched an interactive website version of the map. With Flash technology, a visitor can use a mouse to "roll over" areas of the map allowing multiple visual and political layers of the site to be exposed and entered.

Satellite photographs, Nordenson's GIS mappings, and Kurgan's interactive tour are all ways of seeing. New technologies thus facilitated a collective sensing. While lawyers argued about the conflicting property rights of the complex ownership and leaseholding structure of the site, New Yorkers engaged in a search for the properties of the site. In this exploration, they made collective discoveries about the characteristics, the features, the demography, the history, and the future possibilities of Lower Manhattan. Among these many reconnaissance missions, we highlight the following:

• With detailed drawings in the *New York Times* digital version, reconnaissance looked below to see that beneath the broken streets were miles of telephone cable, water mains, sewer pipes, subway tracks, and electrical lines.

• Looking up, various groups posted information about environmental pollutants in the air over New York. With data and interpretations independent of the Environmental Protection Agency (EPA), this reconnaissance essentially allowed New Yorkers to monitor the official monitors.[8]

• Looking over the site, a group of volunteer architects designed a viewing platform from which visitors could view the site. This physical platform was followed by virtual viewing platforms—webcams positioned atop buildings adjacent to the WTC recovery and reconstruction site.

• Looking in, the Sonic Memorial Project website posted aural recordings of sounds from the World Trade Center.[9] Academic research posted on an "After September 11th" site by the Social Science Research Council looked behind the façade of the WTC, showing that it had been a virtual portal linking global trade in intangible derivatives and warning of the new problems of a financial district in an era when proximity is a function of bandwidth.[10]

• Looking back, historians rediscovered an archeological record of the electronics merchants displaced by the WTC and before that a long-ago Arab market. In virtual exhibits organized by the New York Historical Society and the Skyscraper Museum, New Yorkers learned of the role of the Rockefeller family, of Robert Moses, and of backroom deals in the story of the planning, design, and construction of the world's tallest buildings for which it was often difficult to find nonsubsidized, nongovernmental agency tenants (Sorkin and Zukin 2002).

• With maps on the websites of Rebuild Downtown Our Town (r.dot), a newly formed civic association, reconnaissance (figure 7.2) looked out to display the employment catchment basin that brought workers from New Jersey, Long Island, and Connecticut, illustrating the complexities of the Lower Manhattan transportation hub and showing the possibilities of restoring the former street grid that had been in place prior to the WTC's construction in 1970.[11]

• Looking across the political landscape, public radio station WNYC posted an interactive map of the power structure of the political field. Scrolling over the map, the user could identify network ties of director interlocks and other political alliances among key decision makers in the rebuilding process.[12]

Public debate about projects such as that in Lower Manhattan are replete with discussions about "transparency." Typically, these refer to a desire that important decisions be made with full publicity, open to public view. In these and other reconnaissance missions, we see that transparency can have another moment. The study of science and technology frequently refers to processes by which the socially constructed character of a given artifact or technology has receded out of view, it becomes "black boxed" (Latour 1987). In "opening the black box," we become aware of possibilities that were incipient but not developed. Crisis can create open-

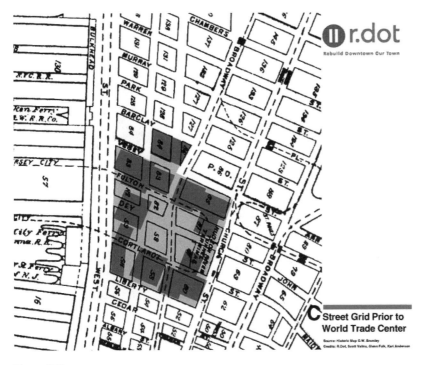

Figure 7.2
Reconnaissance.

ings of the black box. Cold and sleek on the skyline, whether we warmed to the twin towers or resisted their long shadows, they were part of the taken for granted. Tragically, in ruins, they, their histories, and the histories and social dynamics of Lower Manhattan became more transparent. In rediscovering the site, in re-knowing, indeed, re-cognizing the site, reconnaissance missions increasingly opened possibilities about what it might become.

Sense Making

Assemblies of Imagination

Even while fires still smoldered in the WTC ruins, citizens joined together to begin the process of memorializing and rebuilding in Lower Manhattan. Within weeks, literally dozens of civic associations were formed. If you were an architect or an urban planner, it would be no exaggeration to say that you could attend a meeting every

Figure 7.3a,b
Imagine New York.

evening at some venue or another. In place of coordinating the energies of specialists, several newly formed civic organizations saw their mission as soliciting views from the general citizenry. One of these, Imagine New York (figure 7.3), convened more than 230 "imagine workshops" across the city. Meeting in schools, places of worship, community centers, firehouses, and living rooms, they invited the public's ideas and visions. These face-to-face meetings were augmented by an online submission form that made it easy to contribute an idea and/or image. Posters and electronic announcements for the meetings emphasized the following: "Anyone—regardless of artistic ability or any sort of training—can participate in a workshop." The meetings and website collected people's ideas by addressing three questions: "What have we lost? How have we changed? What should be done on the World Trade Center site, in your community, and in the tri-state region to move forward from September 11?"

Trained Imagine New York facilitators wrote down citizens' ideas on large sheets of butcher block paper. These ideas were captured on digital cameras. Altogether some 19,000 statements were solicited from over 3,000 meeting participants and 850 online submissions.[13] Imagine New York then aggregated these 19,000 ideas into 49 "vision statements," which they distributed to the press, presented to official agencies and other civic groups, and re-presented to the community participants on the website. As a means of demonstrating that "we will make sure that your voice is heard" Imagine New York (n.d.) informed contributors that its "online Idea Gallery contains all of the ideas generated in workshops, submitted online, in the mail, and created on murals. We thank you for your lending the project your thoughts."

Searchable by keyword, theme, or workshop location, as the Idea Gallery emphasized, "You can locate your idea." Digitalization, therefore, not only facilitated collection and distribution of the citizens' "visions" but also supported a simple accountability: a given participant could see that her idea had been posted. And while doing so, she could see the similar and differing ideas of others. As figure 7.4 suggests, these ideas were thoughtful, playful, and extraordinarily heterogeneous. Onto the WTC ruins, citizens projected their images of the good city.

Assemblies of Deliberation

Whereas Imagine New York deployed protocols and technologies not for deliberative purposes but for expressive practices, Listening to the City (figure 7.5), an "electronic town meeting," used a different set of protocols and technologies to assemble an explicitly deliberative forum. Sponsored by the Civic Alliance in conjunction with

Rebuild taller and more magnificent than before as a symbol of resilience.

From now on we should listen to other countries problems and try to help so that they don't feel that America is a rich giant.

More kids on more swings.

It should be a place that everyone can go to.

Life without trucks, barricades—restore beauty and businesses.

I want the WTC to look big but not be so big, baby blue with yellow sprinkles.

Try to maintain the sense of community that has flowered in the aftermath of 9/11.

A neutral zone: no IDs, no paperwork.

Use the money to create community centers so the kids can stay out of trouble.

A universal United Nations community for people to sit, talk, and have coffee.

Let go, but not forget. No made-for-TV movies, etc., about 9/11.

We must find a way to celebrate what we've learned about each other and the city.

In the museum, what makes war, and how everyone thinks that they're right.

Global village—the UN for people, not diplomats.

DO SOMETHING RADICAL so people come from all over to see the beautiful structure.

I'd like to see affordable housing included.

Think 'public good' rather than 'private greed.'

Reconnect WTC site to the world by tying it to the river, harbor, and ocean.

A beautiful park is possible, with trees representing each country from which people came who lost their lives on 9/11 and open spaces filled with native greenery—a tribute to all life. We need to be part of nature and of the city at once. We need to see the sun and the sky.

Opportunity to develop new models for nontoxic; sustainable architecture; and redevelop not just finance and biotech; but incorporate industries for language and cultural learning and effective treatment of trauma at WTC site.

Figure 7.4
Examples of some of the 19,000 statements gathered by Imagine New York.

Figure 7.5a,b
Listening to the City.

the Lower Manhattan Development Corporation (LMDC) and the Port Authority, Listening to the City brought 4,500 people to the Javits Center for an all-day meeting on July 20, 2002, to review proposed plans for the WTC site and to deliberate more broadly on the redevelopment of the area. The Civic Alliance had canvassed widely before the meeting, and subsequent analysis indicates that the participants were largely representative of the major demographic contours of the city.

After arriving at the cavernous convention center, participants were dispersed, ten each to hundreds of round tables. At these tables they introduced themselves, and facilitators guided discussion. Participants at Listening to the City thus began by listening to each other. With keyboards hooked to a wireless local area network, each table entered opinions, goals, and means. A central clearinghouse synthesized themes that were projected onto giant screens. Using personal computerized keypads, participants were then asked to indicate their priorities among these themes with polling results displayed on the large screens in an iterative process. In a similar manner, participants also rated six proposals for redeveloping the WTC site. In overwhelming numbers, they rejected each of the proposals. At the end of the day, each participant was given a printout including graphs of the demographics of the attendees and the polling outcomes. Shortly after the July 20 event, 800 people began two weeks of online discussion in a second phase of Listening to the City organized around similar themes (Polletta and Wood 2005).

Widely publicized, the electronic town hall was decisive in discrediting the uninspiring plans sponsored by the Port Authority. In its wake, the LMDC seized the planning initiative. Promising that it would be more responsive than the bureaucrats at the Port Authority, the LMDC invited a set of international star architects to submit proposals to its Innovative Design competition and sponsored a series of offline and online forums, viewings, and hearings through which it solicited public feedback.

Demonstrating

Although relatively few street rallies and other contentious events occurred, the debate over the future of Lower Manhattan was not lacking in demonstrations. Like many of the important issues of our day, the political and the technical were intertwined in the matters of concern in the New York case. Accordingly, the relevant *demonstrations* involved charts, graphs, and visualizations—indeed, a wide panoply

Figure 7.6
Demonstration.

of materials in which participants attempted to offer proof of the validity of their claims. As our research proceeded, we realized that it was pointless to identify some demonstrations as "political" and others as "technical," so entwined were the two in almost every instance.[14]

Exemplary in this respect were the demonstrations of the architects. The signature architects who participated in the Innovative Design competition did not, of course, take to the streets. But, in their own way, each was a kind of social movement attempting to mobilize popular opinion. Starting with their PowerPoint presentations at the Winter Garden where they unveiled their plans in December 2002, the architects demonstrated (figure 7.6). Each showed that his project was inspired. See, for example, Daniel Libeskind's energetic sketches or the shadow cast by Peter Eisenman's crisscrossed hands as attempts to capture the unique moment of inspiration (figure 7.7). Using technical drawings and digital animations, they demonstrated that their buildings could be safely evacuated. With digital renderings of their models placed on the Manhattan skyline or at a city streetscape, they demonstrated that their project would exist on both a monumental and a human scale (all

Figure 7.7a,b
Demonstrations.

Figure 7.7c
(continued)

but one architect showed his building with a child in the image) and that it could be projected far into a future from which New Yorkers would look back with nostalgia. What better evidence that a building could exist than that it already did exist—as a postcard purchased by a tourist. And so each PowerPoint presentation concluded with postcard images—"shot" from helicopters or from a ferry on a calm evening with the Statue of Liberty, the Brooklyn Bridge, or the moon nestled in front, nearby, or hovering over the virtual buildings.[15]

On October 12, 2001, just a month after the WTC attack, people who lived and worked in Lower Manhattan engaged in a demonstration more typical of our conventional ideas of a social movement. Hundreds of people, many wearing surgical masks, assembled not far from Ground Zero at Pace University to demand specific details about the types and levels of toxins in the air and in their residences and workplaces. In press releases during that first month, Christine Whitman, administrator of the federal EPA, had reassured the public that there was no cause for health concerns. Early statements referred to air quality:

EPA is greatly relieved to have learned that there appears to be no significant levels of asbestos dust in the air in New York City." (Governor Whitman, EPA Press Release, 9/13/01)

I am glad to reassure the people of New York and Washington, DC that their air is safe to breathe and their water safe to drink. (Whitman, 9/18/01)

Subsequent statements referred specifically to homes and workplaces:

New Yorkers and New Jerseyans need not be concerned about environmental issues as they return to their homes and workplaces. (Whitman, 9/21/01)

[There is] no evidence of any significant public health hazard to residents, visitors or workers beyond the immediate World Trade Center area. (Whitman, 10/3/01; all quotations available at www.epa.gov/epahome/newsroom.htm)

But the demonstrators at the October 3 meeting told of their children coughing and wheezing and of other symptoms: " 'All I know right now is that there are irritants. What are these things?' said one resident. 'For some people, that meeting might have been soothing, but I'm still thirsting for more information'" (Ramirez, 2001).

Sadly, good information was not forthcoming from the EPA. In fact, the early official statements that conditions were safe put the residents and office workers of Lower Manhattan in a terrible double bind. Because the federal agency had declared that there was no health hazard, other agencies used these rulings as justifications for not making rigorous inspections inside homes and workplaces. Yet it was precisely in these interiors that levels of contamination would be most dangerous when pulverized debris and toxic fibers were stirred up during cleanup (Carpenter et al. 2005).

Over the course of the fall of 2001 and spring of 2002, numerous civic organizations mobilized to pressure government agencies to provide information on health conditions. These included 911 Environmental Action, AsthmaMoms, the WTC Community/Labor Coalition, the Lower East Side-Chinatown Consortium, and the Lower Manhattan Tenants Coalition. Initial efforts were directed at demonstrating that the relevant agencies were engaged in a kind of jurisdictional nonaccountability, each agency claiming that some other was responsible.[16] As they strove to force accountability, residents and workers came to learn that they would have to acquire technical knowledge—for example, about the difference between long and short asbestos fibers, about the toxicity of dioxin, lead, arsenic, mercury, and other contaminants, and about established standards for schools and workplaces. At the meetings of local community groups, we heard discussions that were not only about how to prod elected officials but how to comprehend measurements at the micron level.[17] Some groups focused on the unique conditions in which the towers had collapsed vertically on themselves. That tremendous force produced new forms of ultrafine particle contaminants—for example, cement dust pulverized to microscopic size or inordinate ratios of small to long asbestos fibers—in structures and at levels that had not been observed before (Chatfield and Kominsky 2001). In their demonstrations, the community groups provoked members of the "technical community" to acknowledge that on some matters there were no agreed-upon standards because the types, levels, and combinations of contaminants were so unprecedented in the Lower Manhattan case.

At the end of 2001, new and disturbing information became available to citizen groups. In their initial efforts to learn how to read and interpret technical reports, the local community had been assisted by experts at nongovernmental organizations such as the New York Committee on Occupational Safety and Health (NYCOSH) and the New York Environmental Law and Justice Project. Now they found allies inside the government agencies. For example, in a memorandum of December 3, 2001, Cate Jenkins, an environmental scientist in the Office of Solid Waste and Emergency Response of the EPA, systematically documented discrepancies between official press releases and internal information obtained by the EPA. For instance, while Governor Whitman was reassuring the public based on outdoor air samples, scientists at the EPA were looking at reports of elevated levels of indoor contamination that greatly exceeded the agency's own standards; similarly, the agency was recommending cleanup procedures that directly violated its own safety guidelines. Later the Office of the Inspector General of the EPA issued a finding that the EPA's blanket statements about air safety had not been based on sufficient data and analyses (EPA Office of the Inspector General 2003). Meanwhile, hearings conducted by the EPA's ombudsman concluded that the agency had abdicated its responsibility for monitoring indoor cleanup.[18] Finally, the Sierra Club issued a major study that systematically documented instances where government agencies, including the EPA, had misled the public (Mattei 2003). Agencies responsible for public safety had not simply given poor information but had knowingly given the public deliberately misleading information.

With these technical findings, the various civic organizations sought to demonstrate that the EPA was engaging in a cover-up. Because the dominant print media fell in line with the EPA story (the *New York Times*, e.g., ran no fewer than thirteen stories between September 12 and February 24, 2002, emphasizing the safety of the site) (Katz 2002), these demonstrations were made online. Civic websites directed

What Was Known, What Was Said

A comparison of known information on World Trade Center pollution and health effects
with statements made or actions taken by federal administration

Date	Information on Pollution/Health Effects Available	Statements Made/Actions Taken by Federal Administration
August 1, 1994	EPA advises schools not to use polarized light microscopy (PLM) analysis for asbestos testing, urging them to use the "improved" transmission electron microscopy (TEM). EPA explains that the new method identifies "thin asbestos fibers below the limits of resolution of the polarized light microscope."	In September 2001, the EPA uses the old PLM method to test for asbestos in the dust generated by the WTC disaster.
September 12, 2001	Regarding a White House request to produce fact sheets re asbestos, Dr. Ed Kilbourne tells the CDC, "We are concerned about even being asked to write a document for the public about reentry at this point," and warns, "We are aware of other potential toxic hazards in the WTC area about which you haven't asked." (Federal experts know the typical products of building demolition and burning of mixed materials.)	EPA's September 13, 2001, press release states that pollution tests "have been very reassuring about potential exposure of rescue crews and the public to environmental contaminants... the general public should be very reassured by initial sampling."
September 14, 2001	On September 13, 2001, Drs. Philip Landrigan and Stephen Levin of Mount Sinai warn that Ground Zero workers need training and "protective equipment." Dr. Levin warns that surgical masks do not protect against asbestos and urges use of a mask with a special filter. EPA data shows asbestos in dust ranging from 2.1 percent to 3.3 percent—above the 1 percent level at which material must be managed under asbestos standards. A Federal test of EPA's Region 2 office building lobby at 290 Broadway using the more sensitive TEM method finds asbestos. EPA does not even wait for these results; it conducts an environmental clean-up of its lobby based only on the presence of visible dust.	The White House Council on Environmental Quality changes EPA staff's September 14 draft release, which had stated, "The concern raised by these samples would be for the workers at the cleanup site and for those workers who might be returning to their offices on or near Water Street on Monday, September 17, 2001." This sentence is deleted. Instead, the September 16 release quotes OSHA saying, "Our tests show that it is safe for New Yorkers to go back to work in New York's financial district." The EPA office building testing and clean-up information is not made public at the time.
September 16, 2001	The EPA tells *New York Newsday* that its highest recorded asbestos reading for dust contamination was 4.5 percent.	*New York Newsday* quotes the EPA administrator as saying that "there is no reason for concern," based on airborne asbestos tests in the financial district. The stock market reopens on September 17; tens of thousands of workers return to work in the Ground Zero area.

Figure 7.8
What was known, what was said.

citizens' attention to reports that showed inconsistencies and falsehoods.[19] Typical of these demonstrations were timelines or tables that juxtaposed what was known and what was said by federal administrators (figure 7.8).

With these demonstrations, civic organizations were able to fix the attention of elected officials to their grievances. In the spring of 2003, Senator Hillary Clinton threatened to block the nomination of Governor Whitman's successor at the EPA. In exchange for her vote, she secured public hearings by an expert panel to review the agency's work and make recommendations for corrective action. With the establishment of this panel, citizen groups were eligible for public funds to hire independent experts to monitor the monitors. With vastly superior resources, the EPA launched a counterdemonstration on its own website in a public relations campaign designed to convey that it was, after all, a caring public agency (figure 7.9).

Conclusion

Our overview of the deliberations and demonstrations in rebuilding Lower Manhattan is doubly inconclusive. First, this chapter outlines an analytic strategy and is too brief to examine the topic in depth. Second, the rebuilding of Lower Manhattan is still very much a work in progress (Sagalyn 2005). Although architects have been chosen for the WTC site, the memorial, and the transit hub, there is much dispute about the overall design. Moreover, as we saw, the public's involvement has been less about this or that architectural design than over the use of the site and its relationship to neighboring districts and the city as a whole. Many, indeed most, of these issues remain unsettled.[20]

What has been learned? New Yorkers demonstrated that civic participation can be revitalized and that new technologies can be an important resource in organizing that participation. New civic associations were mobilized, and existing ones were repurposed. The Municipal Art Society spun off Imagine New York, the American Institute of Architects sponsored New York New Visions, the Regional Planning Association provided leadership in forming the Civic Alliance, and professional networks coalesced into more formalized, albeit temporary, organizations. In these and other assemblies, tens of thousands of lay citizens actively participated in the extended processes of collective sense making. In nearly every case, websites, list-servs, and other digital technologies were critical in mobilizing energies, providing information, and supporting collaborative, interpretive work. Aware that the interest of lay citizens and engaged professionals might wane as the sense of immediacy diminishes, dozens of civic organizations formed a new umbrella, New York 2050, to debate the city's future as a lasting legacy to the democratic momentum forged after 9/11. Thus, the most important consequences might lie in yet another stage of sense making when citizens reflect on the process and draw conclusions about the limitations of their own experiments.

The information government paradigm, as applied to the case of post-9/11 New York, highlights how new technologies were less important in facilitating intra-governmental coordination than in fostering the generation of information at a vast number of sites and the circulation of this information among citizens themselves

We Protect More Than the Environment...

Home is where we live our lives and feel safe with our loved ones. For some living in lower Manhattan, the possibility that dust from the collapse of the World Trade Center may linger in their homes has raised concerns.

That is why the EPA, along with FEMA, New York City, New York State and OSHA is offering residents of lower Manhattan — south of Canal, Allen and Pike Streets — the option of having their homes professionally cleaned and/or tested for airborne asbestos contamination free of charge.

While scientific data does not point to any significant long-term health risks, people should not have to live with uncertainty about the future.

Call **1-877-796-5471** or visit **www.epa.gov/wtc** to schedule an appointment to have your apartment cleaned and/or tested or for further information.

www.epa.gov/wtc
1-877-796-5471

Created by Fenn & King Communications • 202-337-6995

Figure 7.9
EPA advertisement.

(Johnson and Bimber 2004). However, we contend that of even greater significance was the interpretative dimension of information government. In our era, information abounds. Faced with a deluge of information, a multiplicity of evaluative principles, and myriad features that could be potentially salient, what is taken into account? What counts? To that challenge, New Yorkers deployed new technologies not only to increase the flow of *information* among a greater number of nodes but to build communities of *interpretation*.

As a large and amorphous project ecology, civic engagement in the New York case shares an important challenge with other "project" forms: given that projects are by definition temporary, how is the knowledge that is gained from one project made available to future projects? This problem is especially acute in the digital era. As our own research indicates, many of the websites and other digital formats from which we collected data are no longer in operation and, therefore, that particular knowledge base is no longer accessible to citizens. If public officials are to be held accountable, the public needs access to records of its own accountings. How will libraries, museums, and universities respond to this challenge?

Notes

Research for this paper was supported by a grant from the National Science Foundation #IIS-0306868. Our thanks to Daniel Beunza, David Lazer, and Fabian Muniesa for helpful criticisms and suggestions on an earlier draft.

1. For useful introductions to these ideas, see the essays "The Pattern of Inquiry," "Analysis of Reflective Thinking," and "The Place of Judgment in Reflective Activity" collected in Dewey 1998.

2. In place of the debate about online versus offline forms, our observations in New York lead us to think about actual organizational forms that recombine virtual and conventional modalities (see Barney 2004; Woolgar 2002).

3. In a study of an abitrage trading room, Beunza and Stark (2004), for example, show how calculation is not a function of the solitary trader but socially distributed across persons, desks, mathmetical models, visualization techniques, automated algorithms, and other instrumentation. See Callon and Muniesa 2005 for a more general discussion of calculation.

4. Our emphasis here on the the networks, protocols, and technologies should not imply that participation happens just by assemblying people in a forum. As Agre (2004) argues, performance requires a set of skills—making associations, building issues, and forging alliances, for example.

5. Burkhalter, Gastil, and Kelshaw (2002) offer an instructive summary: "In sum, deliberative groups build a strong information base, consider a range of solutions, establish representative evaluative criteria, and apply those criteria equally to all solutions" (405). Sanders

(1997) argues against deliberation as necessarily exemplary: "Deliberation is a request for a certain kind of talk: rational, contained, and oriented to a shared problem. Where anti-democrats have used the standards of expertise, moderation, and communal orientation as a way to exclude average citizens from political decision-making, modern democrats seem to adopt these standards as guides for what democratic politics should be like. And the exclusionary connotations of these standards persist" (370).

6. Examples of these images are available at http://www.globalsecurity.org/eye/wtc-imagery.htm.

7. http://www.bu.edu/prc/6months/aroundgroundzero.htm.

8. 911 Environmental Action (www.911ea.org); New York Environmental Law and Justice Project (www.nyenvirolaw.org); Asthma Moms (www.asthmamoms.com).

9. www.sonicmemorial.org/.

10. www.ssrc.org/sept11/essays/.

11. www.rebuilddowntownourtown.org.

12. http://www.wnyc.org/sixmonths/.

13. See Kutz et al. 2005 for a preliminary analysis of these statements using computer-assisted interpretation algorithms.

14. Science and technology studies have been fascinated by the similarities between the repertoires of science and politics (Latour 1987). Most recently, Barry (2001) has shifted attention from processes of representation to practices of demonstration, highlighting the entanglement of the political and the technical. For a concise but extraordinarily rich discussion of these issues, see Callon's (2004) review essay.

15. Unlike physical models, the digital renderings by the architects in the Innovative Design competition were available to the public at any time on dozens of websites.

16. See "EPA National Ombudsman First and Second Investigative Hearings on World Trade Center Hazardous Waste Contamination." Convened by Jerrold Nadler, Congressman; Robert Martin, EPA Ombudsman; Hugh Kaufman, EPA Ombudsman Chief Investigator in New York City, 2002. Available at www.nyenvirolaw.org/PDF/ Transcript-EPA-OmbudsmanHearing-2-23-2002.pdf and www.nyenvirolaw.org/PDF/ Transcript-EPA-OmbudsmanHearing-3-11-2002.pdf.

17. Technical materials posted on community organization websites were often more informative than those of official agencies. See, for example, the "Question & Answer for NYC Residents Specific Safety Precautions" section of ImmuneWeb 911 launched within weeks after 9/11, http://www.immuneweb.org/911/.

18. "EPA has not fully discharged its duties under PDD (Presidential Directive) 62, the National Contingency Plan (NCP) and the 2001 OMB Annual Report to Congress on Combating Terrorism. EPA has abandoned its responsibilities for cleaning up buildings (both inside and out) that are contaminated, or that are being recontaminated, as a result of the uncontrolled chemical releases from the WTC terrorist attack" (Martin 2002). Available at http://www.nycosh.org/environment_wtc/Ombudsman_Findings_WTC.pdf. After issuing his report, National Ombudsman Robert Martin was fired by the EPA.

19. www.911ea.org/.

20. Nonetheless, the collaborative sense making that we described did have consequences in its establishment of success criteria: an outcome can be judged to fail if it does not harmonize commercialization, memorialization, cultural institutions, and new residential development.

References

Agre, Philip E. 2004. "The Practical Republic: Social Skills and the Progress of Citizenship." In *Community in the Digital Age: Philosophy and Practice,* ed. Andrew Feenberg and Darin David Barney, 201–223. Lanham, MD: Oxford: Rowman and Littlefield.

Barney, Darin. 2004. "The Vanishing Table, or Community in a World That Is No World." In *Community in the Digital Age: Philosophy and Practice,* ed. Andrew Feenberg and Darin David Barney, 31–52. Lanham, MD: Oxford: Rowman and Littlefield.

Barry, Andrew. 2001. *Political Machines: Governing a Technological Society.* London and New York: Athlone Press.

Beunza, Daniel, and David Stark. 2004. "Tools of the Trade: The Socio-Technology of Arbitrage in a Wall Street Trading Room." *Industrial and Corporate Change* 13, no. 1: 369–401.

Beunza, Daniel, and David Stark. 2005. "Resolving Identities: Successive Crises in a Trading Room after 9/11." In *Wounded City: The Social Impact of 9/11,* ed. Nancy Foner, 293–320. New York: Russell Sage Foundation Press.

Burkhalter, Stephanie, John Gastil, and Todd Kelshaw. 2002. "A Conceptual Definition and Theoretical Model of Public Deliberation in Small Face-to-Face Groups." *Communication Theory* 12, no. 4: 398–423.

Callon, Michel. 2004. "Europe Wrestling With Technology." *Economy and Society* 33, no. 1: 121–134.

Callon, Michel, and Fabian Muniesa. 2005. "Economic Markets as Calculative Collective Devices." *Organization Studies* 26, no. 8: 1229–1250.

Callon, Michel, Pierre Lascoumes, and Yannick Barthe. 2001. *Agir dans un monde incertain. Essai sur la démocratie représentative.* Paris: Seuil.

Carpenter, David O., Paul W. Bartlett, Liam O. Horgan, and Richard A. Lemen. 2005. "CBPR Expert Advisory Committee Review of the Document Entitled, Draft Proposed Sampling Program to Determine Extent of World Trade Center Impacts to the Indoor Environment." Available at http://www.911ea.org/3Final_WTC_Synthesis.pdf (accessed September 27, 2005).

Chatfield, Eric, and John Kominsky. 2001. "Summary Report: Characterization of Particulate Found in Apartments after Destruction of the World Trade Center." Available at http://www.epa.gov/wtc/panel/GroundZeroTaskForceReport108.pdf (accessed September 27, 2005).

Civic Alliance. 2002. "A Planning Framework to Rebuild Downtown New York." Available at www.civic-alliance.org/pdf/Framework0827.pdf (accessed January 22, 2007).

Culbertson, Frank. 2001. "Letter from Expedition Three Commander Frank L. Culbertson (Captain, USN Retired), Reflecting on the Events of September 11." September 12, 19: 34

hours. Available at http://spaceflight.nasa.gov/station/crew/exp3/culbertsonletter.html (accessed January 1, 2007).

Dewey, John. [1927] 1991. *The Public and Its Problems.* Athens: Swallow Press/Ohio University Press.

Dewey, John. [1939] 1993. "Creative Democracy—The Task Before Us." In *The Political Writings,* ed. Debra Morris and Ian Shapiro, 240–248. Indianapolis and Cambridge: Hackett Publishing Company, Inc.

Dewey, John. 1998. *The Essential Dewey Volume 2: Ethics, Logic, Psychology,* ed. Larry A. Hickman and Thomas M. Alexander. Bloomington and Indianapolis: Indiana University Press.

Dorf, Michael, and Charles Sabel. 1998. "A Constitution of Democratic Experimentalism." *Columbia Law Review* 98: 201–267.

Eliasoph, Nina. 1996. "Making a Fragile Public: A Talk-Centered Study of Citizenship and Power." *Sociological Theory* 14: 262–289.

EPA Office of the Inspector General. 2003. "Evaluation Report EPA's Response to the World Trade Center Collapse: Challenges, Successes, and Areas for Improvement." Report No. 2003-P-00012, August 21. Available at http://www.epa.gov/oig/reports/2003/WTC_report_20030821.pdf.

Fishkin, Jeremy. 2004. "Deliberative Democracy in America: A Proposal for a Popular Branch of Government." *Political Science Quarterly* 119: 544–545.

Foucault, Michel. 1979. *Discipline and Punish: The Birth of the Prison.* New York: Vintage Books.

Friedland, Lewis A. 2001. "Communication, Community, and Democracy—Toward a Theory of the Communicatively Integrated Community." *Communication Research* 28: 358–391.

Gibson, James J. 1979. *The Ecological Approach to Visual Perception.* Boston: Houghton Mifflin.

Girard, Monique, and David Stark. 2002. "Distributing Intelligence and Organizing Diversity in New-Media Projects." *Environment and Planning A* 34, no. 11: 1927–1949.

Grabher, Gernot. 2004a. "Learning in Projects, Remembering in Networks? Communality, Sociality and Connectivity in Project Ecologies." *European Urban and Regional Studies* 11, no. 2: 99–119.

Grabher, Gernot. 2004b. "Temporary Architectures of Learning: Knowledge Governance in Project Ecologies." *Organization Studies* 25, no. 9: 1491–1514. Special issue on Project Organizations, Embeddedness and Repositories of Knowledge.

Hutchins, Edwin. 1995. *Cognition in the Wild.* Cambridge, MA: The MIT Press.

Imagine New York. n.d. Idea Gallery Website. Available at http://www.imaginenyideas.org/Projects/Imagine/ideaGallery.asp.

Johnson, Diane, and Bruce Bimber. 2004. "The Internet and Political Transformation Revisited." In *Community in the Digital Age: Philosophy and Practice,* ed. Andrew Feenberg and Darin David Barney, 239–261. Lanham, MD: Rowman & Littlefield.

Katz, Alyssa. 2002. "Toxic Haste: New York's Media Rush to Judgment on New York's Air." *The American Prospect Online* 13, no. 4, February 25. Available at http://www.prospect.org/print-friendly/print/V13/4/katz-a.html.

Kurgan, Laura. 2002. "Around Ground Zero." *Grey Room* 1: 96–102.

Kutz, Daniel, Javed Mostafa, Monique Girard, and David Stark. 2005. "Using Moral Worlds to Understand Citizen Input." Paper presented at the Sixth Annual Meeting of the Association of Internet Researchers, Chicago, October 6.

Latour, Bruno. 1987. *Science in Action: Following Scientists and Engineers through Society.* Cambridge, MA: Harvard University Press.

Latour, Bruno, and Peter Weibel, eds. 2005. *Making Things Public: Atmospheres of Democracy.* Cambridge, MA: The MIT Press.

Lazarsfeld, Paul, and Harry H. Field. 1946. *The People Look at Radio.* Chapel Hill: The University of North Carolina Press.

Lisle, Debbie. 2004. "Gazing at Ground Zero: Tourism, Voyeurism and Spectacle." *Journal for Cultural Research* 8: 3–21.

Martin, R. 2002. "Findings to Date, Recommendations to Data, and Second Round of Interrogatories related to the National Ombudsman World Trade Center Hazardous Waste Case." Memo to Jane Kenny, EPA Administrator for Region 11, March 27. Available at http://www.nycosh.org/environment_wtc/Ombudsman_Findings_WTC.pdf (accessed September 27, 2005).

Mattei, Suzanne. 2003. "Pollution and Deception at Ground Zero." The Sierra Club Report. Available at http://www.gothamgazette.com/rebuilding_nyc/sierraclub_report.pdf (accessed September 27, 2005).

Merton, Robert K. 1952. *Reader in Bureaucracy.* Glencoe, IL: Free Press.

Mische, Ann, and Harrison White. 1998. "Between Conversation and Situation: Public Switching Dynamics Across Network-Domains." *Social Research* 65: 295–324.

Pea, Roy. 1993. "Practices of distributed Intelligence and Designs for Education." In *Distributed Cognition*, ed. Gabriel Salomon, 47–87. Cambridge: Cambridge University Press.

Polletta, Franscesca, and Lesley Wood. 2005. "Public Deliberation after 9/11." In *Wounded City: The Social Impact of 9/11*, ed. Nancy Foner, 321–350. New York: Russell Sage Foundation.

Rabeharisoa, Vololona, and Michel Callon. 2002. "The Involvement of Patients' Associations in Research." *International Social Science Journal* 54, no. 171: 57–63.

Ramirez, Margaret. 2001. "America's Ordeal Seeking Answers about Air Quality in the Aftermath, Uncertainty Lingers." *Newsday*, October 12, p. A18.

Sack, Warren. 2005. "Discourse Architecture and Very Large-Scale Conversation." In *Digital Formations: IT and New Architectures in the Global Realm*, ed. Robert Latham and Saskia Sassen, 242–282. Princeton, NJ: Princeton University Press.

Sagalyn, Lynne. 2005. "The Politics of Planning the World's Most Visible Urban Redevelopment Project." In *Contentious City: The Politics of Recovery in New York City*, ed. John Mollenkopf, 23–72. New York: Russell Sage Foundation.

Sanders, Lynn M. 1997. "Against Deliberation." *Political Theory* 25, no. 3: 347–376.

Schuler, Douglas. 2004. "Toward Civic Intelligence: Building a New Socio-technological Infrastructure." In *Community in the Digital Age: Philosophy and Practice*, ed. Andrew Feenberg and Darin David Barney, 263–285. Lanham, MD: Oxford: Rowman & Littlefield.

Sorkin, Michael and Sharon Zukin. 2002. *After the World Trade Center: Rethinking New York City*. London: Routledge.

Sydow, Jörg, Lars Lindkwvist, and Robert DeFillippi. 2004. "Project-Based Organizations, Embeddedness and Repositories of Knowledge: Editorial." *Organization Studies* 25: 1475–1489.

Woolgar, Steve. 2002. "Five Rules of Virtuality." In *Virtual Society? Technology, Cyberbole, Reality*, ed. Steve Woolgar, 1–22. Oxford: Oxford University Press.

Case Illustration

The Rise and Fall (?) of Participatory Electronic Information Infrastructures

Åke Grönlund

Around the turn of the century, several "e-democracy" projects existed across the world. They were usually found at local levels of government, but there were also efforts at the national level (e.g., Hansard 2002; Macintosh et al. 2001). One such endeavor was the ambitious Swedish Official Committee on Democracy (SOCD), initiated, like many others in other countries, as a measure to tackle the decreasing popular participation in democratic processes and the associated, as it was perceived, decreasing legitimacy of the democratic system (SOCD, 2000).

The SOCD, in line with *strong democracy* (Barber 1984; see also Premfors 2000) concluded that there was currently too much focus on information and services, and too little on the individual's political role as a citizen. In the wake of the SOCD, Sweden created the position of minister of democracy, and several e-democracy projects aimed at active citizen participation were set up on government funding. There were national awards and a general euphoria around the reinvigorating effects of these projects. Some of them were very ambitious and created considerable change locally over the first couple of years. But then what? To what extent did these "e-democracy" projects lead to lasting change? Were different communication patterns established? Did the information infrastructure within the field of democratic decision making change?

What follows is a description of two of the then leading projects, in Bollnäs and Kista. Both jurisdictions had twenty to thirty thousand inhabitants; one is a Stockholm district, the other a rural town. Both had the standard technical components in place, such as websites, feedback systems, "citizen proposals," the formal right of citizens to make proposals directly to the city/borough council, etc., and both had a long-term strategy. Yet the foundation of each initiative was quite different, one focusing on political leadership, the other on administrative reform.

Bollnäs had chosen a "municipal community network" approach, where personal touch was key. Citizens could directly e-mail the two municipal commissioners and be guaranteed an answer. On the web "The Dialogue," an open forum, has been running since 1998 and contains discussions in several predefined categories. City council meetings were video-broadcasted live on the web. Viewers could send questions via e-mail during the break halfway through the meeting, which were answered after the break. The municipal commissioners were the champions of the activities, very active in the discussion forums and prompt when it came to answering questions from citizens. They felt politics was too party centered, that the important discussions took place at party meetings with only a few people present. They wanted to more broadly involve citizens in political discussions. The goal was simply to engage citizens in local politics. They did so in a very political way, by becoming more visible as political leaders. However, this eventually raised concerns, and resistance, as it changed the traditional Swedish politics model: the political parties were largely invisible in the discussion forums, which is not customary in Swedish political debates where parties rather than individual politicians are in focus.

Since it was so heavily dependent on two champions, the Bollnäs model was vulnerable, as the 2003 local election demonstrated. The new political majority viewed the e-democracy project as an effort of the social democrats, not something of value for the citizens, and did not pursue it. The Dialogue is still available on the web, but questions from citizens go unanswered (and of course there are not as many anymore).

Kista chose a more businesslike approach. Since the mid-1990s, the information technology (IT) manager and a couple of civil servants at the district management office had been championing Web development in close cooperation with local businesses. There were several externally funded projects in the e-democracy genre underpinning the effort, and the then-mayor was supportive. These projects were initiated and owned by the City of Stockholm, not by Kista politicians. The agents of change were therefore the project management team with support from central IT and development functions. Hence, initiative came from the administrative side, not from politicians. The latter were engaged in the process as that became necessary.

The goal was to involve people active in Kista in local development. Kista is a commuting suburb. People come there to work, while many residents commute elsewhere for work. Hence stakeholdership rather than residency was the focus. Indeed this new view of politics was in fact openly discussed, not only in Kista. As opposed to Bollnäs, there was no political leader championing the Kista effort. Rather, it was the administration that tried to open new communication channels between citizens and politicians. They drew on e-democracy best practice of the time, but as civil servants they could of course only champion the channels, not the political agenda.

The Kista Portal opened in 1997. In 2000, democracy was given more focus by means of a designated Web department for "e-democracy," with video broadcasting of council meetings and discussion forums involving politicians both online and at physical meetings. In 2002, e-democracy activities were again upgraded by the opening of the "Kista e-parliament," an effort to create a larger and more permanent forum that could be addressed as a sort of citizen panel on a more regular and deliberative basis in the local development. The Kista web developed rapidly over some five years. The small initiator team enrolled several important networks of actors: first, local businesses; second, the city administration; and third, local politicians—exactly the opposite sequence of Bollnäs.

The Kista trial broke down due to a combination of several changes. The political support was too dependent on the then mayor, who was replaced after the 2003 election. Political support from the new majority in central Stockholm was also wavering. Support from civil society was not strong or organized enough to be used as a counterforce. Little active support existed within the administration beyond the core group of champions. Support from Stockholm central management was also dependent on key people who left as the new majority moved in. There was at the time—after the IT bust at the stock market—a negative feeling toward "flashy IT projects" (a quote from the new mayor, who preferred to direct resources to health care and education). At the same time, external project money drained, which meant there was no immediate business motivation for continuation. Moreover, a centralizing process in Stockholm required all districts to become more similar. E-democracy was one of the things that were streamlined, and so today districts only have political contact information online. Over the process of change, key people left. The IT manager died. The researchers tied to the different externally funded projects left when the money was depleted, and other people in the key group relocated or took early retirement.

Conclusion

In my 2002 review of the previous cases, and of two more (Grönlund 2002), I saw them as precursors in the quest for making good use of IT in local democratic practices. They had made a difference locally; however, not only was implementation still an issue, but the cases also represented different models of democracy. It was clear that e-democracy was not determined by technology; it can come in many shapes. But I also issued a warning: "We found conflicts between local e-democracy and global e-government developments. It appears unlikely that the methods can come much further—locally as well as in terms of becoming role models for others on a more general scale—without a more well-defined relation between the e-democratic activities and policy, as institutions will have to be reshaped. This restructuring is a fundamental one, involving a rethinking of the government model as such." (Grönlund 2002)

As we have seen, the warning was warranted. Today, all Swedish projects, not just the two presented here, have been scaled down or abandoned. Websites are still there, but participation is no longer championed. In all cases, the main reason is that champions, however successful over a considerable period, did not manage to implant the ideas into the political sphere well enough to survive an election. Other factors played a role, too, including the national government's abandonment of its project of revitalizing democracy. Project funds dried up, and the Minister of Democracy was given other tasks. Today, efficient service delivery is at the top of the national agenda, and municipal economy is generally worse than ever. E-democracy is an obsolete word. This, of course, does not necessarily mean that citizen participation will go away, only that it is more likely to take other forms, such as e-lobbying and interaction in service processes.

References

Barber, Benjamin. 1984. *Strong Democracy*. Berkeley: University of California Press.

Grönlund, Åke. 2002. "Emerging Electronic Infrastructures: In Search of Democratic Components." *Social Sciences Computer Review* 21, no. 1 (Fall): 55–72.

Hansard. 2002. Hansard Society—Promoting Effective Parliamentary Democracy. Publications list available at http://www.hansardsociety.org.uk/publications.htm.

Macintosh, Ann, Elisabeth Davenport, Anna Malina, and Angus Whyte. 2001. "Technology to Support Participatory Democracy." In *Electronic Government: Design, Applications, and Management*, ed. Åke Grönlund, 226–248. Hershey, PA: Idea Group Publishing.

SOCD. 2000. *A Sustainable Democracy: Policy for Rule by the People in the 2000s.* SOU 2000: 1. Stockholm: Fritzes.

Premfors, Rune. 2000. *Den starka demokratin (The strong democracy)*. Stockholm: Atlas.

Additionally, interviews and discussions with actors in Bollnäs and Kista, as well as Stockholm central management, have been conducted at several occasions during the period 2000–2002. Follow-up interviews were made in 2005. Further websites and discussion forums were visited on several occasions.

8

"Open-Source Politics" Reconsidered: Emerging Patterns in Online Political Participation

Matthew Hindman

Introduction

The 2004 election in the United States was a watershed for online politics. Online fund-raising was far more successful in 2004 than in previous election cycles, bringing in hundreds of millions of dollars in small donations. With the encouragement of presidential hopeful Howard Dean and other candidates, hundreds of thousands of citizens in hundreds of cities used Internet sites like Meetup.com to organize local advocacy groups. Practically unknown four years earlier, political weblogs or "blogs" helped shape traditional press coverage, with the most popular blogs far exceeding the readership of traditional opinion journals. In addition to candidate fund-raising, independent activist groups like Moveon.org solicited millions of dollars in contributions through e-mail and web appeals.

How are we to make sense of these highly visible, interrelated changes in American political practice? One answer came from elites who were themselves intimately involved in these political innovations. The 2004 election cycle, several suggested, marked the emergence of "open-source politics." Joe Trippi, Howard Dean's campaign manager, declared that Dean had attempted to duplicate "that same collaboration that occurs in Linux and open source" (Lessig 2003). As an article in *The Nation* enthused, "New tools and practices born on the Internet have reached critical mass, enabling ordinary people to participate in processes that used to be closed to them" (Sifry 2004). Markos Moulitsas Zuniga, publisher of the most popular political blog, wrote, "When I'm asked about blogging's legacy, I talk about open source. Open-source politics, open-source activism, open-source journalism—the aggregation of thousands on behalf of a common cause...the ability to pool our efforts on issues that capture the collective imagination is what really gets me excited" (Moulitsas Zuniga 2005). On the other end of the ideological spectrum, a group of prominent conservative political bloggers even renamed its media company

Open Source Media, only to relent when it found that the name was already taken (Johnson and Simon 2005).

Based on "information government"—the flows of information within government and between government and society—this chapter examines "information politics," the flows of information within the political sphere. In particular, it focuses on assertions that network technologies (and especially the Internet) are fundamentally transforming the flows of information regarding politics within the United States. In this chapter, I consider three prominent examples of "open-source" activism: the Dean campaign, the left-leaning political advocacy group Moveon.org, and the most popular political weblogs. In each case, I suggest, forms of community-based production similar to those used in open-source software development have played an important role. Yet this is not the whole story. Media accounts often provide a romanticized and incomplete view of open-source development, suggesting that open-source software is a scrappy underdog, a grassroots effort cobbled together by amateurs and college students. In reality, as I argue here, most of those who work on open-source software are professional programmers with more than a decade of coding experience. Open-source software has thrived, in part, because giant companies like IBM, Sun Microsystems, and Netscape have invested billions of dollars in its success.

Similar contradictions have already emerged in these early examples of open-source politics. If we want to fully understand how open-source methods are changing the political landscape, we must not overlook key investments by traditional players. I argue that we should be particularly careful about the rhetoric of "openness" that continues to pervade discussion of online politics. Many have asserted that open-source politics will flatten traditional hierarchies and help equalize political participation. Consistent with Coglianese (chapter 5), I find that this is not true. Rather, open-source politics has quickly produced its own set of political elites. In short, open-source politics does resemble the open-source software movement—just not in the way that many think.

The Internet and Political Participation

Political scientists have long hoped that new communications technologies would improve American citizenship. Ben Barber's *Strong Democracy* (1984) imagined that new forms of electronic communications media might raise levels of participation and give citizens greater voice in governmental decision making. Similarly, in Robert Dahl's *Democracy and Its Critics* (1989), computerized communications technologies were seen as the only viable solution to disparities in access to political information. Many popular accounts argued that the Internet would perform much as Dahl and Barber had hoped: citizens would become better informed, levels of engagement would rise, and political elites would be made obsolete (e.g., Morris 1999).

Yet when social scientists began to look more closely at the emerging link between the Internet and politics, their conclusions were skeptical. Many scholars focused on the so-called digital divide, in which many traditionally disadvantaged groups lagged behind in Internet use and access. Some worried that the growing importance of information technologies would exacerbate the gap between citizens of industrialized nations and those in the developing world (e.g., Norris 2001; Warschauer 2003). Data from the United States found sharp disparities in Internet access along the lines of race, gender, education, income, age, and locality (e.g., Margolis and Resnick 2000; NTIA 1995, 1998). More recent research suggests some initial gaps have narrowed: women now outnumber men online, age differences are less profound, and rural use more closely matches that in urban and suburban areas (Lenhart et al. 2003; Mossberger, Tolbert, and Stansbury 2003; NTIA 2002). Nonetheless, Internet use remains closely correlated with education and income. Race still matters online: according to 2002 Pew data, 55 percent of blacks and 46 percent of Hispanics say that they do not use the Internet, compared with 40 percent of whites (Lenhart et al. 2003). Other research has debated the relative role of race versus the concomitant problem of concentrated poverty in the digital divide (Mossberger, Tolbert, and Gilbert 2006).

Increasingly, scholars have demonstrated that user skills follow much the same social cleavages as patterns of access. Hargittai's (2003) experimental work showed that many users lack basic skills; political tasks (including finding a campaign website) prove particularly difficult (see also chapter 5). Moreover, according to several studies, the number of Americans online also has plateaued at between 60 and 70 percent of the American public (Bimber 2003b). In the short term, it does not seem that rising overall Internet use will close the digital divide.

Despite concerns about the digital divide, some scholars did conclude that Internet usage had political effects. While finding little relationship between Internet use and other forms of political behavior, Bimber (2001) did observe that Internet use was closely connected to citizen political donations. Tolbert and McNeal (2003) argued that, controlling for other factors, those with access to the Internet and online political news were more likely to vote in the 1996 and 2000 elections. Krueger (2002) similarly suggested that, if Internet access were to expand, the Internet would indeed mobilize many previously inactive citizens. Some scholars also concluded that, at least for younger citizens, Internet use was associated with increased production of social capital (Shah, Kwak, and Holbert 2001; Shah, McLeod, and Yoon 2001).

Amid this Internet scholarship, one of the most persistent and intriguing themes concerns the Internet's ability to permit novel forms of collective action. While Mancur Olson (1965) had famously argued that small groups have organizational advantages over large groups, some researchers hypothesized that new technologies made it possible for broad, diffuse networks of citizens to find each other and pursue common goals (Bimber 1998, 2003a; Lupia and Sin 2003). Bimber (2003a) argued that examples like the Million Mom March and the Libertarian Party–led opposition to changes in banking rules were surprising breaks with previous patterns. The Zapatista movement and 1999 Seattle protests against the World Trade Organization (WTO) were also seen as exemplifying new forms of "networked politics" particularly advantageous to resource-poor actors (Bennett 2003; Kahn and Kellner 2004; Langman 2005). In Bennett's (2003) analysis, a transnational network of activists managed to build a large, diverse coalition across geographic and ideological boundaries, but they struggled to make collective decisions and forge a common identity. And while events like the Million Mom March and the "Battle of Seattle" represented the fusion of technology with traditional protest activities, some scholars focused on a form of political activity that was wholly new: "hacktivism," defined as the writing of software code with the goal of promoting a political ideology (Deibert 2000, 2003; Denning 2001; Taylor and Jordan 2004). According to Deibert (2003), much hacktivist activity has focused on preserving the "openness" of the Internet architecture against the efforts of commercial and security interests to improve online surveillance, censorship, and control.

New forms of political protest also connect with other recent scholarship on the proper role of the public sphere. The past decade has seen many scholars argue for a renewed emphasis on reasoned civic debate (e.g., Bohman and Regh 1997; Elster 1998; Gutmann and Thompson 1996; Habermas 1996). According to theorists, "deliberative democracy," properly pursued, produces benefits at once epistemological, normative, and practical. Scholars of politics, in particular, argued that deliberative debate should generate greater democratic legitimacy, higher levels of social capital, and better public policies (Gutmann and Thompson 2004; Sunstein 2001b; see also chapter 7). Some scholars, drawing on the deliberative democracy literature, have concluded that the Internet will undermine societal deliberation. Sunstein's book *Republic.com* (2001a) suggested that by making broadcasters and other general-interest intermediaries "largely a thing of the past," the Internet would promote political polarization and a coarsening of public debate. Wilhelm (2000) likewise concluded that online political discussions were "neither inclusive nor deliberative," and were particularly likely to silence already marginal voices. Even Benjamin Barber (2003), the early prophet of electronic democracy, worried about the Internet undermining the public sphere.

Yet despite a few novel examples of political organization and some concerns about online discourse, the preponderance of scholarship argued that the Internet would only modestly impact political participation. Richard Davis (1999) declared that the movement of traditional actors and institutions into cyberspace meant that the Internet would perpetuate previous patterns of political influence. In the same vein, Margolis and Resnick (2000) suggested that Internet politics was "politics as usual"; citizens would ignore online political information just as they ignored political information in traditional media. Using longitudinal data, Jennings and Zeitner (2003) found that Internet use had little effect on civic engagement. Norris (2000) similarly highlighted citizens' disinterest in politics, arguing that the Internet "probably has had the least impact on changing the motivational basis for political activism" (22). As Bimber (2003a) summarized the evidence, "It does not appear, at least so far, that new technology leads to higher aggregate levels of political participation" (5).

It was all the more surprising, then, that the Internet played a key role in the 2004 elections. In 2000, Gore and Bush had used the Internet to raise only $2.7 million and $1.6 million, respectively; John McCain raised $1.4 million through his website in the three days after he won the New Hampshire primary (Bimber and Davis 2003, 39). The 2000 experience was consistent with recent history, where most presidential campaign funds for both parties have come from large donations, with the Democrats especially dependent on a few wealthy donors. 2004 marked a sharp break with this pattern. Howard Dean raised roughly half of his $52 million campaign war chest online, with most Internet funds coming from small donations.[1] Wesley Clark, Dennis Kucinich, and (after winning the New Hampshire primary) John Kerry also raised a considerable portion of their funding from small, online donations. Dean convinced more than 640,000 supporters to provide their e-mail addresses and zip codes, so that they could be informed of local pro-Dean "meetups"; roughly 175,000 supporters attended events in more than 600 cities (Hindman 2005c). Survey evidence suggests that meetup attendees were less experienced than typical primary volunteers, consistent with claims that Dean mobilized many previously inactive citizens (Hindman 2005b; Williams, Weinberg, and Gordon 2004; also see Klotz 2003).

The 2004 campaign also provided a larger role for nontraditional interest groups who organized themselves online. Most prominent was Moveon.org, who by November 2004 claimed on its homepage to have more than 2,750,000 members.[2] Moveon.org had been founded largely accidentally in 1998 by Wes Boyd and Joan Blades, two software entrepreneurs. Boyd and Blades created an online petition calling on Congress to halt the impeachment of President Clinton, and instead to "censure and move on." An e-mail Boyd and Blades sent to fewer than 100 friends and acquaintances spread rapidly, ultimately gathering more than 500,000 signatures. The e-mail list, website, and social networks assembled in the anti-impeachment campaign served as the core for future efforts. According to the Center for Responsive Politics, Moveon.org's 527 political organization disbursed $20 million during the 2004 calendar year, ranking it eighth among all advocacy groups.[3]

Third, the 2004 election cycle highlighted the growing importance of political weblogs. Virtually unknown four years earlier, in 2004 blogs were an important source of political news and commentary, particularly among the most politically engaged. According to the Pew Internet and American Life Project, 9 percent of the online population reported visiting political weblogs during the 2004 campaign, with 4 percent visiting "regularly" (Ranie 2005); a more recent Gallup survey found that 12 percent of the U.S. public read political blogs at least several times a month (Saad 2005). Both scholars and popular observers suggested that blogs had helped set the larger media agenda, citing bloggers' role in the resignations of Trent Lott and Dan Rather (Bloom 2003; Drezner and Farrell 2004; Guthrie 2004; Drum 2005; but see Scott 2004). While most political weblogs get little traffic, a handful of hypersuccessful blogs get hundreds of thousands of visitors a day.

Making Sense of These Changes

The 2004 electoral cycle was not a wholesale break with previous writings about Internet politics, but it did challenge prevailing sentiment among social scientists that previous patterns of political participation would persist largely unchanged. In one key area—fund-raising for presidential candidates—there is overwhelming evidence that the Internet raised participation levels. Dean's success at using Meetup .com suggests, too, that the Internet will enable some candidates to recruit many volunteers online. Millions of Americans every day are reading a genre of political opinion that did not exist a few years ago, providing another potential avenue for political mobilization. These phenomena force us to revise, at least in part, previous null findings on the Internet and political participation.

Some have suggested that these Internet-driven changes in the political landscape are part of a consistent pattern. No one received more credit for Dean's online successes than Trippi. Trippi was responsible for many of the campaign's large online investments: the development of the candidate website, the focus on online fundraising, the creation of the campaign blog, and the use of Meetup.com to organize pro-Dean groups all across the country. Trippi saw the Dean campaign as part of much larger shift toward what he termed "open-source politics."

The open-source label, as Trippi explained, came from software development. Most commercial software is proprietary: it is developed in a top-down manner by professional programmers paid by the company that owns the software, and the software code that makes up these programs remains a closely guarded secret. Open-source software, by contrast, allows the underlying software code to be seen by all. Programmers anywhere in the world can view the source code, distribute the code freely, and (in most cases) modify the software program as they see fit (Perens 1999).

The most famous example of open-source software is the Linux kernel, which forms the heart of the GNU/Linux operating system. Linux was originally started "just for fun" by a Finnish computer science graduate student named Linus Torvalds. As Torvalds announced on a mailing list in October 1991, Linux was a "program for hackers by a hacker," a project that "somebody might enjoy looking at it and even modifying it for their own needs" (Torvalds 2002). A decade and a half later, Linux runs 60 percent the world's five hundred fastest supercomputers (Lyons 2005). Most sites on the World Wide Web are hosted on Linux servers; every visitor to Google.com, for example, is using Linux (Broersma 2003).

Trippi had worked for open-source software companies, including a company that packaged and sold a version of Linux. As Trippi explained, "I always wondered how you could take that same collaboration that occurs in Linux and open source and apply it [in politics] ... What would happen if there were a way to do that and engage everybody in a presidential campaign" (qtd. in Lessig 2003). In contrast to traditional campaign work, which was usually carefully stage-managed by paid campaign professionals, Trippi hoped to empower a diffuse network of Dean supporters to work on the governor's behalf. The official campaign blog was designed to build enthusiasm and community sentiment: said Trippi, "We wanted to have a blog where people could comment—where there was interaction, and where we were building a community and a narrative of the campaign" (qtd. in Lessig 2003). Supporters were encouraged to create their own pro-Dean websites and content, and to organize local pro-Dean gatherings. With events such as the "Cheney Challenge," the Dean campaign emphasized the contrast between the $2,000-a-plate fund-raising dinners that provided most of Bush's early campaign funding and the large network of small donors who provided most of Dean's funds (Trippi 2004). Trippi even credited participatory online discussions with a key role in many of the campaign's most important strategic choices; the decision to encourage Dean supporters to organize events using Meetup.com "came straight from a blog—MyDD.com" (qtd. in Lessig 2003).

Trippi's version of open-source politics has been echoed by numerous other observers. Just as Dean did, the Wesley Clark campaign released open-source software to help partisans build their own pro-Clark websites; as Clark TechCorps project manager Josh Hendler explained, "Open source for us symbolizes organizational transparency" (Ulbrich 2005). An article in the *Christian Science Monitor* concluded that open-source methods meant that "the importance of the campaign organization itself has waned...effective message building means that the election campaign is now a collaborative effort among far-flung groups that never have to talk" (Rourke 2004). Moulitsas Zuniga (2005) has also popularized the "open-source" label, arguing that that blogging allows "the aggregation of thousands on behalf of a common cause."

The Theory of Open Source

The term *open-source politics*, then, has been applied to many new forms of activism. But if we are to evaluate whether that label is appropriate, it is important to know more about the open-source movement.

One of the best-known theorists of open-source software—and someone who helped coin the label (Raymond 1998b)—is Eric S. Raymond. In his seminal essay "The Cathedral and the Bazaar," Raymond contrasted two different approaches to software development. Before Linux, many software developers—including Raymond—had believed that complex software projects required a "centralized, a priori approach": "The most important software...needed to be built like cathedrals, carefully crafted by individual wizards or small bands of mages working in splendid isolation" (Raymond 1998a). Linux turned that logic on its head; instead of clear command-and-control structures, "the Linux community seemed to resemble a great babbling bazaar of differing agendas and approaches . . . out of which a coherent and stable system could seemingly emerge only by a succession of miracles" (Raymond 1998a). Yet far from flying apart as Raymond and others had expected, Linux "seemed to go from strength to strength at a speed barely imaginable to cathedral-builders" (Raymond 1998a).

The success of Linux has led to an explosion of scholarly interest in open-source methods. The literature has focused on a number of important questions. Many scholars have explained the open-source movement through the extension of well-known economic principles (Benkler 2002; Lerner and Tirole 2000; Raymond 1998a; Weber 2004). Economists have sought to understand the incentives that allow open-source projects to attract talented programmers, some focusing on career concerns (Haruvy, Wu, and Chakravarty 2003; Lerner and Tirole 2000), others on ego gratification, political values, or programmers' desire to solve their own problems in a creative way (Bitzer, Schrettl, and Schroder 2004; Escher 2004; Lakhani and Wolf 2005; Raymond 1998a; Stewart and Goswain 2004; von Hippel 2005). Others have examined the coordination mechanisms and software structures that allow large-scale open source projects to function, as well as the means by which open source leaders are created (Baldwin and Clark 2004; Fleming and Waguespack 2005; Gonzalez-Baharona, López, and Robles 2004; MacCormack, Rusnak, and Baldwin 2005; Iannacci 2005; O'Mahony and Ferraro 2004). Still others have looked at firm incentives and behavior in supporting open-source development (Bonaccorsi and Rossi 2003; West and Dedrick 2001).

Amid all of this writing, one widely shared expectation is that the same methods that have helped to create the open-source software movement may work in other realms. As Steven Weber (2004) puts it, "Open source is not a piece of software, and it is not unique to a group of hackers. Open source is a way of organizing production, of making things jointly" (224). Some research has looked at the parallels between open-source software and user-driven innovation in areas such as sports equipment, as well as more distant historical examples of "community-centered" innovation processes (Shah 2005; von Hippel 2005). Other work has focused on potential open-source methods for biotechnology (Boettiger and Burk 2004; Hope 2005). Yet many open-source scholars have voiced even broader aims for open source. Indeed, Benkler suggests that the World Wide Web itself should be viewed as an example of "peer production" in action (Benkler 2002).

In light of this research, is the "open-source politics" label an apt one? In many respects, the answer seems to be yes. For our purposes here, we focus on what are arguably the three most celebrated examples of open-source politics: the Dean campaign, MoveOn.org, and the rise of political weblogs. Like Linux, all three examples are unimaginable in a pre-Internet age.[4] Limiting the discussion to these three prominent cases at least partially reduces the danger of arguing by anecdote.

The issue for both open-source theorists and political scientists is not the relative success of these examples, nor is it the fact that all relied heavily on the Internet. The key question, rather, is whether these three cases have produced organizational transparency and large-scale collaboration. Many of the Dean campaign's efforts do seem consistent with claims of "community-centered innovation" or "peer production." Though Dean's campaign blog was run by professional staffers, much of the content (and certainly the comments) was generated spontaneously by individual supporters. By encouraging partisans to start their own pro-Dean sites—and even providing them with the software to accomplish this task—the Dean campaign used community production to build an online presence. Dean meetups relied on the initiative and leadership of local attendees. Even Dean's fund-raising model, which relied on small donations, might be loosely construed as a method of community-based production.

Similar patterns can be seen with Moveon.org. As of January 2004, MoveOn.org had only six paid staff members, forcing much of the burden of organizing onto members themselves. MoveOn.org's online forums are a key part of this process. As CNN explains, "Any member can propose priorities and strategies to which others can respond, and the most-supported ideas rise to the top. That means ceding control over much of the content to motivated online participants, producing interactivity that adds grass-roots credibility."[5] MoveOn.org turned to community-based production for its "Bush in 30 Seconds" contest, in which members were asked to produce a television ad critiquing the president's performance. More than 1,500 ads were submitted, and more than 175,000 Moveon.org supporters voted to determine the five finalist ads (Simon 2004). This was a significant departure from the traditional process of producing television spots, generally limited to a small number of political and technical elites.

Last, there is also evidence of community-based production in the blogging world. It is common to refer to blogging as an "ecosystem," and user comments, reader e-mail, and cross-links with other bloggers all strongly shape blog content. In many cases, the result is an interactive, back-and-forth conversation where bloggers comment on one another's work, and where readers critique what is written and point bloggers to other relevant material.

Open-source politics also seems, in a few cases, to have demonstrated similar strengths to that of open-source software development. Errors in software are an endemic problem; according to an April 2004 report by the National Cyber Security Partnership, commercial software averages between 1 and 7 bugs for every 1,000 lines of code (NCSP 2004). Many claim that open code makes it easier to find and fix software errors. Raymond dubs this principle "Linus's Law": "given enough eyeballs, all bugs are shallow" (Raymond 1998a). Some empirical evidence supports this idea. One recent audit found fewer than 1,000 bugs in the 5.6 million lines of code that make up the Linux kernel—far below the average in commercial software (Lemos 2004).

One possible political analogue to finding software bugs comes from blogs' ability to fact-check media reports. As one journalist concluded, "Blogs' biggest strength has been double-checking and counter-punching the mainstream media" (Seper 2004), and the top blogs can draw on the collective expertise of tens of thousands of readers every hour. Some scholars have argued that blogs played a key role in the resignation of then Senate Majority Leader Trent Lott, focusing attention on initially overlooked remarks, and showing that Lott's seemingly nostalgic statements about racial segregation were part of a longstanding pattern (Bloom 2003; Drezner and Farrell 2004). Even clearer is blogs' role in exposing problems with CBS News's reporting on George W. Bush's National Guard service. The night of CBS's broadcast, an anonymous user on FreeRepublic.com claimed that key documents could not have come from a 1970s-era typewriter. This post was quickly referenced by popular blogs and online news outlets. As one Democratic activist summarized, "It was amazing…to watch the documents story go from [a comment on] FreeRepublic.com, a bastion of right-wing lunacy, to Drudge to the mainstream media in less than 12 hours" (Wallsten 2004).

Key features of open-source development, then, do seem to be mirrored in these new types of political participation. At the same time, there are other, far less emphasized parallels—parallels that complicate claims that open-source politics is the antidote to elite-driven politics. A complete understanding of open-source politics should consider the role of investments by traditional players, the dominance of a few collaborative efforts over all the rest, and the elite nature of emergent participants in the system.

Investments by Traditional Players

Just as election coverage often emphasizes the "horse race" between competing candidates (e.g., Patterson 1995), the open-source movement is often portrayed in opposition to traditional technology companies. In fact, much recent growth in the open-source software movement has come from massive investments by giant firms. IBM, which remains the world's largest technology company, is one prominent contributor: in 2001 alone, IBM's contribution to open-source projects was valued at more than $1 billion (Shankland 2002). IBM's donated code added key functionality to the Linux kernel, under the theory that a more robust Linux would help IBM sell more of its hardware, software, and services.

Other open-source projects owe their very existence to large corporate investments. In 1998 Netscape had lost the browser wars to Microsoft's Internet Explorer; it faced steady erosion of its market share, and the threat that Internet Explorer's dominance would lead the web toward proprietary standards. Netscape's response was to release the code base of Netscape Navigator under an open-source license. Similarly, in July 2000, Sun Microsystems made the decision to release its existing office suite, called StarOffice, under an open-source license. According to contemporary media reports, this move was aimed at attracting developers and reducing the market share of Microsoft Office (e.g., Abreau 2000). Other large technology companies have also been key contributors to open-source projects: Motorola, SAP, Intel, Oracle, and Apple, to name just a few.

The growth of open-source software is thus, in large part, the result of competition *within the technology industry*. Supporting open source has allowed some companies to leverage otherwise unproductive investments in order to sell complementary products, to gain the attention and trust of software developers, and to undercut their competitors.

Similar patterns have governed the emergence of open-source politics. Dean's campaign innovations were less the result of a spontaneous online groundswell, and more a consequence of intense competition among the eight men and one woman vying for the Democratic presidential nomination. Prior to 2004, scholarship on online campaigning observed that candidates avoided interactivity and kept rigid control over their online presence; for strong candidates, there seemed little incentive to risk losing control of the campaign's message (Stromer-Galley 2000). In this context, Dean's experiments with open-source campaign practices has a similar strategic logic to Sun Microsystems' decision to release an open-source version of

StarOffice. As a minor candidate in a crowded Democratic primary, Dean had little to lose.

And just as in software, it seems that successful open-source political advocacy projects can attract large financial investments from traditional players. MoveOn .org's 527 political organization raised more than $12 million in 2004, a feat some viewed as proof that small, online donations were reinvigorating grassroots politics (e.g., Cornfield 2003). Actually, three billionaires—George Soros, Herbert Sandler, and Peter Lewis—provided more than 60 percent of MoveOn.org's 2004 funding.[6] Ultimately, Moveon.org's fund-raising successes in 2004 depended as much on the patronage of a few ultra-wealthy liberals as it did on the contributions of average citizens.

Winners-Take-All Patterns

In talking about open-source politics, one key issue concerns the relative importance of large vs. small groups. Many early visions of the Internet emphasized "pointcasting" or "narrowcasting," and argued that the Internet's most important impact would come from removing the barriers to entry that kept smaller players out (e.g., Gates 1999; Negroponte 1995; Shapiro 1999). This vision of small-scale production lay behind the critiques of Sunstein, Barber, and Wilhelm, all of whom argued that an explosion of information outlets might degrade public discourse (Barber 2003; Sunstein 2001a; Wilhelm 2000). Similarly, many social scientists have suggested that the Internet might be a more level playing field for third parties or other marginalized interests.[7]

Though there is still much to learn about political organization online, early evidence suggests that the Internet's most important political effects—and certainly its most novel ones—come not from a large number of small online groups, but from a handful of really big ones. Here again, the example of open-source software is instructive.

Sourceforge.net is the largest online repository of open-source projects; as of July 2005, it contained 102,933 projects available for public download. In almost any category of software, from games to text editors, Sourceforge hosts dozens or even hundreds of projects. Yet a closer look reveals that diversity in the open-source world is shallower than it appears. Most of the 100,000 software packages listed on Sourceforge are small pet projects with few users and just one programmer. At the other end of the scale are a handful of open-source megaprojects that dwarf the rest, such as the Linux kernel, the Apache web server, the Firefox web browser, the Gnome and KDE desktops, and the OpenOffice.org office suite.[8] On a smaller scale, the same sort of winners-take-all patterns can be found in almost any well-defined software niche, where a few open-source programs get the majority of users and development effort.

Empirical research on open-source development exposes these patterns starkly. Looking at more than 42,000 Sourceforge projects, Healy and Schussman (2003) find that the open-source community is "spectacularly stratified" (see also Krishnamurthy 2002). The number of changes to the source code, the number of times a project is downloaded, and the number of developers a project attracts all follow strong winners-take-all patterns, with a few projects receiving more attention than the rest combined.

Inequalities exist not just between projects, but within them. Mockus, Fielding, and Herbsleb (2000) found that the Apache server was far more concentrated than typical commercial software efforts: while the project as a whole had 388 developers, a group of fifteen programmers were responsible for 88 percent of the added lines of code. A related study of the Mozilla project, a far larger piece of software than the Apache server, found similar (though slightly less extreme) inequalities among contributors (Mockus, Fielding, and Herbslub 2002). In both projects, the group of programmers who wrote bug fixes was an order of magnitude larger than the core development team, and the group who submitted bugs was an order of magnitude larger still. In short, successful open-source software (OSS) projects typically rely on a narrow core development team, augmented by an extremely broad group of marginal contributors.

Similar winners-take-all patterns seem to have emerged in online politics—both within organizations and between them. As Lerner and Tirole (2004) explain with regard to software, "While the leader of an open source project has no formal authority—that is, he cannot direct any one to do any thing—the leadership often has considerable 'real authority.' Leaders play a key role in formulating the initial agenda, setting goals as the project evolves, and resolving disputes that might lead to the splintering and outright cessation of the project" (11). Much the same can be said for the Dean campaign and MoveOn.org, where a small group had a great deal of influence in setting the agenda, coordinating the efforts of supporters, and smoothing over internal disagreements. Dean's campaign was organized by Trippi and a few Dean staffers, particularly Zephyr Teachout and Matthew Gross (Trippi 2004). MoveOn.org, as we noted earlier, relied on Boyd, Blades, and just a handful of other staff.

The other winners-take-all aspect of open-source politics concerns the Internet's tendency to favor a few sites and organizations over all the rest. By the late 1990s, computer scientists, applied physicists, and others had noted that traffic over the entire web followed a power law distribution (Barbási et al. 2000; Faloutsos, Faloutsos, and Faloutsos 1999; Huberman 2001). Despite the incredible vastness of content offered, online audiences remained highly concentrated, with a tiny portion of websites responsible for most of the traffic. Many subcategories of content, such as online retailers or online news outlets, showed the same highly skewed pattern, with a few winning sites receiving more traffic than all the rest combined (Huberman 2001; Pennock et al. 2002). Even when the content available online and offline is largely identical—as with newspaper websites—online audiences are more concentrated than offline readership (Hindman 2006).

As previous research by the author has shown, the winner-take-all patterns seen in other areas of the web also shape online political advocacy (Hindman, Tsiontsionliklis, and Johnson 2003). Using automated web crawling and web page classification techniques, this research explored six very different communities of political websites, groups of pages focused on topics such as abortion, gun control, and the U.S. Congress. In every community, the amount of relevant content identified was vast—thousands upon thousands of web pages. Nonetheless, in every case the top twenty websites in a category received more links than the rest combined.

The same pattern—where a few online outlets get most of the attention—is particularly noteworthy when it comes to blogs. The number of blogs is vast; one survey suggested that, by November 2004, 8 million Americans had started their own blogs (Ranie 2005). Nonetheless, an enormous divide exists between the few hypersuccessful political blogs and all the rest. According to March 2005 traffic data compiled by N.Z. Bear (2005), the top 10 blogs get 48 percent of all blog traffic.[9] A small number of megablogs are thus responsible for most of what citizens read in the blogosphere. Just as with the Dean campaign and MoveOn.org, a tiny group of individuals are the de facto leaders of a large, loose coalition.

Blogs are not the only place we see this pattern. In March 2005, an e-mail from Senator Barack Obama (D-IL) to MoveOn.org's listserv raised $833,000 for the reelection campaign of Senator Robert Byrd (D-WV) (Nyden 2005; Whittington 2005). Moveon.org's fundraising prowess has been seen by many as a prime instance of how online organizing is impacting traditional political concerns. Yet in one respect, this success is shallow. Moveon.org is by far the most successful organization of its type; by mid-2005, its home page claimed more than 3,000,000 members. At the moment, it is difficult to imagine any other online advocacy group raising this amount of money so quickly. While online politics has certainly helped create thousands of small-scale advocacy groups, most evidence of its political impact comes from a handful of large organizations like MoveOn.org.

Elite Professionals

A small number of people on a small number of projects thus wield a hugely disproportionate influence in open-source software—and similar patterns can be seen in the most widely cited examples of open-source politics. The obvious next questions are these: Who are the leaders of these open-source software projects? Does open-source politics promote similar sorts of individuals into its leadership ranks?

For Linux, the common suggestion is that the operating system has been cobbled together by students living in their parents' basements. Empirical studies have consistently challenged this portrait. One recent study by Lakhani and Wolf (2005), which surveyed developers from a random sample of open-source projects on Sourceforge.net, found that a solid majority of contributors were experienced, skilled individuals with jobs in the technology industry. The average contributor had more than a decade of programming experience; 55 percent worked on open-source projects as part of their job.

In much the same way, leadership in open-source politics has a distinctly elitist cast. Political scientists have long documented disparities in political participation—as E. E. Schattschneider (1960) famously put it, "The flaw in the pluralist heaven is that the heavenly chorus sings with a strong upper-class accent" (see also Rosenstone and Hansen 1993; Verba, Schlozman, and Brady 1995). Much the same accent can be heard in the most prominent examples of open-source politics. Dean's online efforts were coordinated by paid staff; Trippi himself was a veteran of four previous presidential campaigns. Moveon.org's Boyd and Blades were not traditional political elites, but, by the same token, they were hardly ordinary citizens. They had strong academic credentials; Boyd had worked as a research programmer for UC Berkeley, while Blades had a law degree and was the author of two books. They were wealthy, having sold Berkeley Systems in 1997 for $13.8 million (Hawkes 2003). They had executive experience, having managed a company with 120 employees and $30 million in annual revenue. And they certainly had computer expertise far beyond that of the average citizen.

Even stronger evidence about the elite-focused character of open-source politics comes from the blogging community. Popular accounts of blogs have emphasized that, for better or worse, blogs give greater voice to ordinary citizens. Some observers have celebrated blogging as "a more democratized form of commentary" (Campbell 2002), while others have worried that blogging gives too much power to "a guy sitting in his living room in his pajamas" (Colford 2004). Previous research by the author shows, however, that bloggers are hardly average Joes (Hindman 2005a). This work looked at the eighty-six political bloggers who, as of December 2004, averaged more than two thousand visitors a day; together these bloggers accounted for 78 percent of blog traffic.[10] There was little ethnic or gender diversity in this group, which included only one African American blogger, one Asian blogger, and five women.

Moreover, in terms of their education and occupational backgrounds, bloggers are an unquestionably elite group. Nearly two-thirds of the sample had attended one the nation's top colleges or universities.[11] More than 60 percent had done postgraduate study. The large majority of these popular bloggers are lawyers, professors, journalists, professional writers, business executives, and information technology (IT) professionals. Startlingly, more than half of all blog traffic goes to bloggers with a PhD, JD, or MD.

Some of the top bloggers, such as former *New Republic* editor Andrew Sullivan or radio host and former news anchor Hugh Hewitt, were well known before their blogging success; other now prominent bloggers might otherwise have had their political commentary limited to letters to the editor or conversations around the water cooler. Yet as of July 2005, the five most widely read political weblogs were published by a professional political consultant with a law degree, a law professor with a JD from Yale, a former economics professor with a PhD from Brown, a journalist with a PhD from Brown, and a trio of Dartmouth-educated lawyers. That is not a random cross-section of the American citizenry. Open-source politics has succeeded in adding a few new faces to the ranks of the politically influential. But it is also clear that, thus far, leadership in open-source politics has been more open to certain sorts of citizens than to others.

Conclusion

As with Henry Ford's assembly line, the central innovation of the open-source movement has been not a product, but a process. A decade and a half after Linus Torvalds sent a brief e-mail to an obscure computer science listserv, the success of Linux and other large open-source projects is undeniable. However, as a few political elites have tried to make open-source methods work in politics, some lessons have been misunderstood.

On the one hand, Trippi, Boyd, Moulitsas Zuniga and others have shown that forms of community-based production can take root in American political life. Previous scholarship had suggested that the Internet could allow the creation of unusual forms of broad-based, ad hoc collective action. The 2004 election demonstrated that these efforts could scale to include millions of citizens and impact traditional campaign concerns. In two core areas of political participation—fund-raising and campaign volunteer work—open-source campaign methods seem to have dramatically altered the previous status quo.

Other important parallels between open-source politics and open-source software have been largely overlooked. In politics as in software, open source methods have created strong winners-take-all patterns. Early evidence suggests that open-source politics particularly favors a few large, loosely joined organizations and a handful of ultrasuccessful websites. Moreover, the small core of individuals who run these organizations and websites are not a representative snapshot of the American public. They are elites: campaign staffers, wealthy entrepreneurs, political consultants, professors, and Ivy league–educated lawyers.

The three examples discussed in this chapter are hardly a complete account of open-source politics. Even if they were, online politics continues to evolve rapidly. One thing that *is* clear, however, is that the egalitarian rhetoric used to justify open-source politics is increasingly in tension with the elite nature of its leadership. Open-source politics can already claim some remarkable successes, but it has not made political elites obsolete.

Notes

1. Matthew Gross, Dean's director of Internet communication, reports that Dean raised $25 million online (Christensen 2005).

2. Archive of http://www.moveon.org as of November 1, 2004, accessed through Archive.org.

3. http://opensecrets.org/527s/527cmtes.asp?level=C&cycle=2004.

4. As Raymond (1998a) states, "I don't think it's a coincidence that the gestation period of Linux coincided with the birth of the World Wide Web."

5. http://www.cnn.com/2004/TECH/internet/01/12/moveon.org.

6. http://opensecrets.org/527s/527cmtes.asp?level=C&cycle=2004.

7. In general, the conclusions in this regard have been mixed. See Bimber 2003a and Norris 2001.

8. Note that large and successful projects, such as these examples, are usually not hosted at Sourceforge.net.

9. Bear's traffic numbers are aggregated from the Sitemeter.com service, which most (though not all) of the highest-traffic bloggers use to measure site visitors.

10. The list of political bloggers was taken from N.Z. Bear's Blogging Ecosystem project at Truthlaidbear.com. Bloggers who did not use Sitemeter to track hits to their sites were excluded from the analysis. Using e-mail surveys and publicly available documents, background information was gathered on seventy-six of the eighty-six bloggers.

11. For the purposes of this census, an elite educational institution was defined as one of the nation's top 30 universities or one of the top 20 liberal arts colleges, according to the 2004 *U.S. News and World Report* rankings.

References

Abreau, Elinor. 2000. "Sun Takes Aim at Microsoft Office." *The Industry Standard*, July 31.

Baldwin, Carliss, and Kim Clark. 2004. "The Architecture of Cooperation: How Code Architecture Mitigates Free Riding in the Open Source Development Model." Working paper, Harvard Business School.

Barabási, Albert-Laszlo, Reka Albert, Hawoong Jeong, and Ginestra Bianconi. 2000. "Power-Law Distribution of the World Wide Web." *Science* 287: 12–13.

Barber, Benjamin. 1984. *Strong Democracy: Participatory Politics for a New Age*. Berkeley: University of California Press.

Barber, Benjamin. 2003. "Which Technology and Which Democracy?" In *Democracy and New Media*, ed. Henry Jenkins and David Thorburn, 33–48. Cambridge, MA: MIT Press.

Bear, N. Z. 2005. "Weblogs by Average Daily Traffic." Available at http://www.truthlaidbear.com/TrafficRanking.php.

Benkler, Yochai. 2002. "Coase's Penguin, or Linux and the Nature of the Firm." *Yale Law Journal* 112: 369.

Bennett, Lance W. 2003. "Communicating Global Activism: Strengths and Vulnerabilities of Networked Politics." *Information, Communication & Society* 6, no. 2: 143–168.

Bimber, Bruce. 1998. "The Internet and Political Transformation: Populism, Community, and Accelerated Pluralism." *Polity* 31, no. 1: 133–160.

Bimber, Bruce. 2001. "Information and Political Engagement in America: The Search for Effects of Information Technology at the Individual Level." *Political Research Quarterly* 54, no. 1: 53–67.

Bimber, Bruce. 2003a. *Information and American Democracy*. New York: Cambridge University Press.

Bimber, Bruce. 2003b. "Notes on the Diffusion of the Internet." Report, University of California at Santa Barbara, July 22. Available at http://www.polsci.ucsb.edu/faculty/bimber/Internet-Diffusion.htm.

Bimber, Bruce, and Richard Davis. 2003. *Campaigning Online*. New York: Oxford University Press.

Bitzer, Jurgen, Wolfram Schrettl, and Philipp J. H. Schroder. 2004. "Intrinsic Motivation in Open-Source Software Development." Working paper, Free University, Berlin.

Bloom, Joel David. 2003. "The Blogosphere: How a Once Humble Medium Came to Drive Elite Discourse and Influence Public Policy and Elections." Paper presented at the Annual Meeting of the American Political Science Association, Philadelphia, PA, August 28–31.

Boettiger, Sara, and Dan L. Burk. 2004. "Open Source Patenting." *Journal of International Biotechnology Law* 1: 221–231.

Bohman, James, and William Regh, eds. 1997. *Deliberative Democracy: Essays on Reason and Politics*. Cambridge, MA: MIT Press.

Bonaccorsi, Andrea, and Cristina Rossi. 2003. "Altruistic Individuals, Selfish Firms? The Structure of Motivation in Open-Source Software." Working paper, Sant'Anna School of Advanced Studies, Italy.

Broersma, Matthew. 2003. "At Web Sites, Windows Outpaces Linux." *CNET News.com*, July 18. Available at http://news.com.com/2100-1016-1027188.html.

Campbell, Kim. 2002. "You, Too, Can Have a Voice in Blogland." *Christian Science Monitor*, June 19, p. 10.

Christensen, Rob. 2005. "Insurer and Doctors Wage E-Combat." *The News and Observer*, July 24.

Colford, Paul D. 2004. "Big Blog Bucks." *New York Daily News*, October 5, p. 52.

Cornfield, Michael. 2003. "Moveon.org Does It Again." *Campaigns and Elections* 24, no. 5 (May): 36.

Dahl, Robert A. 1989. *Democracy and Its Critics*. New Haven, CT: Yale University Press.

Davis, Richard. 1999. *The Web of Politics*. Oxford, UK: Oxford University Press.

Deibert, Ronald J. 2000. "International Plug n' Play?: Citizen Activism, the Internet, and Global Public Policy." *International Studies Perspectives* 1: 255–272.

Deibert, Ronald J. 2003. "Black Code: Censorship, Surveillance, and the Militarization of Cyberspace." *Millennium: Journal of International Studies* 32, no. 3 (December): 501–530.

Denning, Dorothy E. 2001. "Activism, Hacktivism, and Cyberterrorism: The Internet as a Tool for Influencing Foreign Policy." In *Networks and Netwars: The Future of Terror, Crime, and Militancy*, ed. John Arquilla and David Ronfeldt, 239–288. Santa Monica, CA: Rand Corporation.

Drezner, Daniel W., and Henry Farrell. 2004. "The Power and Politics of Blogs." Paper presented at the Annual Meeting of the American Political Science Association, Chicago, IL, September 2–5.

Drum, Kevin. 2005. "Of Blogs and Men." *Washington Monthly*, blog entry, February 18. Available at http://www.washingtonmonthly.com/archives/individual/2005_02/005685.php.

Escher, Tobias. 2004. "Political Motives of Developers for Collaboration on GNU/Linux." Master's thesis, University of Leicester & Freie Universität Berlin.

Elster, Jon, ed. 1998. *Deliberative Democracy*. New York: Cambridge University Press.

Faloutsos, Michalis, Petros Faloutsos, and Christos Faloutsos. 1999. "On Power-Law Relationships of the Internet Topology." *SIGCOMM* 29: 251–262.

Fleming, Lee, and David Waguespack. 2005. "Penguins, Camels, and Other Birds of a Feather: Brokerage, Boundary Spanning, and Leadership in Open Innovation Communities." Working paper, Harvard Business School and SUNY-Buffalo.

Gates, Bill. 1999. *Business at the Speed of Thought: Succeeding in the Digital Economy*. New York: Warner Business Books.

González-Barahona, Jesús M., Luis López, and Gregorio Robles. 2004. "Community Structure of Modules in the Apache Project." Working paper, Universidad Rey Juan Carlos, Spain, June.

Guthrie, Julian. 2004. "Fellow Anchors Defend Rather on Forged Papers." *The San Francisco Chronicle*, October 3, p. A2.

Gutmann, Amy, and Dennis Thompson. 1996. *Democracy and Disagreement*. Cambridge, MA: Harvard University Press.

Gutmann, Amy, and Dennis Thompson. 2004. *Why Deliberative Democracy*. Princeton, NJ: Princeton University Press.

Habermas, Jürgen. 1996. *Between Facts and Norms*. Cambridge, MA: MIT Press.

Hargittai, Eszter. 2003. "How Wide a Web?: Inequalities in Accessing Information Online." Ph.D. diss., Department of Sociology, Princeton University, Princeton, NJ.

Haruvy, Ernan E., Fang Wu, and Sujoy Chakravarty. 2003. "Incentives for Developers: Contributions and Product Performance Metrics in Open Source Development." Working paper, University of Texas at Dallas.

Hawkes, Ellen. 2003. "Joan Blades." *Ms. Magazine*. Available at http://www.msmagazine .com/dec03/woty2003_blades.asp.

Healy, Kieran, and Alan Schussman. 2003. "The Ecology of Open-Source Software Development." Working paper, University of Arizona.

Hindman, Matthew. 2005a. "The New Elite Media: The Politics of Blogs." Working paper, Arizona State University.

Hindman, Matthew. 2005b. "The Real Lessons of Howard Dean." *Perspectives on Politics* 3, no. 1: 121–128.

Hindman, Matthew. 2006. "Measuring Media Diversity Online and Offline." In *Localism and Media Diversity*, ed. Philip Napoli, 327–348. Mahwah, NJ: Lawrence Erlbaum and Associates.

Hindman, Matthew, Kostas Tsiontsionliklis, and Judy A. Johnson. 2003. "Googlearchy; How a Few Heavily Linked Sites Dominate Politics Online." Paper presented at the Annual Meeting of the Midwest Political Science Association, Chicago, IL, April 3–6.

Hope, Janet. 2005. "Open Source Biotechnology." PhD diss., Australia National University.

Huberman, Bernardo. 2001. *Laws of the Web*. Cambridge, MA: MIT Press.

Iannacci, Federico. 2005. "Coordination Processes in Open-Source Software Development: The Linux Case Illustration." Working paper, London School of Economics.

Jennings, M. Kent, and Vicki Zeitner. 2003. "Internet Use and Civic Engagement: A Longitudinal Analysis." *Public Opinion Quarterly* 67: 311–334.

Johnson, Charles, and Roger L. Simon. 2005. "Excuse Us While We Change Back into Our Pajamas." *PajamasMedia.com*, November 21. Available at http://v10.pajamasmedia.com/site/story/copy_of_11212005namechange.

Kahn, Richard, and Douglas Kellner. 2004. "New Media and Internet Activism: From the 'Battle of Seattle' to Blogging." *New Media and Society* 6, no. 1: 87–95.

Klotz, Robert J. 2003. *The Politics of Internet Communication*. New York: Rowman and Littlefield.

Krishnamurthy, Sandeep. 2002. "Cave or Community: An Empirical Examination of 100 Mature Open Source Projects." Working paper, University of Washington.

Krueger, Brian S. 2002. "Assessing the Impact of Internet Political Participation in the United States: A Resource Approach." *American Politics Research* 30, no. 5: 476–498.

Lakhani, Karim R., and Robert G. Wolf. 2005. "Why Hackers Do What They Do: Understanding Effort and Motivation in Free/Open-Source Software Projects." In *Perspectives on Free and Open Source Software*, ed. Joseph Feller, Brian Fitzgerald, Scott A. Hissam, and Karim R. Lakhani, 3–21. Cambridge, MA: MIT Press.

Langman, Lauren. 2005. "From Virtual Public Spheres to Global Justice: A Critical Theory of Internetworked Social Movements." *Sociological Theory* 23, no. 1: 42.

Lemos, Robert. 2004. "Security Research Suggests Linux Has Fewer Flaws." *CNET News .com*, December 13. Available at http://news.com.com/Security+research+suggests+Linux+has+fewer+flaws/2100-1002_3-5489804.html.

Lenhart, Amanda, John Horrigan, Lee Rainie, Katherine Allen, Angie Boyce, Mary Madden, and Erin O'Grady. 2003. "The Ever-Shifting Internet Population." Pew Internet and American Life Project, Washington, DC, April. Available at http://www.pewinternet.org/pdfs/PIP_Shifting_Net_Pop_Report.pdf.

Lerner, Josh, and Jean Tirole. 2000. "The Simple Economics of Open Source." Cambridge, MA: National Bureau of Economic Research. NBER Working Paper no. 7600, March.

Lerner, Josh, and Jean Tirole. 2004. "The Economics of Technology Sharing: Open Source and Beyond." NBER Working Paper no. 10956, Cambridge, MA, December.

Lessig, Lawrence. 2003. "Interview with Joe Trippi." *Lessig.org*, blog entry, August 19. Available at http://www.lessig.org/blog/archives/001428.shtml.

Lupia, Arthur, and Gisela Sin. 2003. "Which Public Goods Are Endangered? How Evolving Communications Technologies Affect *The Logic of Collective Action*." *Public Choice* 117: 315–331.

Lyons, Daniel. 2005. "Linux Rules Supercomputers." *Forbes*, March 15. Available at http://www.forbes.com/home/enterprisetech/2005/03/15/cz_dl_0315linux.html.

MacCormack, Alan, John Rusnak, and Carliss Baldwin. 2005. "Exploring the Structure of Complex Software Designs: An Empirical Study of Open Source and Proprietary Code." Harvard Business School Working Paper no. 05-016.

Margolis, Michael, and David Resnick. 2000. *Politics as Usual: The Cyberspace "Revolution."* Thousand Oaks, CA: Sage Publications.

Mockus, Audris, Roy T. Fielding, and James Herbsleb. 2000. "A Case Illustration of Open-Source Software Development: The Apache Server." In *Proceedings of the 22nd International Conference on Software Engineering*, 263–272.

Mockus, Audris, Roy T. Fielding, and James Herbsleb. 2002. "Two Case Illustrations of Open-Source Software Development: Apache and Mozilla." *ACM Trans. Software Engineering and Methodology* 11, no. 3: 309–346.

Morris, Dick. 1999. *Vote.com*. New York: Renaissance Books.

Mossberger, Karen, Caroline J. Tolbert, and Michele Gilbert. 2006. "Race, Place, and Information Technology." *Urban Affairs Review* 41, no. 5: 583–620.

Mossberger, Karen, Caroline J. Tolbert, and Mary Stansbury. 2003. *Virtual Inequality: Beyond the DigitalDivide*. Washington, DC: Georgetown University Press.

Moulitsas Zuniga, Markos. 2005. "The Rise of Open Source." *DailyKos.com*, blog entry, February 11. Available at http://www.dailykos.com/story/2005/2/11/115012/410.

"MoveOn.org Becomes Anti-Bush Powerhouse." 2004. *CNN.com*. Available at http://www.cnn.com/2004/TECH/internet/01/12/moveon.org.ap/.

NCSP. 2004. "Security across the Software Development Lifecycle." National Cyber-Security Partnership, Report, April 1.

Negroponte, Nicholas. 1995. *Being Digital*. New York: Knopf.

Norris, Pippa. 2001. *Digital Divide*. New York: Cambridge University Press.

NTIA. 1995. "Falling Through the Net: A Study of the 'Have Nots' in Rural and Urban America." National Telecommunications and Information Administration, Washington, DC, July.

NTIA. 1998. "Falling Through the Net II: New Data on the Digital Divide." National Telecommunications and Information Administration, Washington, DC, July.

NTIA. 2002. "A Nation Online: How Americans Are Expanding their Use of the Internet." National Telecommunications and Information Administration, Washington, DC, February. Available at http://www.ntia.doc.gov/ntiahome/dn/anationonline2.pdf.

Nyden, Paul J. 2005. "Senator Gives Big Boost to Byrd." *Charleston Gazette*, March 31, p. 1A.

O'Mahony, Siobhan, and Fabrizio Ferraro. 2004. "Hacking Alone? The Effects of Online and Offline Participation on Open Source Community Leadership." Working paper, Harvard Business School.

Olson, Mancur. 1965. *The Logic of Collective Action*. Cambridge, MA: Harvard University Press.

Patterson, Thomas. 1995. *Out of Order*. New York: Random House.

Pennock, David, Gary Flake, Steve Lawrence, Eric Glover, and C. Lee Giles. 2002. "Winners Don't Take All: Characterizing the Competition for Links on the Web." *Proceedings of the National Academy of Sciences* 99, no. 8: 5207–5211.

Perens, Bruce. 1999. "The Open Source Definition." In *Open Sources*, ed. Chris DiBona, Sam Ockman, and Mark Stone, 171–188. Sebastapol, CA: O'Reilly Publishers.

Ranie, Lee. 2005. "The State of Blogging." Data memo, Pew Internet and American Life Project, Washington, DC, January.

Raymond, Eric S. 1998a. "The Cathedral and the Bazaar." *First Monday* 3, no. 3 (March 2). Available at http://www.firstmonday.org/issues/issue3_3/raymond/.

Raymond, Eric S. 1998b. "Goodbye, 'Free Software'; Hello, 'Open Source.'" E-mail, February 8. Available at http://www.catb.org/~esr/open-source.html.

Rosenstone, Steven J., and John Mark Hansen. 1993. *Mobilization, Participation, and Democracy in America*. New York: Macmillan.

Rourke, Brad. 2004. "Ethics of Open Source Campaign Era." *Christian Science Monitor*, September 22. Available at http://www.csmonitor.com/2004/0922/p09s02-coop.html.

Saad, Lydia. 2005. "Blogs Not Yet in Media Big Leagues." Report, The Gallup Organization, Princeton, NJ, March 11.

Schattschneider, Elmer Eric. 1960. *The Semi-Sovereign People*. New York: Holt, Rinehart and Winston.

Scott, Esther. 2004. "'Big Media' Meets the 'Blogger': Coverage of Trent Lott's Remarks at Strom Thurmond's Birthday Party." John F. Kennedy School of Government Case Program, Case 1731, March. Available at http://www.ksg.harvard.edu/presspol/Research_Publications/Case_Illustrations/1731_0.pdf.

Seper, Chris. 2004. "For Good or Ill; Blogs Make Waves." *Cleveland Plain Dealer*, October 7, p. A1.

Shah, Dhavan V., Nojin Kwak, and R. Lance Holbert. 2001. "'Connecting' and 'Disconnecting' with Civic Life: Patterns of Internet Use and the Production of Social Capital." *Political Communication* 18, no. 2: 141–162.

Shah, Dhavan V., Jack M. McLead, and So-Hyan Yoon. 2001. "Communication, Context, and Community: And Exploration of Print, Broadcast, and Internet Influences." *Communication Research* 28, no. 4: 464–506.

Shah, Sonali. 2005. "Open Beyond Software." In *Open Source 2*, ed. Danese Cooper, Chris DiBona, and Mark Stone, 339–360. Sebastopol, CA: O'Reilly Media.

Shankland, Stephen. 2002. "IBM: Linux Investment Nearly Recouped." *News.com*, January 29. Available at http://news.com.com/2100-1001-825723.html.

Shapiro, Andrew L. 1999. *The Control Revolution*. New York: Public Affairs.

Sifry, Micah L. 2004. "The Rise of Open-Source Politics." *The Nation*, November 4. Available at http://www.thenation.com/doc.mhtml?i=20041122&s=sifry.

Simon, Mark. 2004. "Anti-Bush Ad Contest Proves Popular Online." *San Francisco Chronicle*, January 14, p. A1.

Stewart, Katherine J., and Sanjay Gosain. 2004. "The Impact of Ideology on Effectiveness in Open-Source Software Development Teams." Working paper, University of Maryland, College Park.

Stromer-Galley, Jennifer. 2000. "On-Line Interaction and Why Candidates Avoid It." *Journal of Communication* 50: 111–132.

Sunstein, Cass. 2001a. *Republic.com*. Princeton, NJ: Princeton University Press.

Sunstein, Cass. 2001b. *What Constitutions Do*. New York: Oxford University Press.

Taylor, Paul, and Tim Jordan. 2004. *Hacktivism and Cyberwars: Rebels with a Cause?* London: Routledge.

Tolbert, Caroline J., and Ramona S. McNeal. 2003. "Unraveling the Effects of the Internet on Political Participation?" *Political Research Quarterly* 56, no. 2: 175–185.

Torvalds, Linus. 2002. *Just for Fun: The Story of an Accidental Revolutionary*. New York: Harper Collins.

Trippi, Joe. 2004. *The Revolution Will Not Be Televised*. New York: Regan Books.

Ulbrich, Chris. 2003. "Clark Campaign Going Open Source." *Wired News*, December 24. Available at http://www.wired.com/news/politics/0,1283,61723,00.html.

Verba, Sidney, Kay Schlozman, and Henry E. Brady. 1995. *Voice and Equality*. Cambridge, MA: Harvard University Press.

von Hippel, Eric. 2005. *Democratizing Innovation*. Cambridge, MA: MIT Press.

Wallsten, Peter. 2004. "No Disputing It: Blogs Are Major Players." *The New York Times*, September 12, p. A22.

Warschauer, Mark. 2003. *Technology and Social Inclusion*. Cambridge, MA: MIT Press.

Weber, Steven. 2004. *The Success of Open Source*. Cambridge, MA: Harvard University Press.

West, Joel, and Jason Dedrick. 2001. "Open Source Standardization: The Rise of Linux in the Network Era." *Knowledge, Technology and Policy* 14, no. 2: 88–112.

Whittington, Lauren. 2005. "Byrd Raises $1.2 Million for Next Year's Election." *Roll Call* (April 14).

Wilhelm, Anthony. 2000. *Democracy in a Digital Age: Challenges to Political Life in Cyberspace*. New York: Routledge.

Williams, Christine, Bruce Weinberg, and Jesse Gordon. 2004. "Meetup Survey." Available at http://www.meetupsurvey.com/Study/ReportsData.html.

Case Illustration

Cyberprotesting Globalization: A Case of Online Activism

Sandor Vegh

The annual summits of the World Bank (WB) and the International Monetary Fund (IMF) and other financial institutions lend themselves as political opportunities for transnational protests. Responding to the ubiquitous demonstrations at their major gatherings as well as the threat of terrorism, the 2001 Barcelona WB/IMF meeting was held online. It quickly became clear, however, that this would enable Net-savvy protesters to disrupt the meetings using online activism tools, such as Denial of Service (DoS) attacks or e-mail spams. Consequently, meetings of many leading international organizations are not held online, but in remote locations like the Canadian mountains in Alberta (G8) or the desert state of Qatar (WTO) to minimize chances for protest. The 2003 WB/IMF Annual Meetings took place in Dubai, United Arab Emirates, while the 2006 meetings are scheduled for Singapore, countries known for political, social, and media control. Furthermore, the annual meetings in Washington, DC, have been more controlled by authorities as security forces have become better prepared post-9/11.

The anti-WB/IMF protests have been orchestrated by such umbrella organizations as Anti-Capitalist Convergence (www.abolishthebank.org), 50 Years Is Enough (www.50years.org), and Mobilization for Global Justice (www.globalizethis.org). This last one, for example, is made up of fifteen groups, and their campaign has been endorsed by several hundred other organizations. For the protests against the WB/IMF in 2000, the organization managed to call 20,000 people to the streets. Many of them were from the college population who could not have been reached and mobilized without the Internet.

In the anti-globalization protests, the Internet is used mainly for information distribution, mobilization, and organization, as well as carrying out action. The Internet enables the large number of activist groups and individual protesters involved to establish a time- and cost-efficient communication channel.

Protestors' conscious and efficient use of the Internet is exemplified by the centralized website and e-mail distribution list that is set up for each major protest (usually referring to the date of the action in the domain name, such as www.a16.org or www.s29.org) to bring together the scores of participating activist organizations, coordinating their actions and providing practical information that ranges from shared accommodation to methods of nonviolent resistance against police brutality. Collecting online donations is the primary source of funding for many of these groups. The more sophisticated sites also operate as news portals, and they provide event calendars as well as separate sections for the news media.

"Hacktivism," the utilization of hacking toward political goals, is another, sometimes complementary, pathway to political protest. For example, website defacements are acts of cyberprotest seeking public attention and visibility by "painting" cybergraffiti on the virtual entrance of the target institution. "Virtual sit-ins," as the name suggests (with all its historic connotations), aims to block access to a service, usually a website. The same effect can also be reached with the combined jamming of more traditional communication channels, as recently demonstrated by the coordinated call, fax, and e-mail campaign to the White House and Capitol Hill protesting the Iraq War.

There is another less radical, innovative type of Internet-based activism. During the Summit of the Americas meeting in Quebec City in April 2001, people who could not be physically present at the protests were invited to participate in a virtual walk on the www.marchedespeuples.org website by registering their names and nationalities. During the World Economic Forum (WEF) Meeting in Davos in January 2001, activists from all over the world could send short messages over the Internet either from the www.hellomrpresident.com website or over SMS messaging that were then projected onto a snow-covered hillside in 240 × 15 meter size with a laser beam. The projections could be checked real-time through a webcam. In the case of activism against the WB and WTO, "spoof" websites were set up with similar-sounding domains, criticizing and parodying the target entity (e.g., www.worldbunk.org or www.whirledbank.org, and www.gatt.org).

The spectacular and sensationalist nature of these activities almost guarantees wide-scale media reporting, which is key in the strategy of the activists.

Media attention means wide visibility and the most effective forum for publicizing the issues in contention. Both the activists and the corporations are aware of the power of the image. Given the rich resources of corporate entities to fight hacktivism on the technological level, their main vulnerability lies in their public image.

However, antiglobalization activists do not rely entirely on the corporate media. In addition to the numerous protest websites and alternative press publications online, activists established their own globally organized voice by creating the Independent Media Center in Seattle, initially to cover protests against the WTO in November 1999. Indymedia (www.indymedia.org) is a collective of independent media organizations and hundreds of journalists offering grassroots, noncorporate coverage.

The other technologies in political activism, especially mobile phones and video recording devices, are also gaining significant importance. For example, protesters used balloons outfitted with tiny cameras to take shots of protesting crowds to be analyzed later for headcounts. Sympathetic lawyers advised protesters to document possible police misconduct by immediately leaving detailed voice messages on cell phones and portable music devices. Instant text messaging is now also an indispensable tool in protest coordination. The true power of these technologies, however, is realized when they are linked with the Internet. One example is TxtMob (see www.txtmob.com), a mobile phone group text messaging service that enables one-to-many text messages, originally created to aid the protestors at the Republican and Democratic National Conventions in 2004. During the antiglobalization protests, scores of media activists were equipped with digital cameras, distributing their footage over the Internet shortly after it was shot.

Whether the protests against the WB/IMF were successful or not depends on what goal was set out. If it was to disrupt the meetings, the protests were unsuccessful. In Washington, the police seemed to be better prepared on every occasion, while in Prague in 2000, for example, the message got lost among the newspaper reports on violence and property destruction. If the objective was to convey that there is at least some controversy about the aims or operations of WB/IMF, then these protests were at least moderately successful.

If the goal was to influence the decisions and conduct of these two entities by delivering a message and engaging in dialogue, staging these protests have not proved to be a successful strategy since the WB did not give in to their demands. The WB has, however, reached out to legitimate nongovernmental and community-based organizations. Yet these attempts—along with the Development Gateway Internet Initiative launched in 2001 to provide a forum for dialogue and a source of information on global issues—have been skeptically received by many NGOs that asserted that the true agenda behind these initiatives for the WB was to reach even more people with its perspectives, thereby countering the backlash against corporate globalization. In other words, they were seen as a public relations tool that promoted the privileged view of development professionals rather than that of the poor and disadvanted.

Hacktivism against the WB has been less successful than some of the other tactics enumerated earlier. The only successful hack whose news made it beyond the walls of the WB system administrators was the alleged break-in on June 25, 2001, in which hackers allegedly stole documents and compromised several hundred passwords in an attempt to use them for to send out antiglobalization messages. This lack of success results from the responses by the WB to potential hacktivism. In part, this reflects an avoidance strategy—keeping some things offline to avoid becoming a target for hacktivists. More generally, the World Bank is very much prepared to defend its computer system against online attacks (website defacements, DoS attacks, and viruses). Defacements almost never succeed, but even if they do, there is a little chance it will be publicly noted since the original site will be automatically back up in minutes.

III

Evaluating the Impact of Reengineering Information Flows

The Challenge of Evaluating M-Government, E-Government, and P-Government: What Should Be Compared with What?

Robert D. Behn

In his original "reengineering" article, Michael Hammer distinguished between automating business processes and reengineering them. Automation has "delivered disappointing results," he argued, because it consisted merely of using "technology to mechanize old ways of doing business." In contrast, to implement Hammer's concept of reengineering, firms would "use the power of modern information technology to radically redesign our business processes in order to achieve dramatic improvements in their performance" (1990, 104). Similarly, under the rubric of e-government, public agencies have both automated existing processes and reengineered them.

Indeed, some public agencies have done more than convert manual government (m-gov) into electronic government (e-gov). They have gone beyond using technology to automate or even reengineer m-gov into e-gov. In some cases, public agencies have employed the power of statistical analysis and the advantage of data distribution, which all of those little electrons make possible, to create information-based innovations. They have moved beyond manual government and electronic government to what is truly innovative: performance government (p-gov).

E-gov is more efficient—and often more effective—than m-gov. But it is p-gov that can be truly innovative.

Automation, Reengineering, and Innovation

Every year, the Ash Institute for Democratic Governance and Innovation at Harvard's John F. Kennedy School for Government presents several awards for "Innovation in American Government." Over a thousand public agencies apply for this award annually, and it is amazing how many apply for the mere electronic automation of one of their existing, manual activities. They have taken their old paper processes and put them online. At the same time, they may have streamlined these processes. Still, these public agencies are seeking to be recognized as "innovative" for merely converting from m-gov to e-gov. The work that these agencies are now doing electronically is not fundamentally different from what they were doing with their old manual, paper-intensive processes.

Hammer's article contained in its subtitle his key admonition: "Don't Automate, Obliterate." Nevertheless, much of what has been touted as e-government is little more than the automation of some manual process: do not send employees their payroll checks through the mail; deposit their pay in their bank accounts electronically. Then, do not send employees their pay stubs through the mail; send these notices to them electronically or, even better, send them an electronic notice telling them how to download their pay stub. What Hammer worried was happening in business has also happened in government. For most of what is called e-government is little more than the automation of what had previously been manual processes. M-gov has become e-gov, but the fundamental, underlying nature of what government is doing remains unchanged (though citizens *may* find the electronic version more convenient[1]).

Thus, six years into the twenty-first century, any state government or any good-sized local government would be embarrassed not to have created several e-government websites—as well as its own portal.[2] For example, several states, including North Carolina, Kentucky, and Virginia, have an easily found "e-procurement" website.[3] Michigan has a website for purchasing hunting or fishing licenses online from its Department of Natural Resources and another for renewing a professional license from either its Bureau of Commercial Services or its Bureau of Health Professions.[4] And Sunnyvale, California, has a website for obtaining building and planning permits.[5] Such e-government initiatives (and there are thousands of them) are little more than Hammer's automation. They are not his reengineering.

Some e-government initiatives are, however, true reengineering. Chicago's 311 call system did radically redesign a core activity of city government: accepting, tracking, and responding to citizen requests for service. Prior to the development of computer networks (for entering, reading, and modifying data in a central database), nothing like Chicago's 311 e-government system would have been possible.[6] Now, however, citizens can call a single number to request any one of the multiple services that the city provides. If citizens want the city to tow away an abandoned vehicle, to fill a pothole, or to trim a tree, they just need to call a single three-digit telephone number: 311. Moreover, city employees—from the frontline worker who is responsible for handling the service requests, to the local alderman who wants to know what is happening in his or her ward—have access to such information. Chicago figured out how to use information technology to make the kind of "dramatic improvement" in an existing activity that Hammer had advocated.

From E-Government to P-Government

Further, in a few situations, public agencies have employed the advantages of computer technology not merely to reengineer an existing process but to originate totally new processes that enhance the performance of government. Indeed, Chicago's 311 system not only is an example of e-government reengineering. Chicago's system also created the service-request data that permitted some p-gov innovation.

Yes, Chicago did "obliterate" each of its city agency telephone numbers that were designed to receive service requests from citizens. Yes, Chicago did "radically redesign" the "business processes" by which it took citizen requests, stored such requests, responded to such requests, and accounted for its response to such requests—"to achieve dramatic improvements in their performance." But Chicago did more. Analysts in city departments and the mayor's office studied the data collected through the 311 system to detect patterns and develop different ways of responding to standard, frequent, or difficult requests. For example, in an effort to detect potential outbreaks of West Nile Virus, Chicago analyzed calls to 311 to find areas of the city with concentrations of dead crows. Then, it sent city crews to these locations to find and kill mosquito larvae (Kiviat 2005). This is more than electronic government. This is performance government.

To move from m-gov to e-gov requires automation or, at most, reengineering. To move from e-gov to p-gov, however, requires true innovation.

Two other examples of p-gov are the Compstat process invented by the New York Police Department and the similar CitiStat process created by the City of Baltimore. In both cases, computer technology has been indispensable to assembling and organizing the data necessary for the innovation. William Bratton, who as police commissioner drove the creation of Compstat, has emphasized that he was following a management strategy similar to Compstat while a young police lieutenant in Boston, Massachusetts (Bratton 1998, 99–100); yet, without the technology, he could not have expanded his data-driven approach to fighting crime from a single precinct to an entire city as big as New York. Similarly, without the technology, Baltimore could not have created its CitiStat strategy, which is driven primarily by the service-request data from its 311 system (Behn 2005). For both Compstat and Citi-Stat, computer technology was an enabler. Technology, however, is not, by itself, the core of these p-gov innovations.

Nevertheless, many reports on CitiStat have emphasized the technological aspects of the innovation. *The Baltimore Sun* labeled it a "new high-tech program for government efficiency" (Shields 2000). *The Windsor Star* of Ontario, Canada, said it is "a computer program" (Sacheli 2003). *The Buffalo News* called it "a computer tracking system" ("The State of the City" 2004). *The Daily Standard* termed it "a computerized accountability program" (DiCarlo 2004). *Time* magazine called it "a computerized score sheet" (Thompson 2005, 20).

Indeed, if you visit a Compstat or CitiStat session, you can easily be mesmerized by the dazzling technology—particularly the constant flashing of new maps and graphs on the walls during a session. Moreover, the folks who manage Compstat and CitiStat are proud of their technology and love to feature it when making a presentation. But this focus on the technology misses a more fundamental point: Compstat and CitiStat were created neither by automating a standard government process nor by reengineering an existing government process. Rather both are essentially new governmental undertakings, virtually new governmental functions, fundamentally new governmental strategies. Both are true innovations.

Compstat and CitiStat do more than collect and organize data in electronic form so that it can be entered, observed, and retrieved by a variety of government employees—and by citizens too. Compstat and CitiStat use the data stored in the electrons to create new forms of information. Compstat and CitiStat convert data into information and use that information to create new strategies for enhancing the performance of either a police department or a city.

This is why Compstat and CitiStat are more than electronic government: they are new, innovative forms of information government. The City of Baltimore and the New York City Police Department have exploited the technology of e-government to create new forms of p-government.

The Four Levels of E-Government (and P-Government)

Obviously, the phrase e-government covers a variety of different public-sector activities that are enhanced or permitted by the data processing capacity of those speedy electrons. I divide these electronically enabled activities into four distinct levels—

beginning with the level that requires the least change in government's behavior and the least amount of technology and progressing up to truly innovative p-government.

Level I. E-Gov Information involves making existing facts and knowledge more widely available to citizens by putting them on the Internet or making them more available to government employees on an Intranet (Mahler and Regan 2002). This information may have to be first collected and organized in a new (searchable) database. Once it is easily available, however, citizens can find this kind of e-government service very valuable in their daily lives, and public employees may find the information very useful in their daily jobs. On May 17, 2000, when New York City put the results of its restaurant inspections online, this website received an average of 23,000 hits per hour from citizens checking out their favorite eatery (Lueck and MacFarquhar 2000).

Level II. E-Gov Automation consists primarily of doing electronically—or, at least, more electronically—work that had previously been done manually. Why make human eyes and fingers (to say nothing of human arms and legs) do the work, when electrons can do the same thing faster and cheaper. For example, to file their federal income taxes, U.S. citizens no longer have to complete a paper form; they can do this electronically. Indeed, in 2005, more than half of all U.S. citizens filing their federal income tax did so electronically (Internal Revenue Service 2005).

Level III. E-Gov Reengineering involves, as Hammer advocated, the radical redesign of an important but existing process. Technology is essential for this reengineering for it makes the process redesign possible. One obvious example is the 311 Call Center, now in operation in many U.S. cities.

Level IV. P-Gov Innovation begins not with the task of either automating or redesigning existing work. P-gov involves more than storing data electronically or putting information on the Internet. Instead, p-gov is an entirely unique, completely unprecedented strategy for achieving public purposes—perhaps even a wholly new public purpose. Technology makes this new performance strategy possible; it provides an inexpensive, highly flexible way to collect, analyze, and then deploy information to supply substantially different or conspicuously better services to citizens.

Table 9.1
The four levels of e-government and the information flows of i-government

E-gov level	Changes in information flows
Level I. E-Gov Information	Broadcasting existing government information that was previously buried in paper files to citizens (or within government to agencies) using modern information and communication technology (ICT)
Level II. E-Gov Automation	Improving existing information flows between government and citizens or among government agencies, in a way that is better, cheaper, faster, but still the same information
Level III. E-Gov Reengineering	Radically redesigning information flows in a way that not only improves these flows but in the process captures or creates additional information
Level IV. P-Gov Innovation	Taking advantage of information and communication technology not merely to improve the flow of existing information or to create new information but also to analyze that information in a way that generates new insights, creates new ways of carrying out existing processes, and/or suggests and provides the basis for entirely new policy and management strategies

Still, no matter how visible such technology may be, the electronic technology is *not* the core of a p-gov innovation. This technology does facilitate the innovation but it is not, itself, the innovation. The innovation lies in the novel use of the information, which the electronic technology makes possible, to enhance performance.

These four levels are, of course, "ideal types" (Weber 1947, 329)—a formal, simplified construct designed to accentuate important differences and to provide a basis for comparisons. Many actual e-government initiatives may have the features of two or more of these levels. Nevertheless, for analytical purposes, these four ideal levels may prove quite useful. Table 9.1 illustrates the relationship between each one of these four levels and information government, focusing on the changes in information flows that distinguish each level.

The Evaluation Question: What Should Be Compared with What?

Evaluation requires a comparison. That comparison may be purely informal and strictly implicit—a comparison of what I see with what I expect or hope to see. I evaluate the color of an automobile by comparing it inside my head with the color

I have either envisioned or desired. When I look at a 1958 MG, I implicitly compare its color with those of other MGs that I have seen, as well as with the colors that I have seen on Austin Healeys, Triumphs, and perhaps even Alfa Romeos. If I find the comparison pleasing, the color gets a smile; if I am disappointed or irritated, it gets a frown. Red or British Racing Green deliver contentment; bright pink or purple elicit a contorted grimace.[7]

Thus, the first task in undertaking a systematic evaluation of anything—whether it is an antique sports car or an e-gov initiative—is to decide on the initial basis of comparison. Before launching any evaluation, the evaluator must first answer the key evaluation question: "What should be compared with what?"

The standard answer to the evaluation question—the answer implied in the technique of cost-benefit analysis—is that the benefits should be compared with the costs.[8] And while the costs may be relatively easy to enumerate, the benefits are often more difficult to specify.[9] After all, the benefits of an e-gov initiative, like the benefits of any management or governance initiative designed to improve the functioning of public agencies, come in a variety of incongruous forms: budgetary savings, increased efficiency, greater effectiveness, process improvements, and enhanced operational capacity (Pollitt 2000).

The cost-benefit answer to the what-should-be-compared-with-what question contains an implicit assumption: the benefits should be compared with the costs by converting all of the different kinds of benefits (and also all of the different kinds of costs) into a single metric: money. Because many of the costs are financial and can be directly measured and compared, the easiest mechanism for comparing what with what is to make this comparison in monetary units.

This is not the only mechanism for making such evaluative comparisons.[10] After all, if you really cared only about the color of a sports car that you were considering buying—if money were not a factor—you would need to consider neither the speed nor styling of the options, let alone compare them in common (monetary) units. You would just pick the car with the most appealing color. But if, in addition to the color, something else were important—maybe you prefer Austin Healeys to MGs—you would need some basis for making the comparison. Thus, you may want to ask: how much would it cost to repaint that Austin Healey in British Racing Green? In a variety of circumstances, money provides a convenient metric for comparing what to what.

When conducting a cost-benefit evaluation of any initiative in the public sector, one core difficulty is to capture fully both the benefits and the costs in common, monetary units. Sometimes the costs are easy to measure; the budget and accounting people can sort out the direct and indirect financial costs for whichever initiative needs to be evaluated. The benefits, however, are traditionally much more difficult to identify, let alone measure. Consequently, when seeking to conduct a cost-benefit evaluation of any of the four kinds of e-government, the biggest difficulty usually lies with the benefit side.[11]

Evaluating Level II, E-Gov Automation: Calculating the Return on Investment

A level I initiative in e-gov information may be the easiest of the four types of e-government to implement. Someone must make some decisions about what kinds of information are to be provided. But once these choices have been made, a level I initiative merely requires someone to put sentences or numbers on a website; any entry-level web designer can lay out the graphics necessary to display all kinds of information on a web page. In contrast, a level II initiative in e-gov automation involves the construction of a new, electronic mechanism for delivering an existing public service (such as renewing your automobile's license) or doing some other form of government's existing business (such as applying for an environmental permit). Level II automation does not require a reconceptualization of the service, though it does require some rethinking about how best to deliver this service electronically.

Indeed, a level II initiative in e-gov automation may be both the easiest to conceptualize and the easiest to evaluate.[12] Envisioning an e-gov automation is relatively easy because this initiative involves—conceptually—nothing more than replacing an m-gov process with its e-gov equivalent. If government buys goods and services, it could do this more efficiently with an automated e-procurement process (Moon 2002). If government sells its surplus property at an auction, it could sell such property through an online auction (Wyld 2001, 2004). If citizens have to register to vote, they could do this online; if citizens vote, they could do this online as well (Done 2002). Yes, numerous technical details must still be worked out: How many bytes should we allocate to this data field? What should we label it so everyone understands what information the field contains? Still, the transition from a manual to an electronic process is conceptually straightforward. Indeed, a variety of vendors are prepared (for a modest fee) to help governmental agencies undertake such automation.

Similarly, evaluating e-gov automation is relatively straightforward. This is basically a question of efficiency; the objective behind the automation is to do whatever is being automated more efficiently. The government is not trying to accomplish anything new or different. It is simply trying to do what it has always done at lower cost (to the government and perhaps to citizens too).

Thus, categories of costs and benefits of the new, automated version of this government activity are the same as the categories of costs and benefits of the old manual version. The nature of the costs and the benefits remain unchanged, though the values in many of the cost categories ought to decrease. Moreover, (most of) the important costs and (most of) the important benefits of automation may be easily captured on the agency's annual expenditure statement. Thus, an evaluation of a Level II, e-gov automation will be based—almost exclusively—on the efficiency savings found in the government's budget.

Consider the Internal Revenue Service's e-gov automation of electronic filing. Any catalogue of the costs and benefits would include those listed in table 9.2. Of course, neither citizen costs nor citizen savings appear on the IRS's annual statement of expenditures. Any e-gov automation will require some change in the behavior of some of the people who work within government to adjust their on-the-job

Table 9.2
The costs and benefits of level II, e-gov automation: E-filing income tax returns

Costs	Benefits/savings
Agency capital expenditures[a]	*Agency capital savings*
Software	Less storage space required
Hardware	
Facilities	
Agency operating expenditures	*Agency operating savings*
Employee training and adjustments	Fewer data-entry processors
Maintenance	Fewer hassles over its own data-entry mistakes
Citizens costs	*Citizens benefits*
Time to learn new system	Time saved
Time to implement new system	Quicker refunds[b]
	Fewer hassles over the IRS's data-entry mistakes

a. Johnson (2002) reports that, although web portals are clearly capital projects, 85 percent of them in state governments "are currently funded as operating expenditures" (41).
b. Some might argue that agency operating expenditures should include the loss of interest on the funds that the government refunded to taxpayers more quickly. This, however, is not a loss to the Internal Revenue Service but to the federal government's general fund. Moreover, neither the refunded money nor the interest that can be earned from it really belong to the government. Consequently, I have not included them in table 9.2.

behavior. And an e-gov automation, like electronic tax filing, would also require some citizens to adjust their behavior. Thus, even for an e-gov initiative that is designed strictly to improve the efficiency of government operations, it may be necessary to consider the costs and benefits to citizens.

Still, it may be possible to make a comparison. After all, in the case of electronic tax filing, every citizen has a choice: he or she can file a paper or an electronic return. And presumably for every citizen who chooses to file an electronic return, the benefits (however he or she calculates them) exceed the costs. (For those citizens who do not file electronically, neither their costs nor their benefits have changed.) Consequently, if the IRS can determine that its own expenditure savings exceed the additional expenditures that it incurs, the cost-benefit evaluation comes out positive. Indeed, Cohen and Eimicke (2001) conclude that "the Internal Revenue Service's electronic filing initiative must be judged a success" (36).

Of course, evaluating an e-gov automation has one last complication. Many of the costs (and savings too) are found in the annual operating budget. But for any e-government initiative, there are also up-front capital costs that must be paid for within the first year or two. Still, this problem has a well-known technical solution: discounting. If all future costs (and future savings) are discounted back to the present, all costs and savings can be converted to their present value, summed up, and compared.

If all of the benefits from an e-gov initiative are foregone expenditures—particularly well-known expenditures that the organization has historically made year after year and that now are certifiably less—then the evaluation is strictly a financial calculation. And for many an e-gov automation, this is indeed the case. There may also be some citizen costs as well as citizen benefits; but if citizen behavior suggests that the citizens' benefits exceed their costs, then the agency may be quite confident that, if its own savings outweigh its own expenditures, then cost-benefit evaluation is, indeed, positive.

Evaluating Level I, E-Gov Information: Estimating the Benefits of Information

An e-government initiative that consists purely of putting information on a website may be easy to implement. The information may already exist; it might even be available to citizens—provided these citizens are prepared to visit city hall or agency headquarters and know what to ask for. Or the information might need to be collected. And this information would have to be reorganized in some kind of electronically searchable database. Still, the task of putting data on the web is not very demanding.

A level I initiative in e-gov information may not, however, be easy to evaluate. After all, this involves more than doing a certain activity more efficiently. Even if the information was already official "public information"—even if it was legally available to any and all citizens—it was certainly neither widely nor easily accessible. Citizens may not have known the information was available. They may not have found it to be simple to obtain. They may also not have found this information to be simple to understand.

The financial costs of a level I, e-gov information initiative may be easy to calculate; they will look very similar to the capital and operating costs listed for e-gov automation. And the financial benefits that accrue from costs saved by not providing the information in the old way may also be easy to calculate. Unlike for e-gov automation, however, these savings may not be greater than the costs; after all, an initiative in e-gov information often consists of a new or expanded service (not just the automation of an existing one).

Thus, when launching an initiative in e-gov information, a public agency may be forced to make a large number of choices about how to organize and present this public information. What information should be included? What information should not? And how should it be presented? What should the structure of the website be? How should this information be distributed among the various web pages, and how should information be presented on each web page? E-gov automation is just that—the more efficient automation of an existing process. Given that the process already exists, there may be few fundamental design choices that need to be made. But unless an initiative in e-gov information is strictly putting on a web page—without any change in format—something that was previously on a paper page, the task may involve a number of pivotal choices.

Moreover, these choices will affect the nature of the benefits that citizens gain from the increased availability of some (but not all) information. And these social benefits are much more difficult to specify. What, exactly, are the social benefits of this new information that is now more widely available to citizens? And are there any new (perhaps unanticipated) social costs?

Consider New York City's e-gov information initiative of putting the results of the Health Department's restaurant inspections on the Internet. Table 9.3 lists the categories of benefits and costs for this level I initiative. What are the benefits to citizens of having this information so readily available? Given that thousands of

Table 9.3
The costs and benefits of level I, e-gov information: Restaurant inspections on the Internet

Costs	Benefits/savings
Agency capital expenditures	*Agency capital savings*
Software	Maybe none
Hardware	
Facilities	
Agency operating expenditures	*Agency operating savings*
Employee training and adjustments	Mailing savings
Maintenance	Telephone-operator savings
Citizens costs	*Citizens benefits*
Time and hassle of going online and finding the desired information	More access to more information

citizens seek out this information daily, we can assume that, for these citizens, the information is worth more than the time and hassle it takes to find the information on the Internet.[13] Thus, for these citizens, at least, the net benefits are positive. But how positive? Without forcing citizens to pay for the service, it is difficult to determine how valuable citizens really think the service is.

Additionally, consider the citizens who obtained restaurant inspection information the old-fashioned way—either by looking it up in some publication or by calling or visiting the Health Department. Are their net benefits positive? We could assume that they are. After all, for them, obtaining the information would appear to be much easier and more convenient. Still, there may be some (how many?) curmudgeons who really do prefer the old system.

Finally, providing information to citizens in different ways has an opportunity cost. Maybe a city's Health Department should devote its limited resources to other ways of providing this information to the elderly and the poor who are not apt to use the Internet (chapter 3). Maybe it should devote its resources to ways of ensuring that the information is available in Spanish and any other language that is spoken by at least 10 percent (2 percent?) of its citizens (Pollitt 2000, 191). The budgetary costs of this initiative in e-gov information do capture these opportunity costs.

Still, this budgetary approach does not produce a definitive answer to the what-should-be-compared-with-what question. Maybe this level of e-gov initiative (indeed, maybe all levels of e-gov) should be compared not with doing nothing—with not spending any money—but with other initiatives that require the same level of expenditures, including those that do not exploit the speed and agility of electrons. Table 9.3, however, implicitly compares a level I initiative in e-gov information with doing nothing. But e-gov information does not have to provide new or better information to the citizens. It could provide new or better information to government employees. For example, the Iowa Department of Revenue created a "data warehouse." With this electronic storage facility, the department collects and organizes in one electronic location information from a variety of state agencies that deal with businesses and citizens who are taxed or regulated by state government; this information includes the Revenue Department's data on businesses and citizens (as well as similar IRS data), unemployment compensation data, and data on vendors that do business with state agencies. This form of e-gov information permits auditors in these various agencies to check for noncompliance.

As usual, calculating the capital and operating costs was relatively straightforward. For Iowa's data warehouse, these totaled $11.5 million over three years. But what are the benefits? In this case, what increased tax revenues did the data warehouse produce? Of course, the data warehouse itself produced no new tax revenues. Instead, its existence permitted some state employees to launch a variety of special programs that did, indeed, collect revenue "above and beyond" the state's traditional "baseline, existing revenues." And, the department estimated, these additional revenues totaled $32 million over the first three years.[14]

Still, this benefit number is an estimate. For it assumes that *none* of the $32 million would have been collected were it not for the analysis that the data warehouse made possible. Yet it is not obvious that government would have done nothing; no one can say for sure that one or two entrepreneurial state employees—if they had not had the data warehouse available—would not have invented some other way to identify and collect one or two additional dollars (or one or two million additional dollars). If the world had not discovered the electronic technology that permitted Iowa to create its data warehouse, financial pressures may well have encouraged other innovators within state government to find other creative ways to identify and collect the state's outstanding revenues.[15]

Nevertheless, it is probably reasonable to assume that the state revenues would have been significantly lower (if not $32 million lower) without the data warehouse. Thus, even if you believe that the state overestimated by a factor of two the value of the additional tax revenues gained by employing its data warehouse, a simple comparison of the cost number with the benefit number still suggests that the state's investment in the data warehouse was worth it.

Evaluating Level III, E-Gov Reengineering: Estimating the Value of Improved Service

If the evaluation of an initiative in e-gov information depends primarily on the estimate of the benefits that citizens receive from more easily obtained information, the evaluation of an initiative in e-gov reengineering depends principally on the estimate of the benefits that citizens receive from significantly better service. Yes, a level II initiative in e-gov automation produces a better—that is, more efficient—service. But a level III effort at e-gov reengineering requires the obliteration and the subsequent redesign and reconstruction of the original services; consequently, the replacement service is not merely "better." The service is now significantly better—and, perhaps, qualitatively different.

This is certainly the case for 311, for which table 9.4 catalogues the benefits and costs. From the citizen's perspective, this service is both significantly better and qualitatively different. The city is accepting—indeed, encouraging—citizen requests for services through a single, simple-to-remember telephone number. By creating this 311 number, the city is not merely making it easier for citizens to call the city. With the 311 number, the city is actually inviting such calls. The city is stimulating additional requests for service.

How much do citizens value this new, improved service? How do they evaluate the ease with which they can now request a service from the city (and check back

Table 9.4
The costs and benefits of e-gov reengineering: 311 call center

Costs	Benefits/savings
City capital expenditures	*City capital savings*
Software	Agencies' telephone lines discontinued or converted
Hardware	to other uses
Facilities	
City operating expenditures	*City operating savings*
Emplyee salaries	Agency telephone operators who are now free to
Employee training and adjustments	perform other tasks
Maintenance	
Citizens costs	*Citizens benefits*
Poorer service for some insiders	Requesting a service is easier
	Obtaining information on the status of a service
	request is much easier
	Requesting a service is encouraged

on its status)? How do they evaluate their city's increased willingness to respond to their requests for service?

For this initiative in e-gov reengineering, what should be compared with what? To estimate the value that the citizens are receiving, the new service is one "what." And, if only implicitly, the citizens would be comparing this new, improved service with the old, decrepit, hard-to-use (or impossible-to-use) service. When citizens estimate the benefits that they receive from the new service, they will not attempt to compare the fancy 311 service with the modest, automated, but not reengineered service that the city might have chosen to provide. They will simply compare the new service with the old.

But how will they do that? How much better will they decide that the new service is? How will they even think about the value of the new service? What kind of thought process will they use? How will citizens go about evaluating a service that government has never before provided?

Economists have created a mechanism for getting citizens to answer this question in monetary terms: ask them how much they are willing to pay for the service. Unfortunately, citizens' hypothetical willingness to pay often differs significantly from their operational willingness to pay.[16] When confronted with a concrete payment decision, the behavior of humans often differs significantly from the hypothetical answer that they gave to a pollster. Thus, any evaluation of an e-gov initiative that requires an estimate of nonfinancial benefits and costs—particularly those that accrue to citizens—depends upon a variety of assumptions that the evaluators make about them.[17]

Thus, this estimate of nonfinancial benefits and costs is just that: an estimate. Sometimes, if the assumptions on which the estimate is based are reasonable and widely accepted, the estimate may be quite good. In other circumstances, the uncertainty or disagreement over the assumptions make the estimate little more than a good guess. Any analyst who conducts such an evaluation should be candid both about the assumptions employed and the uncertainty in the final estimate.

Evaluating a Level IV, P-Gov Innovation: Estimating the Value of a Completely New Service

Evaluating a level III e-gov reengineering is complicated because it requires an estimate of the value citizens gain from the new and, perhaps qualitatively, improved service. At least, however, the citizens have a basis for making this evaluative estimate. For 311, they have a sense (if not personal, operational knowledge) of how their government worked before the city reengineered its telephone-answering and service-request system; they have some understanding (if only implicit and indirect) of how easy or difficult it was to get the city to fill a pothole. They may not be able to give a thoughtful, reliable, monetary estimate of how much they value the re-engineered service. Still, they have, at least, a basis of comparison.

But what basis of comparison may citizens use for a level IV, p-gov innovation? What might they compare with what? What benchmark might they use as the basis from which to compare such an innovation? And what might they conclude are the benefits and costs of the innovation?

For example, in the case of Compstat or CitiStat, citizens do not directly see, feel, or otherwise experience the innovation's benefit. Sure, Compstat may reduce the crime rate, and CitiStat may get the potholes filled more quickly. But how do citizens know? And how do citizens know to attribute any improvement that they perceive in their quality of life to Compstat or CitiStat. Sure, the entrepreneurs who launched these level IV, p-gov innovations are telling the citizens how their newfangled invention is improving everyone's lives. But how much will the citizens believe them? How much should the citizens believe them? For two reasons, the citizens' answer to the economists' willingness-to-pay question become even more chimerical.

First, citizens have no clear benchmark with which to anchor their judgment about any improvement in their quality of life. Maybe it does appear that the pot-hole got filled more quickly. But how much more quickly was that? How quickly was it *before*? How quickly is it now? Maybe it does appear that the neighborhood is safer. But how much safer? How safe was it *before*? How safe is it now? For citi-zens, this is "the measurement question."

Second, citizens have no clear way of knowing how much any quality-of-life im-provement was caused by the p-gov innovation about which the jurisdiction's public officials are constantly speaking. Maybe that pothole was filled quicker not because the CitiStat innovation was keeping the Public Works Department focused on this important service. Maybe that pothole was filled quicker (if it was quicker) because the asphalt truck just happened to be driving past, and the driver bothered to stop. Maybe the crime rate is down not because the Compstat innovation is keeping the precinct commanders and beat officers focused on developing locally effective, crime-fighting strategies. Maybe the crime rate is down (if it is down) because jobs are more plentiful, and criminals now have other economic opportunities. For citi-zens, this is "the attribution question."

Table 9.5
The costs and benefits of p-gov innovation: Compstat and CitiStat

Costs	Benefits/savings
City capital expenditures Software Hardware Facilities	*City capital savings*
City operating expenditures Employee salaries Employee training and adjustments Maintenance	*City operating savings*
Citizens costs	*Citizens benefits* Improved quality of life

The catalog of costs and benefits for a p-gov innovation (see table 9.5) may be quite a bit shorter. For example, neither CitiStat nor Compstat is apt to create any significant savings in either the city's capital or operating budget. Nor are they likely to impose many costs on citizens. Moreover, the costs to the city's capital and operating budgets are relatively easy to specify.

For a level IV, p-gov innovation, the big question concerns the benefits to citizens. These benefits are quite complex, often intangible, and perhaps only ethereal. How large do citizens think these quality-of-life improvements are? And how much do they think governmental innovation caused these improved benefits? These measurement and attribution questions are what make evaluating a level IV, p-gov innovation so difficult.

The Evaluation Challenge

The task of evaluating even a simple level I initiative in e-gov information—for example, New York City's database of restaurant inspections or Iowa's database of the financial interactions that citizens and businesses have with government—is not all that simple. Indeed, the conceptual challenge is the same at level I as at level IV. For any effort to evaluate a new form of m-government, e-government, or p-government confronts the same basic question: *What should be compared with what?*

Often, buried in an evaluation of a government initiative lies the implicit assumption that, had the government not created this initiative, it would have done nothing. Indeed, this is the assumption that the public official would prefer: "Look how much better things are compared with when I took over." Implicit in this declaration is another assumption: "If I had not taken over, nothing would have happened." "If I had not done something, your quality of life would not have improved."

Indeed, our knowledge of organizational behavior suggests that this assumption is quite plausible. After all, the best predictor of what an organization will do this year is what it did last year; all organizations have created routines and standard operating procedures that they continue to employ year after year. Moreover, an organization does not develop its routines and procedures randomly but to solve its own, real problems of coordination, consistency, and predictability. The continuity in the behavior of public agencies is well known and derived from important organizational needs (Allison 1971, chap. 3). Perhaps then we should take seriously at least part of the public official's default basis of comparison. Any change in the operation of government (though not necessarily the presumed consequences) should be compared with what government was doing before the initiative was launched.[18]

Many scholars who specialize in program evaluation would disagree. They would advocate a controlled experiment, which provides a clear answer to the what-should-be-compared-with-what question. One "what" comes from the treatment group that receives the benefits (and costs) of the governmental initiative. The other "what" comes from the control group that is denied access to the initiative.

For example, a controlled experiment of 311 would have involved installing the new system in half the city while continuing the old system in the other half. Such an experimental approach to evaluation confronts, however, some significant practical problems. What will the citizens in the half of the city that does not get the 311 system—to say nothing of their alderman—say about the experiment? Can the mayor justify politically the huge capital cost of the 311 system if it is only an experiment? Can the operators of the 311 system develop a practical method (based on the caller's zip code) for denying half the city access to the 311 number?[19]

Other scholars advocate that any such experiment should introduce only one aspect of an initiative in any experimental jurisdiction (Karmen 2000, 95). But what if the various components of the initiative are expected to not have independent effects, but to reenforce each other synergistically (Behn 1991, chaps. 8, 9)? The 311 system includes not just the single telephone number; it also includes the database of the service requests, plus the tracking and follow-up on these requests. Indeed, it even includes a publicity campaign to convince citizens to call 311. What would the half of the citizenry who could not get through to 311 do? Answer: complain—and loudly.

Conducting a controlled experiment of any e-gov or p-gov initiative (and of many m-gov initiatives in governance and management) would appear to confront some problems of practical and political significance. Thus, for most e-gov and p-gov initiatives, the public official's implicit assumption—that the default baseline from which we should evaluate any initiative is what was happening before the initiative and thus would have continued to happen without the initiative—may be the only realistic basis for a comparison.

Still, even with this as the baseline from which to measure citizen benefits, the second attribution question remains: *What caused what?* If the citizens' quality of life did increase, whose fault is it? Was this improvement caused by the government? How do we know that any improvement was not caused by an unusual change in the intensity of sunspots, by fluoride that was (secretly) added to the water, or by the aliens who visited Area 51 a half-century ago? How can we be confident that a governmental initiative actually caused any improvements?

Indeed, tracing out any cause-and-effect connection is never easy. There exist many possible cause-and-effect theories. Indeed, for every public official who asserts that Compstat reduced crime in New York City (Bratton 1998; Giuliani 2002), there exists a scholar who will assert precisely the opposite (Harcourt 2001; Levitt and Dubner 2005). Thus, without a social experiment, it is impossible to eliminate the competing cause-and-effect theories. Indeed, without such an experiment, someone can always assert that any change from the baseline was somehow caused by sunspots, fluoride, or aliens.

Evaluating an e-gov initiative is hardly different from evaluating any effort to improve the workings of government regardless of whether it seeks to achieve that improvement by deploying electrons or with some other management strategy. Electrons offer a number of advantages. They are speedy, agile, cheap, and versatile. They provide government with the opportunity to do things more efficiently and more effectively. They offer government the opportunity to do new and different things. They offer government the opportunity to develop new strategies for enhancing performance. Moreover, electrons do not talk back.

Electrons, however, are not the only mechanism that government has to increase efficiency, to improve effectiveness, or to foster innovation to enhance performance. We can also improve the workings of government by capitalizing on the motivation and ingenuity of humans. Still, whether we rely on electrons or humans, the core challenges of evaluating such initiatives to improve the performance of government are the same (Blalock 1999; Boston 2000; Denrell 2003; Pollitt 2000). Always, there is the fundamental question that only humans (not electrons) can answer: "What should be compared with what?"

Notes

1. Or, they may find the electronic version less convenient. Personally, I liked the old way. I got my pay stub in the mail, tore it open, discarded the envelope, glanced at the critical number, and filed the document with its predecessors. Now, however, I have to log onto the website, go through multiple screens, enter my password at two different points in the process, get to the document, check Print Preview to see if the document will print onto one page (rather than on 1.05 pages), and then click Print. As with some forms of e-commerce, e-government may gather some of its increased (internal) efficiency by off-loading work onto citizens.

2. Even my own town of Watertown, Massachusetts (pop. 33,000) has its own portal: http://www.ci.watertown.ma.us. For a discussion of U.S. governmental agencies' websites (including its portal, FirstGov.gov), see Stowers 2002. For a discussion of the websites of state governments within the United States, see Gant, Gant, and Johnson 2002.

3. See North Carolina: http://www.ncgov.com/eprocurement/asp/section/ep_index.asp; Kentucky: https://eprocurement.ky.gov; and Virginia: http://www.eva.state.va.us.

4. http://www.mdnr-elicense.com/welcome.asp, and http://www.michigan.gov/elicense.

5. http://ecityhall.sunnyvale.ca.gov/cd/default.htm.

6. Okay. It would—technically—be possible to create a manual 311 system. After all, to calculate the trajectories of V-2 rockets during World War II, Wernher Von Braun organized a gymnasium full of clerks with mechanical desktop calculators.

Similarly, it is conceivably possible to create an m-government version of 311. This m-government would require a large, warehouse-sized room, thousands of telephones, thousands of file cabinets, and a very large staff. Some staff would answer the telephones and record each citizen's service request (SR) on a form in at least quintuplicate. (This form would come prestamped with a service-request number.) Other staff would run these SR forms to the file cabinets. Here, more staff would file one of the forms by its SR number and another by the nature of the service requested while shipping the other three copies to the appropriate agency. When the agency had finished the service request, it would note this on its three copies, keep one, and send the other two back to the warehouse. There, these two copies would be filed next to the first two forms. Then, when the citizen called back to check on his or her service request, the appropriate form could be retrieved, and the citizen informed of what action was taken when.

This manual system for handling service requests requires extensive staff, lots of space, and lots of file cabinets. The advantage of automation is that the electrons occupy less space, move much faster, and can be managed by considerably fewer people. This hypothetical m-government approach is not, however, conceptually different from e-government's new 311 system.

The size, speed, and manageability of the electrons create one more advantage: they permit the easy enhancement of the system. Each service request comes with a number of different characteristics: the nature of the problem, the location of the problem, the time and date that the request was made, and the person who made the request. Ideally, any 311 system—manual or electronic—would permit the government to retrieve the status of any SR by any of these characteristics. For example, it might be desirable or necessary to retrieve all the SRs for problems at the intersection of Third Avenue and Main Street. Electrons make this easy. But the manual system described in this chapter does not permit this. To make this kind of retrieval possible, the system would require some significant expansion: it would require two more copies of the SR forms (one to be filed by location and one to be sent to the department and returned) plus an additional set of filing cabinets so that one copy of all SR forms would be filed according to location.

Electronic technology permits the government to do such things as calculating trajectories or organizing citizen requests for services both faster and more efficiently. Because Chicago could purchase super-high-speed computers with a lot of storage capacity, it could think about incorporating the data obtained from a 311 citizen call-in system into a large, searchable, retrievable database of every request made by a citizen for service as well the status of the city government's response. Thus, this e-government database provided the infrastructure necessary for analyzing the information stored in the computers; indeed, without the existence of such technology, Chicago would have been unable to exploit the analytical, p-gov possibilities created by its 311 telephone system.

7. Yes, there are some electrons involved in this comparison, for it is electrons that are firing the neurons in my brain that are making the comparison. Nevertheless, this evaluation is strictly personal and subjective. Other individuals with different neurons (though identical electrons) will evaluate the color of these objects quite differently. Electrons don't make an evaluation objective.

8. Johnson (Gant, Gant, and Johnson 2002) argues that "governments should conduct studies that analyze the benefits and costs of developing web portals and applications for on-line transactions" (51) but reports that "only one state reported conducting a benefit-cost or return-on-investment analysis prior to investing in a web portal project" (41).

9. For a discussion of many "intangible," hard-to-measure benefits of e-government, such as "improving trust in government," increasing "governmental transparency," helping to "reduce corruption," and reinforcing "a culture of accountability," see chapter 3.

10. For one critique of cost-benefit analysis, see House 2000.

11. For an example of a cost-benefit analysis of e-government, see the Texas Department of Information Resources (2003).

12. Evaluating a level II initiative may be the "easiest" of the four to evaluate. But that does not mean it is "easy." Indeed, the dearth of full-fledged, cost-benefit evaluations of level II, e-government automations suggests that, perhaps, the task is quite complex and expensive.

Yet governments continue to employ all four levels of electronic automation, reengineering, and innovation. Why? This may simply be because citizens and opinion leaders "expect" government to do this. After all, e-business is ubiquitous. Even very small businesses have their own websites. And, citizens may ask, aren't these hard-headed business types making clear, rational calculations of benefits and costs before they make an e-business investment? Finally, continues this logic, if rational business managers are making these kind of investments, government managers should be doing the same. Government may be relying on business to make the generic evaluations that suggest that for many forms of electronic automation, reengineering, and innovation the benefits are greater than the costs.

13. Starting with the search engine Google, I took less than two minutes to find the inspection results of several restaurants in midtown Manhattan. The basic webpage for these restaurant inspections is http://www.nyc.gov/html/doh/html/rii/index.shtml.

14. This information comes from Nucleus Research (2004) plus a telephone conversation on Friday, April 22, 2005, with Rhoda E. Kirkpatrick, project manager, Iowa Department of Revenue and Finance.

15. For example, in the 1980s, without the advantage of a data warehouse, the Massachusetts Department of Revenue found a variety of innovative ways to identify and collect taxes that were legitimately owed to the state. See Behn n.d.

16. Instead of asking citizens for their willingness to pay, we could ask citizens about how much time they saved and then value this time based on their wage rate. This analytical approach might work well for levels I and II. But for level III—which involves a fundamental reengineering of a governmental activity—the citizen benefits are (presumably) more than mere time saved.

17. There is also the question of the costs imposed upon citizens by the new 311 system. There do not, however, appear to be many. Maybe a few citizens (plus a few aldermen) really knew how to make the old system work. They had memorized one (or several) of the city's key telephone numbers and had made friends with the people who answer these telephones. They had devoted the time and energy to figuring out how to make the old system work for them. Consequently, they were able to obtain immediate and personal service. Now, however, their request is no different than any other citizen's. These few insiders would, with the new system, incur a cost in terms of impersonal (i.e., poorer) service.

   And how would they evaluate this deterioration in their own, personal service? Again, willingness to pay—"How much would you pay to have the old system back?"—could provide an answer. Still, we may be a little uneasy about how accurate or meaningful any answer to this question may be.

18. Pollitt (1995) has a (slightly) different answer to this part of the what-should-be-compared-with-what question. He argues that it "should be where the organization is now compared with where it would have been if it had continued developing as it had been immediately prior to reform" (144). Of course, it is difficult to say with any assurance how the organization would have "continued developing." Indeed, this assumes that the organization was indeed "developing" rather than stagnant. Naturally, it is in the current public official's interest to assert that the organization was indeed stagnant. Nevertheless, from what we know about organizational behavior, that may not be such an unreasonable assumption.

19. An alternative would be for two similar cities to flip a coin. Philadelphia installs 311; Cleveland doesn't. But any comparison of citizen services in Philadelphia with those in Cleveland would be so confounded by other differences that the experiment could hardly produce a definitive conclusion.

References

Allison, Graham T. 1971. *Essence of Decision: Explaining the Cuban Missile Crisis.* Boston: Little, Brown.

Behn, Robert D. 1991. *Leadership Counts: Lessons for Public Managers.* Cambridge, MA: Harvard University Press.

Behn, Robert D. N.d. Unpublished. Massachusetts Department of Revenue.

Behn, Robert D. 2005. "The Core Drivers of CitiStat: It's Not Just About the Meetings and the Maps." *International Public Management Journal* 8, no. 3: 295–319.

Blalock, Ann Bonor. 1999. "Evaluation Research and the Performance Management Movement." *Evaluation* 5, no. 2: 117–149.

Boston, Jonathan. 2000. "The Challenge of Evaluating Systemic Change: The Case of Public Management Reform." *International Public Management Journal* 3: 23–46.

Bratton, William, with Peter Knobler. 1998. *Turnaround: How America's Top Cop Reversed the Crime Epidemic.* New York: Random House.

Cohen, Steven, and William Eimicke. 2001. "The Use of the Internet in Government Service Delivery." In *E-Government 2001,* ed. Mark A. Abramson and Grady E. Means, 9–43. Lanham, MD: Rowman & Littlefield.

Denrell, Jerker. 2003. "Vicarious Learning, Undersampling of Failure, and the Myths of Management." *Organization Science* 14, no. 3: 227–243.

DiCarlo, Rachel. 2004. "Irish Times: Baltimore Mayor Martin O'Malley Is Speaking at the Convention Tonight. Is He a Rising Star in Democratic Politics?" *The Daily Standard,* July 28. Available at http://www.weeklystandard.com/Content/Public/Articles/000/000/004/395vcyct .asp.

Done, Robert S. 2002. *Internet Voting: Bringing Election to the Desktop.* Washington, DC: The IBM Center for the Business of Government.

Gant, Diana Burley, John P. Gant, and Craig L. Johnson. 2002. *State Web Portals: Delivering and Financing E-Service.* Washington, DC: IBM Center for the Business of Government.

Giuliani, Rudolph W. 2002. *Leadership.* New York: talk miramax books, Hyperion.

Hammer, Michael. 1990. "Reenginering Work: Don't Automate, Obliterate." *Harvard Business Review* 68, no. 4: 104–112.

Harcourt, Bernard E. 2001. *Illusion of Order: The False Promise of Broken Windows Policing.* Cambridge, MA: Harvard University Press.

House, Ernest R. 2000. "The Limits of Cost Benefit Evaluation." *Evaluation* 6, no. 1: 79–86.

Internal Revenue Service (IRS). 2005. "2005 Tax Filing Season Sets Records." IRS release IR-2005-53, April 28. Available at http://www.irs.gov/newsroom/article/0,,id=138112,00.html.

Johnson, Craig. 2002. "Financing and Pricing E-Service." In *State Web Portals: Delivering and Financing E-Service,* Diana Burley Gant, Jon P. Gant, and Craig L. Johnson, 35–55. Arlington, VA: The PricewaterhouseCoopers Endowment for the Business of Government.

Karmen, Andrew. 2000. *New York Murder Mystery: The True Story Behind the Crime Crash of the 1990s*. New York: New York University Press.

Kiviat, Barbara. 2005. "The Magic Number." *Time* (February 7): 52.

Lau, Edwin. 2006. "E-Government and the Drive for Growth and Equity." In Viktor Mayer-Schönberger and David M. J. Lazer, eds., Brilliant Book, Center of the Universe: Very Distinguished Publisher.

Levitt, Steven D., and Stephen J. Dubner. 2005. *Freakonomics: A Rogue Economist Explores the Hidden Side of Everything*. New York: William Morrow.

Lueck, Thomas J., and Neil MacFarquhar. 2000. "Site Listing Restaurant Inspections Starts a Feeding Frenzy on the Web." *The New York Times*, May 18, p. B1.

Mahler, Julianne G., and Priscilla M. Regan. 2002. *Federal Intranet Work Sites: An Interim Assessment*. Washington, DC: IBM Center for the Business of Government.

Moon, M. Jae. 2002. *State Government E-Procurement in the Information Age: Issues, Practices, and Trends*. Washington, DC: IBM Center for the Business of Government.

Nucleus Research. 2004. "ROI Case Illustration: Teradata" Iowa Case Illustration E60, Department of Revenue, June.

Pollitt, Christopher. 1995. "Justification by Works or by Faith? Evaluating the New Public Management." *Evaluation* 1, no. 2: 133–154.

Pollitt, Christopher. 2000. "Is the Emperor in His Underwear? An Analysis of the Impacts of Public Management Reform." *Public Administration* 2, no. 2: 181–199.

Sacheli, Sarah. 2003. "Francis Vows More Openness at City Council." *The Windsor Star* (Ontario, Canada), September 23, p. A2.

Shields, Gerard. 2000. "City Figures to Improve Efficiency." *The Baltimore Sun*, November 19, p. 1B.

"The State of the City: Masiello Views the Good While Ignoring the Bad in His Annual Speech." 2004. *The Buffalo News*, February 4, p. C4.

Stowers, Genie N. L. 2002. *The State of Federal Websites: The Pursuit of Excellence*. Washington, DC: The IBM Center for the Business of Government.

Texas Department of Information Resources. 2003. *Cost-Benefit Study of Online Services*. Austin: Texas Department of Information Resources.

Thompson, Mark. 2005. "Wonk 'n' Roller." *Time* (April 25): 20–21.

Weber, Max. 1947. *The Theory of Social and Economic Organization*. Trans. Talcott Parsons. New York: The Free Press.

Wyld, David C. 2001. "The Auction Model: How the Public Sector Can Leverage the Power of E-Commerce through Dynamic Pricing." In *E-Government 2001*, ed. Mark A. Abramson and Grady E. Means, 85–161. Lanham, MD: Rowman & Littlefield.

Wyld, David C. 2004. *Government Garage Sales: Online Auctions as Tools for Asset Management*. Washington, DC: The IBM Center for the Business of Government.

Case Illustration

The Swiss E-Government Barometer: Kuno Schedler Feels the Temperature of E-Government Services

Viktor Mayer-Schönberger and David Lazer

The Swiss E-Government Barometer, initiated by Professor Kuno Schedler of the University of St. Gallen, is an annual survey of the Swiss electronic government landscape.

Unlike most surveys on electronic government, the Swiss E-Government Barometer does not focus on citizens as users of online public services. Instead, it surveys public-sector decision makers and implementers of electronic government within the powerful cantonal administrative units in Switzerland, thus offering a unique perspective into the context and mindset of those that ultimately decide what, when, and how to implement a public service online.

Schedler and his team distribute roughly 1,300 questionnaires to decision-making public administrators in all twenty-six cantons every year. Because it has been conducted annually, the barometer provides a rare longitudinal glimpse of the evolution and perception of electronic government by public administrators.

Each round of data collection constitutes a snapshot of the state of electronic government—what public services have been made available online. The survey also includes items on agency information and communication infrastructure and its usage, enabling analysis of whether a particular work context (more or less technologically savvy) influences bureaucratic decision making on electronic government.

The questionnaire stands out in two ways. First, it asks public administrators for their motives and reasoning regarding electronic government. While many other studies assume that if citizens demand public services online they will be provided, the barometer offers a window into how and why public administrators decide to push for electronic government. Second, the barometer assesses the digital information flowing from the executive to the legislative branches by asking public administrators to describe digital information they provide to legislatures.

Survey participants receive free of charge detailed individualized feedback in the form of a cluster analysis. It enables individual agencies to benchmark their responses vis-à-vis their peers. The results of the annual barometer are published both electronically and in hard copy, and are available at http://www.electronic-government.ch.

10

Information Quality in Electronic Government: Toward the Systematic Management of High-Quality Information in Electronic Government-to-Citizen Relationships

Martin J. Eppler

Introduction: The Relevance of Information Quality for Electronic Government

The provision of relevant, timely, consistent, and reliable information to citizens is at the core of many electronic government initiatives. In fact, the improvement of the quality and quantity of information provided to citizens is frequently cited as one of the main motives for electronic government efforts (Grant and Chau 2005, 4–6). The basic belief behind such initiatives is often that information technology by itself can increase the quality of information provided to citizens (7). While interactive online government services, such as electronic government portals, public service search engines, online forms, or notification services, can indeed increase the accessibility, convenience, and timeliness of governmental information, they cannot ensure that the retrieved information is accurate, informative, current, or comprehensive. This may lead to frustrations and unfulfilled expectations on behalf of citizens wanting to complete a certain task or researching relevant public information. As the channels of electronic government become more and more of a commodity that citizens take for granted, there is a need for a shift from a management focus on the delivery mode (electronic government) to the essence of the provided service, which is content. The informational perspective on government highlights not just the different potential architectures of information flows associated with different technologies but the quality of those flows as well. This new focus on information requires more than just deploying state-of-the-art information technology. It calls for clear information-related roles and responsibilities, for reliable review processes, and for an information- and citizen-centric service culture. In this chapter, I outline some of the reasons why the mere reliance on information technology is not enough to warrant high-quality information in electronic government. I do so with a clear focus on government-to-citizen relationships, although many of the discussed insights can be equally applied to government-to-government or government-to-business relations. Following this rationale, it is surprising that electronic government is an area to which the information quality perspective has not been applied yet, although it offers many fruitful approaches to improve electronic government services.

The main premise of this chapter is that only an explicit and systematic effort to manage the quality of government-provided information can lead to successful and sustainable electronic government services. This systematic effort involves various professional groups (Eppler 2003b) within government agencies that need to agree on common quality standards regarding information content, format, delivery process, and infrastructure. If these groups—including managers, content experts, administrators, and information technology (IT) staff—do not cooperate and do not agree on an explicit and common standard for information quality, problems ensue.[1] The Problems resulting from low information quality in electronic government websites include the following:

• Citizens stop using online government platforms to seek information because the online information is *irrelevant*, *outdated*, *of unstated origin*, or *inconsistent*.

• Citizens cannot find relevant information because the interaction process with a government website is *complicated* and *unintuitive*.

• Citizens cannot comprehend how to proceed to complete a certain administrative task because of *unclear* information. They need to phone in and ask for additional instructions, resulting in additional costs in terms of agency staff time.

• Citizens lose valuable time in gathering necessary government-provided information because it is *dispersed*, *incomplete*, or *not well-organized* (i.e., based on a citizen's life situation).

• Citizens do not entrust their personal information to virtual government applications because of unresolved *security* issues (information is not properly protected.)

• Citizens lose interest in public issues because of *lengthy* information that is not concise and does not provide an overview.

• Citizens or their representatives seek legal action against a public institution because apparently signficant but *inaccurate* information that concerns them has been made accessible online *too early* and has thus adversely affected them.

• Citizens cannot participate actively in political processes, because the necessary information is not online on time, due to an *inefficient* publication process and too many bureaucratic barriers.

• The budgets of public ministries can no longer keep up with their growing websites, because *maintainability* issues have not been addressed early and the allocated funding is not sustainable to maintain the online information base.

These problems can be detected by employing *online satisfaction surveys* (Eppler, Algesheimer, and Dimpfel 2003), conducting usability sessions, or conducting *online focus groups* with citizens from different age groups and with differing professional backgrounds. Although these problems may seem unrelated at first sight, they can all be traced back to a missing information quality policy that assures that the right information is made available at the right time, in the right format, through the right communication channels, to the right people, at the right costs.

To address and prevent such problems,[2] I propose first steps toward an information quality management framework for electronic government applications. My chapter is organized as follows: First, I define information quality in the context of electronic government by relying on prior definitions of the concept of information quality and adapting it to the public sector. Then, I outline specific ways to manage—that is to say, to assign accountability—and assure high-quality information in electronic government websites. In the last section, I describe some of the constraints that make information quality improvements difficult to achieve in many electronic government settings. I argue that it is useful to view information quality management (IQM) as an innovation for the public sector, because it requires significant changes in the habits and routines of public servants. As an innovation, IQM is subject to the typical innovation diffusion barriers, elicited elegantly by communication-based approaches of studying innovation. These barriers, and possible ways of overcoming them, are discussed in the final part of this chapter.

Defining Information Quality for Government-to-Citizen Relations

In a recent study on government-to-citizen electronic government initiatives, West (2004) states that "there is no agreement on appropriate benchmarks or what constitutes an effective government Web site" (18). In order to develop such benchmarks, I employ the rich definitions and metrics that exist on the notion of information quality. These definitions can be applied to the electronic government context. They are discussed in this section.

Generally, information quality designates the characteristic of an information product (Wang et al. 1998; Eppler, Gasser, and Helfert 2005) or service—for example, a set of information bundled for a specific purpose, to meet or exceed the requirements of its stakeholders. The stakeholders of an information product or service are its consumers, creators, custodians (or administrators), direct or indirect content providers, intermediaries, and regulators. High-quality information is information that is fit for use and of high value to its consumers, because it is free of errors or other deficiencies. The notion of value in this context is a multidimensional one as the information quality definitions in table 10.1 effectively illustrate.

Besides stressing different quality dimensions (such as content or format) or *attributes* (such as accuracy or timeliness), the previous definitions also highlight different information *stakeholders* (including their value expectations or specifications)

Table 10.1
Select information quality definitions

Information quality definition	Source
The degree to which information has *content, form, and time characteristics* that give it *value* to specific end users.	O'Brien 1991
Information quality is the characteristic of information to be of *high value* to its users. The smaller the difference between information provision and information need, the greater the information quality.	Lesca and Lesca 1995
Information quality can be defined in terms of accuracy, timeliness, conciseness, convenience, and relevance of information.	Rainer and Watson 1995
Quality information is information that meets *specifications* or *requirements*.	Wang and Strong 1996; Kahn and Strong 1998
Information quality can be defined as information that is *fit for use* by information consumers.	Huang, Lee, and Wang 1999
Information quality means consistently meeting all knowledge worker and end-customer *expectations* through information and information services.	English 1999
Data are of high quality if they are *fit for their intended uses*, by customers, in operations, decision making, and strategy setting.	Redman 2001
Information quality relates to the content of the (electronic government) site: the suitability of the information for the user's purposes.	Barnes and Vidgen 2003
Information quality is a condition where the *content and its media* provide *high value* to the information producers, administrators, and consumers. Information quality means providing the right information, in the right format, at the right time, at the right costs, to the right people.	Eppler 2003a, 2003b

and their different *uses* of information. An information quality definition for the electronic government sector can combine these elements and specify them for the public service context. The result of this amalgamation is the following definition of information quality:

Information provided by public agencies to citizens can be considered to be of high quality if the information and its medium meet or exceed citizens' expectations and regulators' specifications and if the information is of high value to citizens because it is fit for their various uses. Information quality can be further defined with attributes that relate to the time, format, content, and media dimension of information (such as timeliness, relevance, conciseness, or convenience). (Eppler 2003a)

In spite of the merit of such definitions (e.g., to facilitate the development of metrics for electronic government effectiveness and benchmarking[3] or to articulate a quality mission statement), it is obvious that it is much easier to define information quality than to actually assure and manage it. Nonetheless, an explicit systematic definition of what a public institution considers to be high-quality information can be a first important step toward more valuable online information. For that purpose, however, the definitions provided here are still too general.

Information quality can be described more specifically with the help of information attributes or structured criteria lists that categorize information characteristics into several meaningful and manageable dimensions. So-called information quality frameworks (e.g., Taylor 1986; Wang et al. 1998) define information quality by categorizing core criteria that make information useful for information consumers. Such information quality frameworks exist for various application domains, ranging from e-commerce websites to printed newspapers. In the context of electronic information, most information quality frameworks consist of two levels: the individual criteria and a category level (which groups the attributes). Among the numerous existing information quality frameworks (for a partial review, see Eppler 2003a), very few use categories that can be used directly for management purposes, namely, for assigning responsibilities to specific professional groups. The framework I present here offers such attribute categories. They can be used to assign specific areas of responsibility for information quality factors in a government agency. Our framework for information quality management in electronic government is depicted in figure 10.1. The framework categorizes the different quality attributes of information into meaningful and manageable groups.

On the highest level of abstraction, the framework distinguishes between content and medium quality—namely, the message and its channel. Media quality is divided

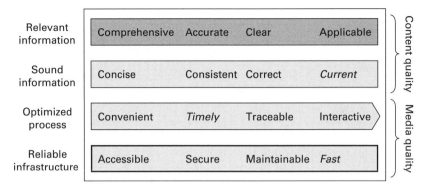

Figure 10.1
A framework for information quality.

into process and infrastructure, while the content itself is viewed in terms of relevance (i.e., relative or subjective information quality criteria) and soundness (i.e., intrinsic or objective information quality criteria). The individual attributes contained in each category reflect the diverse expectations and needs that publicly available information and its media must meet for various information stakeholders. These attributes relate to information format (such as conciseness), time (such as timeliness), and costs (such as maintainability). They are based on web surveys on information quality among 1,200 web users as well as on existing information quality frameworks (Eppler, Algesheimer, and Dimpfel 2003).[4] The main logic behind this framework is a pragmatic one: the categories help assign responsibilities for different prerequisites of information quality within a public agency or institution. This is illustrated by the following figure that shows the same four levels again, but this time labels them according to the professional group that is responsible for each set of criteria. As figure 10.2 shows, the main responsibility for providing the right (relevant) information is with the line managers or department heads. The responsibility to see that this content is right (sound) lies with an agency's content providers themselves, usually subject matter experts. The responsibility for a convenient interaction process lies with the information technology managers (who should not interfere with the content-related matters) and the usability engineers (Nielsen 1993, 2000). The responsibility for a reliable and speedy infrastructure, finally, lies with the IT hard- and software specialists (either inside a public administration or with an outside partner). The main plan for how each set of criteria is consistently met is referred to as a policy. Each policy is briefly described here.

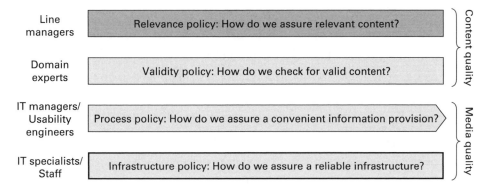

Figure 10.2
Roles and policies derived from the IQ framework.

In order to implement an information quality function based on the previous framework, a public agency needs to institute four kinds of IQM policies:

1. A *relevance policy* based on a profound understanding of the real information needs of citizens. The goal of this policy is to assure that the information that is provided is relevant and comprehensive enough, accurate enough, clear enough, and generally applicable for the targeted citizens.

2. A *validity policy* that outlines how information is reviewed internally in order to avoid information deficiencies, such as documents that are too long, internally inconsistent, incorrect, or outdated.

3. A *process policy* that describes how the interaction process remains usable for various types of citizens. Usable in this context means convenient to use, with timely information delivery that can be adapted to one's needs and where the sources of information are visible.

4. An *infrastructure policy* that describes the necessary preventive measures to assure that the information hard- and software remain reliable. Reliability in this context refers to the requirements of the citizens (they expect an easily accessible infrastructure that is safe and fast), but also to the constraints of the public agency (which must assure that its level of spending for the infrastructure is maintainable in order to offer the services in a sustainable manner).

A sample checklist with some of the key questions that should be answered by each of the four policy documents in a public agency is as follows:

1. Relevance Policy[5]

• What are the main expectations of our citizens with regard to content?

• Which are (derived from the expectations) our main content areas?

• How do we monitor changes in the relevance system of the citizens?

2. Validity Policy[6]

• How and by whom is influential information double-checked before publication?

• Is there an appeal process that citizens can employ to rectify wrong information?

• Does published information have an expiration date or what other mechanisms are there to insure regular updates of information?

3. Process Policy

• Have the navigation trails to find information been tested with user groups and with different user scenarios?

• Is the navigation behavior of the users of the electronic government analyzed? Are log-off points registered and navigation trails improved accordingly?

• How can citizens suggest improvements to the interaction process?

4. Infrastructure Policy

• Is there a backup system for the infrastructure?

• Is there a strategy on how to scale the system's capacity in case the information demand by citizens increases?

• Is there a rights management and a security software installed?

How these policies and responsibilities are implemented is the subject of the next section.

Managing Information Quality in Electronic Government through Roles, Processes, Tools, and Training

The four levels that were previously introduced can now serve not only to distinguish among different *roles* for information quality, but also to distinguish key *processes*, *tools*, and *training* areas that are needed to make high-quality information a reality in government websites.

In terms of *roles*, we have already distinguished among staff who are responsible for content selection (content directors), for content validity or soundness (reviewers or content managers), for the interaction processes (usability engineers, webmasters, etc.) and for reliable base infrastructures (IT specialists, platform managers).

With regard to key quality *processes*, we can—again using the four categories—distinguish among feedback processes that validate whether the provided information is indeed relevant to the citizens, review processes that help validate information before it is published, interaction processes that make the information more easily accessible to citizens, and infrastructure maintenance processes that guarantee the smooth functioning of the underlying hard- and software. Ideally, each such process is assigned to a process owner who oversees its functioning.[7]

As for information quality management *tools* that can be used to improve and assure information quality in electronic government applications, our prior distinction leads to the following types of instruments. For the relevance dimension, we need tools that help us survey and monitor the citizens use of the electronic government applications in order to see what kind of content is most frequently accessed and which areas of an electronic government site are barely used. A great variety of such tools is available on the market, tools aimed primarily at the private sector.[8] Many of them can be easily adjusted to the electronic government context. For the validity dimension, there are so-called workflow tools that help organize a review-based publication process that includes quality checks and update mechanisms. With regard to process quality, monitoring tools similar to those discussed for relevance purposes can be employed. They can be used to analyze the log files of citizens' visits to a government website in order to detect deficits in the current interaction process. The last group of (mostly technical) tools consists of system monitoring and maintenance tools that help prevent security issues or system fallout. Examples of such tools are security software (firewall, anti-virus), code parsers (which detect source code compliance with accessibility standards) or site performance improvement software.

A last vital but often overlooked element of implementing information quality management in an electronic government context is the *training* of public administrators. Training with regard to information quality ranges from generally educating public officers about the most pressing information needs of their citizens, to technically training them to run websites, to training information managers about usability issues. Whereas the training related to the relevance and process dimension focuses on the expectations (in terms of content) and use (in terms of interaction) of the citizens, validity training consists of instructing public officers in how to operate review or control processes for information. Infrastructure training, finally, prepares the technical staff for security concerns or for fallout scenarios.

If these areas are considered beyond just focusing on the information technology, then information quality improvements stand on a much broader base. Public policymakers and public officers, who strive to improve the quality of the information provided to citizens, still face, however, many barriers. These barriers are analyzed in the next section with the help of innovation diffusion theory.

Constraints and Barriers for Information Quality Management in G2C Relations

So far we have focused on the factors that contribute to information quality and foster information quality–oriented behavior. For a realistic assessment of the management of information quality in electronic government, however, we should not neglect the many restrictions that make information quality improvements difficult, and sometimes even impossible in the public sector. In order to systemize and categorize such possible potholes in the road to information quality, we rely on prior findings from innovation diffusion theory (Rogers 1995).[9] Rogers highlights five factors that influence the rate of adoption of a new practice: the *complexity* of the innovation (i.e., how difficult it is to master), the *compatibility* with prior practices (i.e., the degree of change necessary to adopt it), the *observability* of the new behavior (i.e., how easy it is to recognize it), the *trialability* of the new behavior (i.e., whether it is possible to test the innovation first), and the relative *advantage* of the innovation for the people affected by it (i.e., the benefits brought by the innovation).[10] These innovation characteristics are examined for information quality management in the table that follows.

Table 10.2 highlights the problematic compatibility dimension of IQM, because of the many changes required to institutionalize information quality management. Since public administrations are typically geared toward continuity and consistency with previous practices and rules (as their dominant logic), this issue must be addressed in more detail (see Tornatzky and Klein 1982). In the electronic government practices that we have observed (see case illustration), there are often compatibility problems with regard to five areas:[11]

1. Existing *rules* or regulations: Establishing new processes and roles requires at times new regulations or modifications to existing ones.

2. Existing *skills*, expectations, or routines: Implementing the aforementioned policies requires new skills (as indicated in the section on training) and sometimes new attitudes from public workers.

Table 10.2
IQM and its innovation characteristics

Innovation characteristics...	...and their manifestation in information quality management (IQM)
1. *Relative advantage*: The new practice is perceived as better than current practices.	IQM dramatically reduces information scrap and rework (English 1999) and increases citizens' satisfaction with electronic government services.
2. *Compatibility*: The new practice is consistent with existing values, past experiences, and needs.	IQM requires the acquisition of new skills, the design of new processes, the purchase of new tools, and the definition of new roles and may thus often be inconsistent with current habits.
3. *Complexity*: The difficulty of applying the new practice.	The roles, processes, and tools of IQM are indeed complex, as they consist of numerous, interrelated elements, but they can be mastered through differentiated, focused responsibilities (i.e., splitting content and media quality tasks) and through adequate training activities.
4. *Trialability*: The possibility of experimenting with the new practice on a limited basis.	IQM can be gradually introduced, for example, by first focusing on particularly influential information.
5. *Observability*: The results of a new practice are visible to others.	Through citizen surveys and focus groups the changes in information consumer satisfaction can be measured.

3. Existing tools and *infrastructures*: Some of the existing infrastructure might not be able to support information quality management and thus has to be replaced.

4. Existing *resources*, such as staff, budget and available time: Providing high-quality information is just one of many goals of public agencies; thus this objective might be incompatible or at least in conflict with other objectives that require time, budget, and effort.

5. Existing *reference points*—such as official benchmarks or values, established institutional networks, or predefined standards of higher-level public agencies—may result in a conservative bias in the perceptions and attitudes of public servants.

The fifth group of compatibility constraints includes elements that are highlighted in Rogers's theory of innovation diffusion—namely, previous practices (e.g., of citizens or government officials) or norms of the social system (e.g., regarding security issues) (Rogers 1995, 163). As Rogers states in one of his insightful case illustrations: "An important factor regarding the adoption rate of an innovation is its compatibility with the *values, beliefs, and past experiences* of individuals in the social system" (4).

Following this logic, any type of initiative that aims to improve the quality of information provided to citizens must take into account *how to change current reference points* in a way that is not in extensive conflict with the norms of the social system. In figure 10.3, we have summarized these compatibility constraints visually. The main implication for electronic government managers is thus to reflect whether their information quality policy is actually *fundable* (in terms of the budget allocated to assuring high-quality information), whether it is *allowable* (in terms of the existing regulation), whether it is *doable* and *conceivable* with the existing skill base and infrastructure, and how it will influence the relationship with existing *reference points*. Proactively changing these reference points—for example, by comparing an

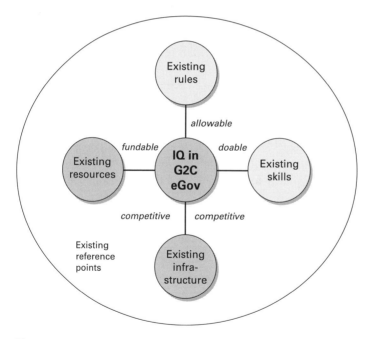

Figure 10.3
Compatibility constraints for information quality improvements in electronic government initiatives.

agency's information quality level with that of a comparable agency in another country—is one effective way of confronting these limitations and motivating public servants to make information quality improvements that lead to truly *competitive* electronic government services.

Conclusion

Information government focuses on the architecture of information flows within and from government. This chapter applies the rich vein of research on information quality and practice to what has emerged as one of the most important media for these information flows—the Internet. Especially in government-to-citizen relationships, the quality of the provided information is a key determinant of the success of electronic government initiatives. This is why information quality approaches can and should be applied to this important area. I have argued that a systematic management of information quality must address at least four levels: content relevance, content validity or soundness, the interaction process, and the underlying infrastructure. Clear responsibilities must be assigned to each of these areas within an agency, and management processes should be designed and deployed accordingly. These processes can be supported by a variety of tools and facilitated by targeted training. In this way, information quality improvements can be iteratively achieved—for example, by first focusing only on highly influential or sensitive information. I have also highlighted that public leaders need to take into account the often considerable barriers to information quality improvements. The factors highlighted by innovation theory, especially the compatibility with past practices, can be useful indicators in that endeavor. To overcome these barriers, government officials must create incentives[12] and competitive reference points to motivate and mobilize public servants to improve their information quality online. Beyond that, they must provide adequate funding, tools, and training so that this motivation can ultimately lead to a government that does not just focus on the electronic channels through which it provides information, but on the actual information itself and the value it provides to citizens.

Notes

1. For similar categorization of authentic citizens' complaints regarding e-government sites, see, for example, Barnes and Vidgen 2003.

2. Accenture's (2004) global e-government survey finds that there are now new efforts to integrate e-government sites vertically across national, state/regional, and local government levels. In this integration process, reliance on the quality of information among the various levels becomes crucial to the effectiveness of the overall system. Thus, large-scale e-government integration may be another driver that raises the importance of the information quality issue in government-to-government contexts. In this chapter, as mentioned, I focus primarily on government-to-citizen applications, but it seems obvious that high-quality information among government agencies is also one prerequisite to information quality provided to citizens.

3. See Barnes and Vidgen 2003 for this use of information quality in e-government.

4. A central challenge in the management of information quality is that many of these attributes are in trade-off relations to one another; namely, the improvement of one attribute (such as security or timeliness) may lead to a reduction in another (such as accessibility or accuracy). Managing these trade-offs requires a clear understanding of the relative importance of these qualities for citizens (Hazlett and Hill 2003, 445). For similar information quality attributes, see, for example, Gilbert, Balestrini, and Littleboy 2004 or Barnes and Vidgen 2003.

5. Two current studies that illustrate the urgent need for such a policy are Dawes, Pardo, and Crasswell 2003 and Marche and McNiven 2003. These authors illustrate that governments are often not sensitive to the information needs and relevancy systems of their citizens.

6. These suggestions are based on the guidelines issued by the U.S. Office of Management and Budget with regard to the implementation of the federal data quality act that requires each federal agency to install an information quality process for its influential publicly released information. See, for example, http://www.whitehouse.gov/omb/fedreg/final_information_ quality_guidelines.html (accessed July 5, 2005).

7. All of these processes rely, of course, on the smooth functioning of the underlying administrative processes. Becker, Algermissen, and Niehaves (2004) show in their recent study of processes in e-government that this is still a major challenge.

8. Commercially available tools that provide such functionalities are, for example, www .opinionpoll.com, www.lets-ask.com, www.infopoll.com, www.websurveyor.com, www .webtrends.com, www.analog.cx, and www.nedstat.com.

9. For a similar application of diffusion theory to e-government (from the citizens' adoption point of view), see Carter and Belanger 2004.

10. A communication approach, such as Rogers's, toward innovation seems a fruitful perspective to understand possible limitations to information quality–induced changes in e-government for two main reasons. First, conceiving of information quality improvements as an innovation diffusion process helps managers *be prepared* for possible negative reactions that occur when current processes or habits need to be modified (it is thus a particularly realistic approach that is sensitive to people's resistance to change). Second, the communication approach to innovation diffusion is, as Rogers has shown (Rogers 1995, 78), open to analyzing *any type* of innovation with the help of proven conceptual tools. In that respect, Rogers himself has used many *public-sector initiatives* as case illustrations for innovation diffusion.

11. "Legislative and *regulatory* barriers, *financial* barriers, *technological* barriers and the digital divide, among others, can impede the uptake of e-government" (OECD 2003, 13).

12. One type of incentive may be to create an online certificate or "ribbon" to label high-quality contributions or government websites. In the private sector, companies and institutions such as Reuters, DeutscheBank, Giga Information Group (now part of Forrester), and MedCertain (a so-called trustmark for online health information) have begun to use labels to explicitly signal quality-assured content to web users.

References

Accenture. 2004. *eGovernment Leadership: High Performance, Maximum Value*. eGovernment Executive Series. New York: Accenture.

Barnes, Stuart J., and Richard T. Vidgen. 2003. "Assessing the Quality of a Cross-National e-Government Web Site: A Case Illustration of the Forum on Strategic Management Knowledge Exchange." In *Proceedings of the 36th Hawaii International Conference on System Sciences* (HICSS'03). Hawaii: IEEE.

Becker, Joerg, Lars Algermissen, and Bjoern Niehaves. 2004. "Processes in e-Government Focus: A Procedure Model for Process Oriented Reorganisation in Public Administrations on the Local Level." In *Proceedings of the Second International Conference on Electronic Government*, 147–150. Berlin: Springer.

Carter, Lemuria, and France Belanger. 2004. "Citizen Adoption of Electronic Government Initiatives." In *Proceedings of the 37th Hawaii International Conference on System Sciences* (HICSS'04). Hawaii: IEEE.

Dawes, Sharon S., Theresa A. Pardo, and Anthony M. Cresswell. 2003. "Designing Government Information Access Programs: A Holistic Approach." In *Proceedings of the 36th Hawaii International Conference on System Sciences* (HICSS'03). Hawaii: IEEE.

English, Larry P. 1999. *Improving Data Warehouse and Business Information Quality*. New York: Wiley and Sons.

Eppler, Martin J. 2003a. *Managing Information Quality*. Berlin and New York: Springer.

Eppler, Martin J. 2003b. "Managing Information Quality: Everyone Has a Role to Play." *Cutter IT Journal* 16, no. 1: 13–17.

Eppler, Martin J., Rene Algesheimer, and Marcus Dimpfel. 2003. "Quality Criteria of Content-Driven Websites and Their Influence on Customer Satisfaction and Loyalty: An Empirical Test of an Information Quality Framework." In *Proceedings of the 8th MIT Information Quality Conference*, 108–120. Cambridge, MA: MIT.

Eppler, Martin J., Urs Gasser, and Markus Helfert. 2005. "Information Quality: Organizational, Technological, and Legal Perspectives." *Studies in Communication Sciences* 2, no. 4: 1–16.

Gilbert, David, Pierre Balestrini, and Darren Littleboy. 2004. "Barriers and Benefits in the Adoption of E-government." *International Journal of Public Sector Management* 17, no. 4: 286–301.

Grant, Gerald, and Derek Chau. 2005. "Developing a Generic Framework for E-Government." *Journal of Global Information Management* 13, no. 1: 1–30.

Hazlett, Shirley-Ann, and Frances Hill. 2003. "E-Government: The Realities of Using IT to Transform the Public Sector." *Managing Service Quality* 13, no. 6: 445–452.

Huang, Kuan-Tsae, Yang W. Lee, and Richard Y. Wang. 1999. *Quality Information and Knowledge*. Upper Saddle River, NJ: Prentice Hall.

Kahn, B. K., and D. M. Strong. 1998. "Product and Service Performance Model for Information Quality: An Update." In *Proceedings of the 1998 Conference on Information Quality*, ed. I. Chengalur-Smith and L. L. Pipino. Cambridge, MA: MIT.

Lesca, Humbert, and Elizabeth Lesca. 1995. *Gestion de l'information, qualité de l'information et performances de l'entreprise*. Paris: Litec.

Marche, Sunny, and James D. McNiven. 2003. "E-Government and E-Governance: The Future Isn't What It Used to Be." *Canadian Journal of Administrative Sciences* 20, no. 1: 74–86.

Nielsen, Jakob. 1993. *Usability Engineering*. Boston, MA: Academic Press.

Nielsen, Jakob. 2000. *Designing Web Usability: The Practice of Simplicity*. Indianapolis, IN: New Riders Publishing.

O'Brien, James A. 1991. *Introduction to Information Systems in Business Management*. 6th ed. Boston: Irwin.

OECD. 2003. "The E-Government Imperative: Main Findings." Policy brief, Paris. Available at http://www.oecd.org/dataoecd/60/60/2502539.pdf (accessed April 12, 2005).

Rainer, R. Kelly, and Hugh J. Watson. 1995. "The Keys to Executive Information Systems Success." *Journal of Management Information Systems* 12, no. 2: 83–98.

Redman, Thomas C. 2001. *Data Quality: The Field Guide*. Boston: Digital Press (Butterworth-Heinemann).

Rogers, Everett M. 1995. *Diffusion of Innovations*. 4th ed. New York: The Free Press.

Taylor, Robert S. 1986. *Value-Added Processes in Information Systems*. Norwood: Ablex.

Tornatzky, Louis G., and Katherine J. Klein. 1982. "Innovation Characteristics and Innovation Adoption-Implementation: A Meta-Analysis of Findings." *IEEE Transactions on Engineering Management* 29, no. 1: 28–45.

Wang, Richard Y., and Diane M. Strong. 1996. "Beyond Accuracy: What Data Quality Means to Data Consumers." *Journal of Management Information Systems* 12, no. 4: 5–33.

Wang, Richard J., Yang W. Lee, Leo L. Pipino, and Diane M. Strong. 1998. "Manage Your Information as a Product." *Sloan Management Review* 39, no. 4: 95–105.

West, Darrell M. 2004. "E-Government and the Transformation of Service Delivery and Citizen Attitudes." *Public Administration Review* (January/February): 15–27.

Case Illustration

Information Quality in Electronic Government Websites: An Example from Italy's Ministry for Public Administration

Lorenzo Cantoni

In 2004 the Italian Ministry for Public Administration, in collaboration with other parties, conducted a pilot program aimed at promoting the culture of user-centered website design and management among public administration officers. A version of the information quality model was developed and tested in two different administration bodies, and then made available to all the others through a CD-ROM, a website, and dedicated training programs.

This case shows how the design and evaluation of public administration websites can fit into an information quality model, and how this can lead to a sustainable virtuous circle of continuous improvements.

1. Project Context and Outline

The Italian law requires that public administrations of a certain kind or size run a Public Relation Office (URP, or Ufficio per le Relazioni con il Pubblico). Recently, Italy adopted a law requiring that all messages foreseen by the statute governing URPs have to be made available through websites.

After the first wave of websites, the URPs came to the realization that simply having a functioning website is inadequate because citizens require high-quality online services that provide high-quality information. In this context, the "Usability CD" project was born—the production of a CD-ROM to be distributed to Italian URPs. Due to the many requests, the content of the CD-ROM has been made available also through a website (http://www .urp.it/cpusabile). In addition, a dedicated training program has been designed and successfully tested with about forty Italian public administration officers.

2. Project Design and Development Phases

In order to assess the quality of the URP websites, two sites were chosen: a website run by the city of Modena, called Unox1 ('one by one') and another by the Campania region. The MiLE, or Milano Lugano Evaluation model, was adopted as a general usability assessment framework (Triacca et al. 2004), in connection with the WCM, or Website Communication Model (Cantoni and Tardini 2006).

"Usability," in this project, has to be understood in a complex information quality framework, including content usability/usefulness; in fact, content usability is becoming an important and challenging usability issue, as stated by Jakob Nielsen (Cantoni, Di Blas, and Bolchini 2003, xiii): "Unfortunately, it is more difficult to study the usability of communication than the usability of navigation. It is pretty clear-cut whether the user can find something or not. It is more difficult to test the quality of information."

Available data about websites' actual use (usages) were analyzed mainly through log files, mailing list subscriptions, and e-mails received; such data helped the project members better understand *what kind of information users were interested in* (relevance dimension). In one case, the results of a research conducted through telephone interviews were used, to assess the level of satisfaction of citizens with respect to public administration communication activities. Front-office personnel were interviewed, and focus groups were run, in order to further focus on what is *relevant* for citizens in their interactions with those public administration online services.

These analyses have enabled the identification of *user profiles*, based on age, profession, Internet access type, and users' goals and expectations. Once the user profiles of the e-government websites were defined (13 different profiles for one website, 16 for the other one), *user scenarios* were developed with the help of all stakeholders. User scenarios are task-oriented vivid descriptions of envisioned use of the electronic government application, expressed in narrative form, as stories of typical users using the site, with their motivations, goals, and expectations (Bolchini and Paolini 2004; Cantoni, Di Blas, and Bolchini 2003). *Inspections* were conducted in order to assess whether user scenarios could be effectively conducted, as well as to measure how easy or difficult it was to conduct them (efficiency). A list of recommendations was compiled for each of the concerned websites, which were eventually modified accordingly. Recommendations for improving the websites were divided into the macro areas of *content quality* and *media quality*. *Content quality* recommendations for improvement ranged from adding missed content, to rephrasing it, to updating it, to improving suitability for the intended target public, etc. *Media quality* recommendations covered navigation, layout, and graphic design. Closely connected to both areas, analyses of work-flow processes and of the labeling system (how active parts/links are labeled, how pages/sections are titled) were conducted. An analysis conducted applying Nielsen's heuristics (Nielsen 2000) and user-testing activities complemented the profiles and scenarios strategy.

3. Some Lessons Learned

The following are key lessons learned from the pilot:

• A process of continuous improvement needs a strong commitment by the involved public administration offices; hence, the importance of having evangelizers in URPs, and of offering them a common forum where to get in contact. The training experience was especially important in this regard.

• Because URPs have frequent personnel turnover, a clear and simple plan needs to be developed, which can easily be followed by people who have not been involved in the process from its very beginning.

• No *pass or fail* approach seems to be viable; instead, a virtuous circle of continuous information quality improvement seems to be more apt, effective, and efficient.

• Working on similar cases greatly helps people better understand procedures, as well as feel more at ease and become more committed.

• Viewing the law as a departure point, not as a constraint, greatly helps operators in devising and running an information quality improvement project.

References

Bolchini, Davide, and Paolo Paolini. 2004. "Goal-Driven Requirements Analysis for Hypermedia-intensive Web Applications." *Requirements Engineering Journal*, Special Issue 9: 85–103.

Cantoni, Lorenzo, Nicoletta Di Blas, and Davide Bolchini. 2003. *Comunicazione, Qualità, Usabilità* (Communication, quality, usability). Milan: Apogeo.

Cantoni, Lorenzo, and Stefano Tardini. 2006. *Internet*. Routledge Introductions to Media and Communications Series. London: Routledge.

Nielsen, Jakob. 2000. *Designing Web Usability: The Practice of Simplicity*. Indianapolis: New Riders Publishing.

Triacca, Luca, Davide Bolchini, Luca Botturi, and Alessandro Inversini. 2004. "MiLE: Systematic Usability Evaluation for E-learning Web Applications." In *Proceedings of the ED-MEDIA 2004*, ed. Lorenzo Cantoni and Catherine McLoughlin, 4398–4405. Norfolk, VA: AACE.

11

It Takes a Network to Build a Network

David Lazer and Maria Christina Binz-Scharf

Introduction

The information government paradigm focuses on how information flows through government. Many of the chapters in this volume concentrate on the potential impact of technology on information flows. This chapter's focus is the converse, asking what the impact of information flows on the use of information technology in government is. The role of the institutions, informal networks, and other mechanisms of information diffusion are critical to understanding how information and communication technology (ICT) is integrated into government because ICT creates a novel malleability to information flows, which poses substantial challenges to government managers. Novelty by its nature poses risks to any manager for two reasons: first, there is the possibility of unanticipated consequences, and, second, there are costs involved in trying to minimize what is unanticipated.

One critical mechanism that individuals use to manage novelty is to learn from others' experiences. People learn from each other by multiple mechanisms—through personal networks, from organizations, through news media. Within the organization, such a learning network generally includes peers and individuals involved in the relevant processes. In addition, organizations rely heavily on others' experiences. Intergovernmental organizations are especially important in bridging distant parts of a diffuse policy community, as well as in aggregating information by offering their take on what constitutes good practice.

In short, it takes a (human) network to process the information involved in building a (transformational ICT) network. Drawing on interview data we collected from e-government projects (see Binz-Scharf 2003; Binz-Scharf and Lazer 2007), we begin by examining the collective (human) information processing challenges that the development of e-government presents to organizations. The implementation of e-government involves, in significant part, a search—for information, solutions, opportunities. Because e-government is a global phenomenon, many individuals are simultaneously engaged in parallel searches to deal with similar issues. How those individuals are connected must have a major impact on the course of development of e-government globally. In this chapter, we begin with a discussion of the challenges of managing novelty. We then turn to the diffusion of information literature to examine how the structure of a network might affect the performance of the system. We break this down into two subsidiary questions: (1) How does the network affect the diffusion of information? (2) How does the system sustain the creation of new information? We then examine the roles of different intra- and interorganizational networks in the e-government arena.

Managing Novelty

Novelty—for example, new and potentially transformational technology—is an enormous managerial challenge for four reasons. First, new technologies pose a problem-solving challenge because the initial array of choices is vast. As one observer from a statewide e-government project stated, "[The state] was, 'Well, we've never been here before. Nobody's ever been here before, so we're gonna have to figure this out on our own.'"[1] There are a finite number of "old ways" of doing things, but an infinite number of possible new ways. This multitude of possibilities is typically forgotten after a choice has been made, but the initial points of decision are potentially paralyzing.

The second reason that novelty is a challenge is—small *p*—political. One can view any organization as an amalgam of interests competing for resources having reached a tenuous accommodation with each other (Cyert and March 1963). Re-engineering information flows disrupts that equilibrium, inevitably increasing the importance of some, and reducing (or eliminating) the relevance of others. Often the incumbent coalition will resist that technology, a pattern seen from the use of ICT to facilitate knowledge sharing (McDermott 1999), to the development of nuclear submarines (Ambrose 1983), to the use of DNA in the criminal justice system (Lazer 2004). This resistance is not due to the complexity of the new technology, as the manager of a large e-government project described: "The technology is not the challenge. That's really pretty easy. It's the people, and it's the policy.... People are going to have to undergo a fundamental change, a total change in the way that they think about their jobs and deliver service, to make this work."

The third reason, which often, but not always, goes hand in hand with politics, is cultural. Existing ways of doing business both shape the perceptions of how things can be done and take on normative overtones (Weick 2001). An organization may have been doing things a particular way for a generation or more. Those routines serve symbolic as well as functional needs (Chetkovich 1997). A new technology may render certain activities obsolete, and yet their elimination resisted because of their symbolic value. The experience of a project member of one of the e-government teams we studied illustrates some of these challenges:

We see people wanting to create an online application that basically mimics the paper process, not taking advantage of what you can do electronically…, not rethinking how that business process can be re-architected….Take [for example]…environmental permits…. There may be paper signatures that are required right now, ink signatures, that are not mandated by any statute or regulation, it's just that for the last hundred years we've done it this way, so they immediately think, 'Oh my god, I need an electronic signature'. So we go back and ask, 'Why do you think you need an electronic signature?' 'Because the paper is signed.' 'Well, where does it tell you that the paper has to be signed?' And when they go back and they look at their regulations and statutes, they say, 'You're right, there's nothing here that says that, so we don't need that, we need to authenticate where the paper's coming from, but we don't need a signature.'

The need for signatures was not a statutory requirement, but had become embedded within the belief systems of those in charge of the permitting system through years of doing business in that particular way.

Finally, new technologies may offer better ways of doing business in the long run, but present substantial transition costs in the short run. In the public sector, funding for new endeavors depends on a—capital *P*—political process rather than capital markets. These political processes may not be responsive to the cyclical financial needs that technological developments sometimes require.

People manage novelty, in significant part by searching for information, in order to reduce uncertainties and unanticipated events. We now turn to one of the key ways that people or organizations search for information—through their networks.

Networks

Novelty at the individual level means that the individual (person or organization) is actively engaged in a search—for information, solutions, opportunities. Novelty at the system level means that many individuals are simultaneously engaged in searches to deal with similar issues (Lazer and Friedman, forthcoming). By parallel, we do not mean independent. Instead, those searches are intertwined, where experiments in one corner of the system provide lessons for other corners of the system. However, of course, not every individual pays attention to every other individual in the system. There are two seemingly contradictory reasons for this: (1) *information deprivation*—that much important information is (semi)private; and (2) *information overload*—there are inherent limits on what people can pay attention to. We discuss each in turn.

First, even in the public sector, much information is private. In part this is because the information is behind organizational boundaries, and there is no reason for the organization to make it more broadly available. In fact, in some cases (e.g., failures) there will be a strong incentive not to make that information public. In this case, the information might be reasonably easy to represent and transfer; however, some information (tacit knowledge—i.e., knowledge residing in people's heads) is inherently difficult to transfer.

Second, it is impossible for any individual person or organization to attend to and process every bit of information available on a given subject. Could an agency evaluating whether to put transactions online examine what every other agency in the world has done? Of course not; it would be a Herculean task, and one with rapidly declining returns. The critical search question is whom to pay attention to and whom to ignore—where there may be very valuable potential lessons that are consequently ignored.

Human networks provide the architecture for systemic search. Network analysis is defined by its focus on *relationships* among individuals/organizations ("nodes") rather than on the nodes (Wasserman and Faust 1994). It is through networks that individuals navigate both information deprivation and information overload. It is through relationships that private information is conveyed. One critical type of relationship is *attentional*—who pays attention to whom?

The configuration of these networks can have a major impact on the long-term success of a system. In this particular case, we define the system as the multitude of government entities that make decisions as to how to implement ICTs within government. The question we examine is exactly how that configuration of relationships might affect the performance of the system. We break this down into two subsidiary questions: (1) How does the network affect the diffusion of information? (2) How does the system sustain the creation of new information?

Diffusion

An enormous body of literature exists on the diffusion of innovations (see Rogers 1995 for the definitive overview). This literature addresses many determinants of diffusion—where the configuration of the network is one of the critical factors. A significant component of this literature focuses on interorganizational diffusion (e.g., Galaskiewicz and Wasserman 1989; Haunschild 1993); here we discuss how the network configuration affects the spread of information, examining in turn factors at the dyadic and systemic levels.

Dyadic

Dyadic factors characterize a particular relationship between two actors. The dyadic factor that has received the most attention, following Granovetter's (1973) "Strength of Weak Ties," is the distinction between "weak" and "strong" relationships (although, as we discuss here, Granovetter's paper was primarily about systemic factors). The strong/weak dichotomy is one that actually bundles quite a few dyadic factors, many of which are likely continuous, including affect, precedence, family ties, interpersonal knowledge, and so forth.

The strength of a tie likely has a significant effect on the volume and type of information conveyed between two actors. For example, Hansen (1999), in his study of knowledge sharing across organizational subunits, found that transfer of complex information and tacit knowledge required strong ties, reflecting the greater costs of transfer. Thus, the additional "bandwidth" of strong ties is likely necessary to convey certain types of complex information (Nelson 1989). Similarly, strong ties are expected to take precedence over weak ties; information will be shared with strong ties before weak ones (Carpenter, Esterling, and Lazer 2003).

Systemic

Dyadic factors affect the transmission of information between any pair of actors. However, whether A shares information with B, of course, is not only dependent on the nature of their relationship, but on the structure of the overall network. Here we discuss three patterns that sometimes characterize the configuration of networks: clustering (triadic closure, homophily, geography), small worlds, and scale-free networks.

Networks tend to be somewhat clumpy, where the probabilities that different dyads communicate are interdependent. Three especially important factors drive this interdependence: triadic closure, homophily, and geography.

Triadic closure means that the probabilities that A talks with B, and B with C, and A with C tend to be strongly interdependent (Heider 1946; Holland and Leinhardt 1977). Thus, for example, friends do tend to talk to friends. How much triadic closure there is in a network tends to be strongly related to how rapidly information diffuses through that network. A high degree of clustering means that a high proportion of the information a node receives will be redundant—A speaks with B and C, who talk to each other and therefore have similar information. In Granovetter's (1973) "Strength of Weak Ties," the key result is that weak ties tend to be structurally superior at providing access to information, because weak tie networks have lower levels of closure than strong tie networks.

Homophily is the tendency of individuals that are similar to each other to communicate more (Lazarsfeld and Merton 1982; McPherson, Smith-Lovin, and Cook 2001). This is an enormously robust, if conceptually underexplored, pattern. It has several informational effects. First, it may reduce the amount of information that individuals receive because it will result in a homogenization of the sources of information that individuals receive, since they largely receive information from individuals like themselves. Second, homophily may be associated with a high utility of information received, because the information received from those in a similar position will likely be more relevant.

Geography may be seen as a special case of homophily, where the relevant index of similarity is distance. Gravity models of international trade suggest that trade drops with the exponential of the distance between two countries (e.g., Frankel 1997); studies of intraorganizational relations suggest a similar pattern operates even at the microlevel scale of distance between offices and cubicles (Allen and Cohen 1969).

Bridging ties are thus especially important both to individuals, who may gain informational advantages if they are tied to others that their contacts do not know (Burt 1992), and to the system. This insight has been highlighted by the "small world" research of Watts and Strogatz (1998), which found that even a small number of bridging ties can dramatically lower the average number of degrees of separation between dyads. That is, a few bridges can greatly accelerate the spread of information within a system. Therefore, if one is looking at a large organization, a few relationships that bridge the silos can have a vastly disproportionate impact on the spread of information within the organization.

There has also been recent attention to the idea of "scale-free" networks (Barabasi and Albert 1999). Scale-free networks are characterized by a strong hub-spoke structure, where a few nodes are highly connected and the large majority are peripheral. Hub-spoke networks can be very effective at rapidly spreading information while minimizing the density of the overall network. All information flows into the hub, and (potentially) right back out to the spokes—although, as anyone who has been stuck in an air terminal can testify, hub-spoke systems are highly dependent on the capacity of their hubs.

While the underlying mechanisms that produce scale-free networks are still under examination, it is likely that a necessary precondition for scale-free networks to emerge is a lack of capacity constraints in terms of connectedness of nodes. That is, it needs to be physically possible for some nodes to have many links in order to produce a scale-free network. Thus, it is unlikely that a network of close friends will be characterized as scale-free, while it is possible that the linkage structure of the World Wide Web would be.

In particular, it is notable that many of what we label "attention" networks may be characterized as scale-free. We define attention networks as networks where the relationships convey attention of one node to another. Thus, for example, the World Wide Web and citation networks might be characterized as attention networks, where both linkage and citation conveys attention of one node to another and does not imply any degree of reciprocity. Attention networks generally fulfill the precondition mentioned earlier for scale-free networks—that there is no limit to the number of links one node may *receive* (outgoing links may be a different story). Attention networks also tend to reflect a reinforcing process, where those who receive attention at time t are more likely to receive additional attention at time $t + 1$—namely, there is a contagion of attention (Barabasi and Albert 1999).

Information Production, Informational Diversity, and Aggregation

Networks thus provide the conduit for information to flow through the system. They also affect the availability and aggregation of information in the system. Information aggregation refers to the capacity of the system to effectively pool the information produced by members of the system. The information cascade literature, for example, highlights how public signals can outweigh private information, resulting in clearly suboptimal collective outcomes (Banerjee 1992; Bikhchandani, Hirshleifer, and Welch 1992; Strang and Macy 2001).

Ironically, the capacity to see what others are doing has the potential to reduce the diversity of alternatives in the system. This reflects, in part, isomorphic pressures to conform to the dominant behaviors observed elsewhere as well as a winnowing out of evidently inferior strategies (DiMaggio and Powell 1983). While this winnowing process may improve performance in the short run, it may also reduce the diversity in the ecology of strategies in the system, reducing long term performance (Lazer and Friedman, forthcoming).

The Role of Institutions in Facilitating the Development of Networks and Aggregating Information

While networks are often referred to as "self-organized," that is a partial truth. System-wide institutions facilitate the development of certain networks and the inhibiting of others. Research on social capital suggests that socially constructed boundaries strongly affect the development of relationships (Bourdieu 1985; Coleman 1990). The emergence of social categories and formal organizations around those categories both reflect and foster the existence of networks.

We now turn to the question of how networks affect the management of a particular form of novelty that government confronts—the integration of ICT.

Managing E-Government through Organizational Networks

How do current interpersonal and interorganizational networks affect the dissemination and aggregation of information on the use of ICT in government? In this section, we offer a survey of some of the mechanisms that have served this function. We should also note that we focus more on formal institutional efforts to interconnect people and information, rather than informal networks, because the former leave more behavioral traces than the latter; further, these institutional mechanisms certainly play a key role in the development of interpersonal ties through which information about e-government flows. We divide our discussion into two parts. The first focuses on intragovernmental efforts at network building, the second on intergovernmental networks.

Intragovernmental Efforts

The reality of large organizations rarely matches the neat hierarchy of organizational charts. The various units and subunits of government must act somewhat autonomously. That autonomy sometimes produces waste due to duplicated efforts, but it also fosters innovation. One of the primary effects of e-government initiatives is to create social networks through which information about innovations flows. As one individual involved in the Massachusetts e-government initiative stated:

> From that whole process of those...workgroups, I got to know more people, and became more familiar with their content, information on their sites and things like that. So now that the workgroup period is completed,...I talk to and follow up with people, and kind of check in with them, take requests, follow up on requests.

Similarly, FirstGov,[2] the initial effort to create a federal-wide portal, catalyzed informal networks among the many people involved in creating portals across the federal government (see the FirstGov case illustration). In the words of its director:

> FirstGov started in 2000 and there were some cross-agency portals already in existence at that time: Seniors.gov, Students.gov, Business.gov. They really came out of NPR [National Performance Review]. So I knew about them because I had been working at NPR and what we did do was to build a network of people who were running cross-agency portals so that they knew who each other were, could support each other, could learn from each other and could help new ones form.

Thus, while FirstGov created a hierarchical view of information—a general top level at the homepage, branching down to progressively more specialized areas of interest—the organizational processes underlying that were bottom-up. As First-Gov's director reports, "[We] started a cross-agency portal group that would meet monthly and it grew over time as the numbers of portals grew, but we really were helping each other and it was all the pioneers who looked beyond agency lines."

These networks also facilitate a critical coordinating role. As Fountain highlights (see chapter 4), while many policy outputs are coproduced, there is a general lack of coordination of that coproduction process. This coordination, in part, can be achieved by increasing awareness of interdependence, as one individual involved in the Massachusetts e-government initiative states: "It's amazing in some of these workgroups, when you sit there and you find agencies that are just figuring out that they are in fact serving the same constituencies, or that they have different pieces of the same continuum of service."

The significance, from the perspective of this chapter, of FirstGov and the Massachusetts project is that both facilitated decentralized peer-to-peer knowledge sharing. As noted previously, creating bridges across the silos should greatly increase the speed with which information spreads. Further, when one is dealing with a change in organizational processes, horizontal networks like these both facilitated the spread of information, but also provided a critical social support role for innovators (Kelman 2005). Social psychology research suggests that unanimity has a particularly stifling effect on dissent (Asch 1951). When innovators are linked to each other (as well as to potential future innovators), for some, the awareness of the efforts of others will be enough to maintain their own efforts (and for the potential innovators to initiate). This is particularly important where research suggests that small changes in individual threshold tendencies to adopt can result in dramatic changes in the system level (Granovetter 1978; Lazer 1999).

An early adopter of ICT in government, Washington State offers a model of a more centralized informational network supporting the integration of technology into government. Washington created a "Digital Government Academy," a system-wide institution that serves as a network hub in facilitating the diffusion of e-government applications. The academy provides a live development environment where course participants from different agencies and organizations come together to learn how to build e-government applications and how to accelerate the deployment of online services. Here, a few nodes are highly connected (academy members), and the large majority are peripheral (agencies).

The contrast between the Washington State and Massachusetts and FirstGov efforts in part reflects the different stages of these respective projects. Research suggests that at their inception e-government projects tend to have more diffuse networks, reflecting the initial exploratory needs of the project. The diffuse networks facilitate a slower, deliberative process. At later stages, these networks are consolidated, through more centralization, creating more of a hub-spoke network (Binz-Scharf 2003). As noted previously, hub-spoke networks, for a given level of density, will tend to be better at disseminating information than decentralized networks. This centralization reflects, in part, a degree of convergence among actors and increased capacity of the hub (essential, if the system is to effectively spread information, and clearly the case in Washington State).

Bridging relationships are also important in providing a conduit for information from the public to decision makers. For example, in Massachusetts particular staff were assigned as "channel managers," each responsible for relations with a particular stakeholder (e.g., citizens, government, business, visitors).

Intergovernmental Efforts

Intergovernmental organizations are critical nodes in the diffusion of e-government knowledge and practices at various levels. The prevailing aim of these efforts is to support e-government decision makers through a variety of measures—for example, by organizing workshops and conferences to foster the exchange of knowledge, by publishing reports and strategy papers, and by identifying best practices. In doing so, these organizations bridge single organizational networks, thus enabling learning across governmental organizations. The intergovernmental organizations themselves function as a hub in an attentional network. Depending on the scope of the organization, the influence on actual practices can be substantial. A number of preexisting, large, "generalist" organizations have been especially important regarding e-government policies—for example, the United Nations, the European Union (EU), and the World Bank.

These organizations also likely have a disproportionate impact on the attentional networks within the e-government community. A case in point is the prominence that Finland's e-government efforts reached due to a 2001 award by the EU for e-government best practices, promoting Finland to the position of international "e-government pioneer." It is difficult to imagine that a geographically remote and non-English-speaking country would otherwise have gained such an impressive amount of attention in the international arena for its use of information technology in government. The EU award, in short, set up a self-reinforcing process by which the EU's attention to Finland made it more likely other entities would pay attention to Finland, and so on.

Like legacy technology, these preexisting organizations can be regarded as "legacy institutions," which shape the path of the introduced innovation. Perhaps the most prominent example along these lines is the OECD e-government project, with a potential to directly reach the thirty OECD member countries and well over seventy other countries with which the OECD has an active relationship, as well as indirectly any decision makers who have Internet access and can download their reports. The OECD thus facilitates the creation of networks and is a central hub into which much (unprocessed) information pours, which it processes and then disseminates widely.

Unsurprisingly, these preexisting organizations focus on features of e-government reflecting their preexisting priorities. For example, in 2001, the OECD's focus on good governance pushed the Public Management Service (today called the Public Governance and Territorial Development Directorate) to launch a long-term project on e-government. This project was aimed at exploring ways in which "governments can best exploit information and communication technologies to embed good governance principles and achieve public policy goals," as stated on the project website,[3] and it was explicitly designed to build on the modernization of public administration. In three seminars, the project brought together government officials with responsibility for e-government initiatives and e-government experts from the private sector, government agencies, civil society organizations, universities, and think tanks to discuss the vision of e-government, its strategic implementation, and its contributions to public-sector reform. The outcomes of these seminars were synthesized in a report entitled *The e-Government Imperative* (OECD 2003), which described problems facing governments today when implementing e-government and laid down guiding principles for successful e-government. In a symposium organized by the OECD to discuss the report, senior e-government officials identified the need for a seamless approach to serving business and citizens as one of the most pressing issues to maximizing the benefits of e-government. As a result, the focus of the OECD e-government project has now shifted to finding solutions of seamless government, a topic that has been addressed in a series of symposia for senior e-government officials.

In addition to providing venues for e-government decision makers to exchange knowledge and ideas, the OECD e-government project conducts country reviews at the request of member countries "to assist . . . in evaluating their e-government policies, ensure international comparability of findings, and systematically build up a body of empirical evidence regarding good e-government practices."[4] These reports obviously reflect extensive communication between the OECD and particular governments. They also facilitate the dissemination of information about the practices of particular countries to other decision makers, even in the absence of direct communication.

Another important example of an intergovernmental organization that both processes information and fosters peer-to-peer interpersonal networks is the EUROCITIES Knowledge Society Forum—TeleCities,[5] a network of over one hundred local authorities from twenty-four European countries (see the TeleCities case illustration). The network provides a platform for members to share their experiences and to develop practical solutions to achieve an "Inclusive Information Society" at both the European and local levels. Embedded in the larger organization EUROCITIES, TeleCities aims to promote e-government and e-citizenship at the local level "to ensure that all citizens can equally gain from the benefits of the Information and Knowledge Society," as it claims on its website. A 2004 benchmark survey report, entitled "eCitizenship for All,"[6] allows local authorities to benchmark themselves against each other and has served as a basis for identifying best practices.

Within the United States, the National Association of State Chief Information Officers (NASCIO),[7] facilitates the spread of information among governments. NASCIO sponsors national annual and midyear conferences, producing proceedings available to members. Moreover, NASCIO facilitates peer-to-peer communication through its Strategic Materials and Resources Tool (SMART), an online resource in which it places both materials it produces as well as materials its members produce. NASCIO also has an information aggregation role, producing reports on best practices in addition to assessments of the state of e-government more generally.

The OECD, TeleCities, and NASCIO are only a few of the many intergovernmental organizations that have critical network functions in the diffusion and aggregation of information. Other intergovernmental organizations in the United States include:

- *The Government Management Information Sciences* (GMIS),[8] whose goal is "to provide an organizational structure and network with associated activities, which may be used by all state and local government agencies and educational institutions which are members in order to help them in their information and automation endeavors and with associated projects and problems." Its members include government agencies from eighteen states, and it has international sister organizations, mainly at the municipal level. It organizes an annual "International Education Conference," and further facilitates the diffusion of information through its newsletter and listserv.

- *The Metropolitan Information Exchange* (MIX),[9] which aims "to promote progress in the IT Profession by providing senior IT Executives of large local government jurisdictions (100,000 citizens or more), of comparable interests in information and communication applications and equipment with the means for learning and exchanging all types of management and information processing matters." It organizes weeklong annual conferences, conducts an annual survey, sponsors a newsletter and listserv, and offers consulting advice.

- *Lgov.org*,[10] a nonprofit organization with the aim of "improving the effectiveness of local government information technology services through the establishment of an active, mutually supportive Internet community of local government IT professionals." It also maintains a listserv, an online "community meeting hall," an online document library with RFPs, contracts, best practices, studies, and reports.

Academic centers devoted to the study of e-government, such as the National Center for Digital Government (NCDG) at the University of Massachusetts and the Center for Technology and Government (CTG) at the State University of New York (Albany), are also an important mechanism in bridging the worlds of academia and practice.

The preceding analysis suggests that this alphabet soup of organizations is important in facilitating information diffusion within the e-government universe. These organizations serve as bridges between otherwise disconnected policy communities at multiple levels—municipal, state, and national. They also facilitate, through conferences and other means, the emergence of peer-to-peer networks of policymakers confronting similar problems across these communities. In addition, they serve as informational hubs, taking in information from many, then aggregating and resending it out to the spokes. The previous discussion suggests that each of these functions should have substantial effects on the flow of information among decision makers.

The Bridging Role of Consulting Companies

Finally, another set of actors that play a critical bridging role within the e-government informational network are the consulting firms. For example, for its e-government initiative, Massachusetts chose to have a strong collaborative relationship with the consulting firm Accenture. Accenture had consulted with several other state governments on how to implement e-government, following a similar approach and thus cementing certain procedures into standards. Furthermore, Accenture publishes regular reports, among them an annual "E-Government Leadership" report, which is highly publicized and widely distributed to government agencies, thus elevating the consulting firm to the hub of an attentional network.

Consulting companies have a distinctive position in the network, in that their objective is to simultaneously disseminate practices, and to make the information regarding those practices proprietary, so that the company can extract rents from their dissemination. The experience that consulting companies produces thus (in larger part) stays within those companies, and does not necessarily spread from the consulting companies to policymakers, and from those policy makers to other policymakers. The diffusion process of the information produced from the experiences of consulting companies is therefore quite different from that of governments. First, those experiences are likely to be focused on areas where the knowledge produced will be proprietary to the consulting companies. Second, this information will hence not easily spread from government to government (except as evaluations of and use of particular vendors). Third, the consulting companies will have a far greater incentive to disseminate information about (proprietary) innovations than governments will have regarding (nonproprietary) innovations.

Consulting companies also bridge government and corporations, which have reengineered their informational architectures using many of the same consulting companies that governments are using. The implication of this is that governments, when using consulting companies, are both taking advantage of the experiences that these consulting companies have gained working with private firms and are potentially captive to models developed for the private sector.

Conclusion

The objective of this chapter was to examine the role that soft networks play in the development of hard networks. Developments in ICT remove many of the constraints in the configuration of information flows within government. The infinite number of possibilities for reconfiguration creates its own set of challenges for decision makers. Each configuration offers its own calculus of benefits and costs, and of opportunities and obstacles. It is impossible for decision makers to evaluate even a small fraction of the alternatives; therefore, the pooling of experiences and knowledge of decision makers becomes critical. Soft networks—person-to-person and institution-to-institution communication—thus become central to understanding the development of information government. This chapter discussed how particular network configurations affect the diffusion and processing of information generally, then turned to an examination of some of the central institutions involved in the spread and aggregation of information among decision makers regarding the use of ICT to reconfigure information flows within government.

Notes

Support from NSF Grant #0131923 and Grant #066298 from the Swiss National Science Foundation is gratefully acknowledged.

1. Unless otherwise noted, the quotations in this chapter are based on personal interviews conducted by Maria Christina Binz-Scharf. See Binz-Scharf 2003 and Binz-Scharf and Lazer 2007 for a full discussion of the methodology.

2. http://www.firstgov.gov.

3. http://webdomino1.oecd.org/COMNET/PUM/egovproweb.nsf.

4. http://webdomino1.oecd.org/COMNET/PUM/egovproweb.nsf/viewHtml/index/$FILE/country_studies.htm.

5. http://www.eurocities.org/.

6. "eCitizenship for All: A European Benchmark Report," 2004 (http://www.deloitte.com/dtt/research/0,1015,cid%253D80902%2526pre%253DY%2526lid%253D1%2526new%253DU,00.html).

7. http://www.nascio.org.

8. http://www.gmis.org.

9. http://www.mixnet.org/.

10. http://www.lgov.org/.

References

Allen, Thomas J., and Alfred P. Cohen. 1969. "Information Flow in Research and Development Laboratories." *Administrative Science Quarterly* 14, no. 1: 12–19.

Ambrose, Stephen E. 1983. *Eisenhower* Vols. 1–2. New York: Simon and Schuster.

Asch, Solomon E. 1951. "Effects of Group Pressure upon the Modification and Distortion of Judgements." In *Groups, Leadership, and Men*, ed. Harold Guetzkow, 177–190. Pittsburgh, PA: Carnegie Press.

Banerjee, Abhijit V. 1992. "A Simple Model of Herd Behavior." *Quarterly Journal of Economics* 107, no. 3: 797–817.

Barabasi, Albert-Laszlo, and Reka Albert. 1999. "Emergence of Scaling in Random Networks." *Science* 286, no. 5439: 509–512.

Bikhchandani, Sushil, David Hirshleifer, and Ivo Welch. 1992. "A Theory of Fads, Fashions, Custom, and Cultural Change as Informational Cascades." *Journal of Political Economy* 100, no. 5: 992–1026.

Binz-Scharf, Maria Christina. 2003. Exploration and Exploitation: Toward a Theory of Knowledge Sharing in Digital Government Projects. Ph.D. diss., University of St. Gallen, St. Gallen.

Binz-Scharf, Maria Christina, and David M. Lazer. 2007. "Information Sharing in Digital Government Projects: Managing Novelty and Cross-Agency Cooperation." KSG working paper, Harvard University, Cambridge, MA.

Bourdieu, Pierre. 1985. "The Forms of Capital." In *Handbook of Theory and Research for the Sociology of Education*, ed. John C. Richardson, 241–258. New York: Greenwood.

Burt, Ronald S. 1992. *Structural Holes: The Social Structure of Competition*. Cambridge, MA: Harvard University Press.

Carpenter, Daniel P., Kevin M. Esterling, and David M. Lazer. 2003. "Information and Contact-Making in Policy Networks: A Model with Evidence from the U.S. Health Policy Domain." *Rationality and Society* 15, no. 4: 411–440.

Chetkovich, Carol. 1997. *Real Heat: Gender and Race in the Urban Fire Service*. New Brunswick, NJ: Rutgers University Press.

Coleman, James S. 1990. *Foundations of Social Theory*. Cambridge, MA: Belknap Press.

Cyert, Richard M., and James G. March. 1963. *A Behavioral Theory of the Firm*. Englewood Cliffs, NJ: Prentice-Hall.

DiMaggio, Paul J., and Walter W. Powell. 1983. "The Iron Cage Revisited: Institutional Isomorphism and Collective Rationality in Organizational Fields." *American Sociological Review* 48, no. 2: 147–160.

Frankel, Jeffrey. 1997. *Regional Trading Blocs in the World Economic System*. Washington, DC: Institute for International Economics.

Galaskiewicz, Joseph, and Stanley Wasserman. 1989. "Mimetic Processes within an Interorganizational Field: An Empirical Test." *Administrative Science Quarterly* 34, no. 3: 454–479.

Granovetter, Mark S. 1973. "Strength of Weak Ties." *American Journal of Sociology* 78, no. 6: 1360–1380.

Granovetter, Mark S. 1978. "Threshold Models of Collective Behavior." *American Journal of Sociology* 83 (May): 1420–1443.

Hansen, Morten T. 1999. "The Search-Transfer Problem: The Role of Weak Ties in Sharing Knowledge across Organization Subunits." *Administrative Science Quarterly* 44, no. 1: 82–111.

Haunschild, Pamela R. 1993. "Interorganizational Imitation: The Impact of Interlocks on Corporate Acquisition Activity." *Administrative Science Quarterly* 38, no. 4: 564–592.

Heider, Fritz. 1946. "Attitudes and Cognitive Organization." *Journal of Psychology* 21: 107–112.

Holland, Paul W., and Samuel Leinhardt. 1977. "Dynamic Model for Social Networks." *Journal of Mathematical Sociology* 5, no. 1: 5–20.

Kelman, Steven. 2005. Unleashing Change: A Study of Organizational Renewal in Government. Washington, DC: Brookings Institution.

Lazarsfeld, Paul F., and Robert K. Merton. 1982. "Friendship as Social Process: A Substantive and Methodological Analysis." In *The Varied Sociology of Paul F. Lazarsfeld*, ed. P. L. Kendall, 298–348. New York: Columbia University Press.

Lazer, David M. 1999. "The Free Trade Epidemic of the 1860s and Other Outbreaks of Economic Discrimination." *World Politics* (July): 447–483.

Lazer, David M., ed. 2004. *The Technology of Justice: DNA and the Criminal Justice System*. Cambridge, MA: MIT Press.

Lazer, David M., and Allan Friedman. Forthcoming. "Parallel Problem Solving: The Social Structure of Exploration and Exploitation." *Administrative Science Quarterly*.

McDermott, Richard. 1999. "Why Information Technology Inspired but Cannot Deliver Knowledge Management." *California Management Review* 41, no. 4: 103–117.

McPherson, Miller, Lynn Smith-Lovin, and James Cook. 2001. "Birds of a feather: Homophily in Social Networks." *Annual Review of Sociology* 27: 425–444.

Nelson, Reed E. 1989. "The Strength of Strong Ties: Social Networks and Intergroup Conflict in Organizations." *Academy of Management Journal* 32, no. 2: 377–401.

OECD. 2003. *The e-Government Imperative*. OECD e-Government Series. Paris: Organisation for Economic Co-operation and Development.

Rogers, Everett M. 1995. *Diffusion of Innovations*. 4th ed. New York: The Free Press.

Strang, David, and Michael W. Macy. 2001. "'In Search of Excellence': Fads, Success Stories, and Adaptive Emulation." *American Journal of Sociology* 107: 147–182.

Wasserman, Stanley, and Katherine Faust. 1994. *Social Network Analysis*. Cambridge: Cambridge University Press.

Watts, Duncan J., and Steven H. Strogatz. 1998. "Collective Dynamics of 'Small-World' Networks." *Nature* 393, no. 6684: 440–442.

Weick, Karl E. 2001. *Making Sense of the Organization*. Oxford and Malden, MA: Blackwell Business.

Case Illustration

TeleCities: Sharing Knowledge among European Cities

Viktor Mayer-Schönberger and David Lazer

TeleCities is a voluntary network of more than 140 European Union-affiliated cities as well as major vendors interested in the opportunities and challenges that information and communication technologies present to local government. TeleCities offers its members a platform for "exchanges of good practice and for cooperation on relevant policy issues in a European framework," according to its website. Organizationally, TeleCities is a forum of EUROCITIES, the European Union (EU) network of major cities.

In 2004 Chris Newby became chair of TeleCities. His background as a councillor of the Liverpool City Council shaped his involvement with Tele-Cities. "Liverpool," he says, "has a history of voting administrations out of office for ignoring that they serve citizens' needs and not their own. That is why when voted into office we put the technology agenda high on the list of priorities to better serve our citizens."[1] Doing so, he reckons, is much easier if one can tap into the experiences of others—to avoid making the same mistakes and to use best practices developed by others. That led Liverpool to become very active in TeleCities.

Sharing expertise, Newby argues, requires giving as much as taking. A case in point, he explains, is Liverpool's service delivery strategy. The aim was to offer citizens an easy way to get in touch with the city council and have 95 percent of their queries answered at the time of their first contact. Liverpool established the largest call center of any UK local government, as well as a decentralized network of fourteen "one-stop shops" across the city. To complement these two channels of communication, Liverpool was looking to install transactional on-street kiosks. While other UK cities had experimented with informational kiosks, nobody had attempted interactive and transactional ones. Through the help of TeleCities, Liverpool discovered that Vienna (Austria) had successfully established a network of exactly the type of kiosks that Liverpool wanted. A team from Liverpool met with its Vienna counterpart and was able to replicate the Vienna system—and success—in Liverpool.

The overall success of Liverpool's service delivery strategy in turn prompted many delegations from other TeleCities members to visit Liverpool for learning and benchmarking—cross-jurisdictional learning facilitated by the TeleCities network. Newby adds that Liverpool's TeleCare initiative, offering assistance through information and communication technology for elders who wish to remain in their homes, has similarly spread through the help of TeleCities.

Note

1. This quotation and others here are from an interview with Chris Newby on May 24, 2005.

12

The Governing of Government Information

Viktor Mayer-Schönberger and David Lazer

We began this volume with the observation that information is foundational to governing. The body of this book examined the implications of information flows (1) between the government and citizens (chapters 5, 6, 7, and 10); (2) between the government and customers (chapters 2 and 3); (3) among citizens/political activists (chapter 8); and (4) among government agencies (chapters 4, 9, and 11). We conclude with a more normatively oriented discussion, focusing, in particular, on three overarching issues: the capacity of government institutions to adapt to the informational flows that are now technically possible; the balance between individual interests in retaining control over information vis-à-vis government and the collective interest in the informational capacity of government; and the role of potential new information flows in transforming (or not) the deliberative space.

Government: Knowing What It Knows

Technology is typically no longer the binding constraint with respect to the sharing and integration of information—institutions are, as Fountain discusses (chapter 4). Consider the FBI's Violent Criminal Apprehension Program (ViCAP). ViCAP was developed to help facilitate information sharing regarding crimes with telltale patterns. The FBI has developed the ViCAP software for local law enforcement agencies to use, where each agency enters into the system details regarding violent crimes. These entries are checked against entries in other jurisdictions, in the hope of linking crimes by the same perpetrator and thus assisting investigators. Strikingly, while ViCAP has had some notable success stories, most law enforcement agencies do not use the ViCAP system, in some cases preferring their own, incompatible systems.

The ViCAP case highlights that while there are substantial potential gains from the adoption of electronic government because of the technological possiblity to route information more effectively, there are significant barriers to systems integration. Our current institutions evolved in an environment where routine sharing of detailed information was, practically speaking, impossible. It would be most unlikely that they would be structured in a fashion that facilitated what was heretofore technically impossible. It is therefore unsurprising that these institutional challenges have been nearly insurmountable in some cases. Here we highlight three key issues with respect to why agencies might underinvest in technology, especially technologies that link them to other agencies and to the public: a collective action problem among organizations with respect to creating information-sharing systems, principal-agent problems raised by sharing information among organizations and between the government and society, and the coalitional politics within organizations.

Investment in compatible systems presents an enormous collective action problem; decisions that benefit the system are made by one organization at a time. Depending on the technology, the various depositories of data may have made investments in incompatible systems. Data integration thus requires significant investments, either by some agencies into the standards of others, or by all agencies into new standards. The benefit of these technologies lies in part in their networked dimension; my information is yours and vice versa, and together they are more powerful than they are apart. The presence of network effects in markets tends to lead to powerful standardizing pressures. Most of the world uses Microsoft Windows and Word not because of the technical superiority of Microsoft software, but because of the benefits of interoperability (Varian and Shapiro 1998)—for example, to be able to share documents.

These same standardizing pressures should operate on public organizations. However, simply because there are benefits to standardization does not mean that the world will converge on a standard. There are significant switching costs for government organizations to change to another organization's standard. These may include substantial hardware, software, and human capital costs. Further, the benefits of switching are proportional to the number of other units that have that standard. In a world of many standards, there may be no one standard that has enough adherents to make it worth switching. To take the preceding example, for a state to abandon its own system of linking information regarding violent crimes for ViCAP requires abandonment of productive investments. If neighboring states have non-ViCAP-compatible systems, it would greatly reduce the benefits to shifting to the ViCAP system. Thus, it is possible that it may not be in the interest of a single state to unilaterally switch, leaving the world stuck in a suboptimal equilibrium.

The second major set of impediments to the adoption of networked technologies we identify is two types of principal-agent (agency) issues. The first involves agency issues of one organization "lending" information to another. The second involves agency issues created in the delegation of power to government.

The very reason that individuals might be worried about government having personal information is the same reason why organizations might be hesitant to share information with each other: there is inherent uncertainty as to how that information might be used. With a few exceptions, it is generally impossible to produce a "single use bit." While A might share information with B with a particular understanding of the limitations of its use, A must be concerned that B might use that information for other purposes. This is one reason why, for example, law enforcement organizations conducting overlapping investigations might not share information—because of the fear that that information might be used in a fashion that would compromise their own investigation.

Additionally, governments have particular interests in preventing information from flowing into the public sphere. Transparency reduces autonomy, where autonomy is an almost universal organizational imperative (Wilson 2000). Transparency both makes clear when policymakers act opportunistically—with respect to either policy (i.e., deviating from the preferences of the public) or abuse of power. Thus, laws permitting citizens to access government information may be a particularly difficult pill for public organizations to swallow, despite (or because of) their salutary effects on deliberation within society.

Finally, control over information is power, and changes in the flow of information will have important political consequences within organizations. There are, for example, major benefits to having a brokerage position within informational networks (Burt 1995). It is plausible, for example, that particular technologies might reduce the power of certain actors through the elimination of a brokerage position ("disintermediation"), and/or increase the power of other actors through increased capacity to monitor. Reengineered information flows thus might reinforce or undermine the ruling "coalition" within the organization, with concomitant support or opposition for those changes (Cyert and March 1963). Actors with veto power might block the implementation of new technologies, or at least shape their implementation in a fashion that they believe augments rather than undermines their power.

Balancing the Informational Interests of the Citizen and Society

Information that flows from citizens to government comes in various types. In many nations citizens are obligated to provide certain information, like earnings for tax purposes. Citizens supply government with other information in order to procure certain privileges (e.g., a license to drive a car) and services. And government collects some data provided voluntarily by citizens (e.g., vast amounts of economic data) to help it govern.

Electronic government has frequently been conceived as obtaining information from citizens in exchange for a public service. Utilizing concepts developed for electronic commerce, electronic government architects frequently ask what lessons government agencies can learn from ecommerce leaders like Amazon.com in creating electronic government successes. From this perspective, citizens are simply customers of public services transacted online.

Interactions between individuals and the government differ, however, in two fundamental ways from their private-sector equivalent. First, in most cases government agencies are the sole providers of a particular service. Customers do not have a choice in selecting their transactional partner. This results in an immanent power differential between government agency and citizens desiring to transact with it. Further, (in theory) government has a monopoly of coercive power in society. Government agencies may use this power differential to compel citizens to supply information, which they may not have been willing to provide to a private-sector partner. As a result, government agencies are uniquely capable of collecting information from citizens as well as organizations.

Government, of course, is not simply another entity with which citizens transact, but it is a creature of the people. The citizenry in a democracy is the sovereign, delegating power to the government as its agent to perform certain tasks. As a voluminous political science literature indicates, this delegation creates an enormous agency problem regarding the actions of government. To reduce the agency problem, citizens as voters require comprehensive information from government agencies on what they are doing, why, and how. This is a central reason for the transparency rules and open access and freedom-of-information legislation Burkert discusses in chapter 6. Without transparency, there is no accountability and citizens cannot make informed decisions about democratic delegations of power. At least equally important is that citizens need access to government information to evaluate policy choices in order to construct their policy preferences.

This puts citizens in a seemingly paradoxical situation. Individually, there is a desire to avoid providing information to the government, which might at some future date prove disadvantageous in some unanticipated fashion. However, citizens as "citoyen," as members of the democratic sovereign desiring to inform themselves and deliberate on public matters, have a strong interest in the collection of information by the government. As sovereign, they have significant incentives to ensure that government procurement of public services is done in an effective and efficient manner. They want the state to collect and process information so that bureaucratic rules including the provision of public services can be evaluated and, if necessary, adjusted. That is, the obligation of citizens to provide information is borne of their reciprocal commitments to each other.

There is thus a subtle balancing act, simultaneously empowering government to achieve collective goals, while at the same time tying the hands of government. The tension between individual and collective, of course, is not new—whether one is looking at public goods or "governing the commons." Generally, if the benefits of a good go to every individual in a collective regardless of whether they contribute, individuals will tend to contribute less than is in their collective interest. Policy interventions are thus necessary to encourage (and sometimes force) individuals to contribute to the common good.

This tension takes on a particular spin with information, however, because of the potential uncertainty of how information might be used, or what it might reveal in the future (Lazer and Mayer-Schoenberger 2006). The consequence of the government having a particular piece of information about someone is uncertain and *ongoing* unless it is somehow anonymized (unlike many other resources, information may be used but not consumed). An extreme example is offered by the development in the 1930s in the Netherlands of a comprehensive population registration system. The objective of the system—to streamline administration and to reduce burdens on citizens—echoes some of the rationales for more sophisticated information technologies today. That system, however, was subsequently used to assist the Nazis in apprehending Dutch Jews and Gypsies, who suffered a much higher death rate than in any other occupied Western European country, or, notably, than Jewish refugees in the Netherlands, who were not in the registration system (Seltzer and Anderson

2001). This case highlights how the same information provided in one context (benign Dutch government) eased the lives of citizens, subsequently, in another context (malignant Nazi regime), could be reused for purposes that were repugnant to citizens and to the architects of that system.

The conceptual lens of *information government*, looking at the flows of information and the controllers of these flows, highlights that these flows predate the online provision of public services. They are the consequence of the presence of a powerful state that reflects the collective desire to achieve a measure of control over individuals. In addition, the rise of the welfare state over the last half-century has prompted government agencies to significantly increase the collection and processing of information from individuals in order to distribute entitlements (Mayer-Schönberger 1997, 222).

The availability of modern information and communication technologies, however, has made the tension become more obvious and troubling. The Internet enables government to have citizens enter the required information for the provision of public services themselves. Because acquiring information through this mechanism is almost costless to government, it creates an incentive to ask for more information. Drastically reduced costs of storage make it possible to not only collect massively more information from citizens than before, but also keep this information in government databases. These databases in turn can be linked, producing greater informational power.

Furthermore, information pertaining to an individual or an organization may be obtained from government through open access legislation. While transparency laws existed long before the Internet, digital networks make it cheaper and easier for government to offer access to government information online, thus reducing the burden on the public sector to fulfill individual access requests. The more government databases become accessible online, the easier it is to look up and combine information about individuals (as well as organizations). What used to be costly, time-consuming, and difficult—to request access to government information from different agencies—may over time become as easy as a few mouse clicks.

To be sure, technology is not the culprit. Digital networks do not create or expand government's control over information flows. Given macrolevel public-sector realities, like constrained budgets for most government agencies in most developed nations, however, these technologies offer government a powerful tool to increase productivity and lower cost. Network and information economics make this an eminently rational decision for government agencies. Its troubling side effect is that it significantly exacerbates the tension between the desire of the citizen as individual to keep information private, especially vis-à-vis the government, and the craving of the citizen as sovereign to have government collect and provide access to citizen information.

Unfortunately, there is no easy means to alleviate this tension. The democratic welfare state will continue to collect, process, store and even distribute information about its citizens. Drastically limiting the informational capacities of the state is not a viable option, as it may lead government to offer fewer services less efficiently. Society would be left with less oversight and a diminished ability to make informed policy decisions. Giving up on individuals' claims to keep a modicum of control over information flows is not an option either. In many nations, these claims are constitutionally protected. They also are at the core of a system of checks and balances in an information society. A key policy objective then is to help citizens negotiate this tension.

The "easy" case is when the threat to the informational balance between citizens and state is obvious to citizens. Citizen pressure may then lead to the adaptation of legal and regulatory frameworks to rectify the imbalance. For example, when governments in Europe as well as Canada and the United States toyed with the idea of integrating citizen information in central databanks, citizens demanded privacy legislation (Miller 1971). The first generation of data protection laws around the world was a direct consequence of citizens' concerns about loss of individual control over information. Similarly, in 1983 the German Constitutional Court found individuals to possess a constitutionally protected right of informational self-determination, which forms one of the foundational bases of the current European Union Directive on data protection. The Court's ruling was a direct consequence of the widespread public outcry opposing the German government's attempt to compel citizens to respond in detail to a nation-wide census (Flaherty 1989, 79–83). In these and similar cases, the objective of public policy is to bring about the informational rebalancing between the individual and society that the citizenry desires.

Unfortunately, many government actions that lead to informational imbalances are less obvious. They may garner little public attention initially, and cause concern only as they accumulate over time. These actions may only affect a certain group of little political power, or affect many individuals but not deeply enough to cause them to mobilize. Further, once investments have been made in the informational capacity of government, reversing course may be costly and difficult, thus weighing in heavily in the public debate against change. Informational rebalancing generally increases regulatory complexity, thus making it less likely that rebalancing will work. More important, perhaps, most of us are largely unaware of the informational power the government already has and how the government's next steps in collecting and processing information may impose on our individual lives. This, in turn, may make it less likely that public deliberation will focus on informational imbalances and demand public polices to address it.

A key policy objective within an information society may therefore be to assist citizens in negotiating this informational Scylla and Charybdis. Some have argued that the very technologies that create the informational imbalances may also hold hope for creating a more inclusive space of public deliberation. By the same token, a revitalized public sphere may also fuel the desire of citoyen to access government information. Injecting government information, obtained through open access legislation, may be seen as a fundamental component of a public deliberative process that ultimately may lead to better decision making. And thus the tension between the individual and the citoyen resurfaces.

Using the *information government* lens thus exposes the importance the conception of the democratic process has not only for the informational tension between individual and citoyen, but also for the design of our institutions to facilitate deliberation regarding this tension.

Deliberative Democracy and the Role of Access to Information

A number of commentators have seen the Internet and similar digital network technologies combined with widespread access to and use of personal computers as an enabler of civic deliberation, creating a virtual deliberative space, a virtual New England town hall meeting, in which a wide spectrum of participants deliberate public issues. For them the Internet represents the revival of a public sphere analogous to revolutionary France, as eloquently portrayed by Habermas: with citoyen coming together in the many cafés of Paris to share the latest information on public issues obtained through their personal connections and sources within government (Habermas 1991). By this view the Internet will involve many of the citizens who have become apathetic and disinterested in public affairs as well as providing a virtual soapbox to those who want to deliberate but so far have been excluded. This anticipated widespread engagement of citizens is sometimes labeled "deliberative democracy" (Gutmann and Thompson 1996), or "strong democracy" (Barber 1998). However, as Coglianese (chapter 5) shows with respect to electronic rulemaking, and Hindman (chapter 8) with respect to online mechanisms for political mobilization, at least in these areas and using these technologies the rise of strong, deliberative democracy has not happened.

Revivals of public deliberation have been predicted before, and predicated on new information and communication technologies. In the 1980s, France's Minitel—a simple, yet very popular terminal connected to a central database through dial-up, and similar services in Britain (Videotex) and Germany (Bildschirmtext) were portrayed as bringing about a revolution in civic deliberation, much like similar experiments based on cable television in Canada and the United States (Haefner 1984). Yet these efforts failed.

In the 1990s the Internet was seen as having significant potential for a deliberative renaissance (Dutton 1996). High hopes accompanied the launches and rises of a number of Internet communication tools, only to be dashed by reality. Newsgroups were not realizing the deliberative potential, and neither were the self-published webzines that followed. At a time, online communities were portrayed as the long-sought tool, only to be replaced by blogging (Froomkin 2004, 9–17). However, as Hindman explains in his chapter, blogs have not been successful either in stimulating "strong democracy." Soon podcasts and vodcasts may turn into the deliberative magic rod of the day.

While it is not impossible that a future yet unknown technology may bring about the drastic change in deliberation that so far we have failed to witness, critics of a deliberative revival have argued that the problem is less technical than human. In fact, Habermas himself, while recreating the vivid picture of civic deliberation in revolutionary France, has made clear that such kind of public deliberation is gone for good. Instead he suggests that industrialized democracies have created a suitable alternative to "strong democracy," an alternative that is different from simple representative democracy, the conventional alternative to deliberative democracy. This alternative is premised on the existence of mass print and broadcast media. Instead of deliberation as the exclusive domain of citizens, the media bear a portion of the deliberative burden: processing, presenting, and criticizing alternate constructions of issues of public concern. Citizens witness this and ultimately cast their votes. A critical goal of public policy, in this view, is ensuring robust deliberation through ensuring that citizens have equal capacity to participate in societal discourse. Significant hope for public discourse is placed in the hands of information intermediaries, enabling an activist public sphere (Habermas 1991).

While none of the contributors to this volume see an imminent rise in strong deliberative democracy, intriguingly, both Hindman (chapter 8) and Coglianese (chapter 5) identify the rise of new information intermediaries. Hindman suggests that bloggers are not the voice of the masses but represent an educated elite that desires to and has the means to engage in public discourse, acting as stand-ins for specific societal views. Coglianese credits electronic rulemaking not with involving the public (even where it does, he reminds us, it is a formal, not a substantive, deliberative exercise). Instead he suggests that electronic rulemaking enables smaller groups with substantive expertise but without necessary lobbying infrastructure in Washington to inject their voices into the debate. These smaller groups act as information intermediaries, resulting in an improved outcome based on an improved information base. Finally, Girard and Stark (chapter 7) suggest that even in the specific cases when online deliberation worked, the value arguably is found less in deliberation and more in the information repository created through the deliberative process.

Burkert (chapter 6) complements this empirical analysis with his normative view of the importance of information intermediaries for open government and transparency. He opines that citizens alone would not be able to exercise access rights and transparency guarantees. Instead they will have to rely on intermediaries, who comprise not just the traditional media and new entrants like bloggers, but also a new caste with specific expertise in obtaining government information, like EPIC.

If one accepts these premises, a number of policy implications may be derived from them. Existing and new information intermediaries that perform central elements of the mediated deliberative process may need to be strengthened and protected. Extending legal protection to new entrants like bloggers may be important, but so is facilitating the tasks of access intermediaries Burkert (chapter 6) mentions and of processing and analysis intermediaries Coglianese (chapter 5) describes. By the same token, the more central a role these information intermediaries play, the more important it may become that information freedom permeate the internal operation of these intermediaries as well.

Moreover, accepting this view may also make addressing the tension of the citizen as customer and citoyen easier. Insofar as information intermediaries take over some of the deliberative duties of citizens, they may reduce the tension citizens feel between their roles as consumer and citoyen. Thus information intermediaries may potentially function as a structural insulation buffer that makes it easier for citizens to negotiate their private and public roles.

Conclusion

Information is necessary to govern. To deliver services to individuals, to make sure that citizens fulfill their obligations, to produce policy that achieves public goals requires information. Further, citizens need information about and from government, both to hold government accountable, as well as to engage in an informed discussion as to what is desirable policy. The development of network technologies over the last generation creates the potential for a vast transformation of governance.

There are, however, two caveats. First, institutions have an enormous impact on information flows. E-mail, for example, does little to facilitate communication if government workers are not connected to the Internet. Simply because a particular technology increases the capacity of the system or an organization does not mean that it will be adopted. Technological decisions that affect the system are often in the hands of constituent organizations, creating a massive collective action problem, likely sometimes yielding undernetworked systems. Further, within organizations, there may be resistance to new information flows, because those new flows may undermine the position of powerful actors within the organization.

Second, information collected by the government potentially does create a burden on individuals and organizations. This chapter examines the balancing between the collective desire to empower government and individual interests in privacy. This leads simultaneously to pushes to increase certain information flows, and pulls to constrain information flows.

We are thus at a pivot point in the role that information may play in governance, because of the development of technologies that make information flows (technically) vastly more malleable than they were a generation ago. Our objective in this volume has been to elucidate what is known about information and government, and, practicing what we preach, to provide a forum for a variety of key perspectives on what can and should be the blueprints for the wiring of information flows within government and between government and society in the twenty-first century.

References

Barber, Benjamin. 1998. "Three Scenarios for the Future of Technology and Strong Democracy." *Political Science Quarterly* 113, no. 4: 573–589.

Burt, Ronald S. 1995. *Structural Holes: The Social Structure of Competition*. Cambridge, MA: Harvard University Press.

Cyert, Richard M., and James G. March. 1963. *A Behavioral Theory of the Firm*. Englewood Cliffs, NJ: Prentice-Hall.

Dutton, William H. 1996. "Network Rules of Order: Regulating Speech in Public Electronic Forums." *Media, Culture and Society* 18: 269–290.

Flaherty, David H. 1989. *Protecting Privacy in Surveillance Societies*. Chapel Hill: University of North Carolina Press.

Froomkin, A. Michael. 2004. "Technologies for Democracy." In Democracy Online: *The Prospects for Political Renewal through the Internet*, ed. Peter M. Shane, 3–20. New York and London: Routledge.

Gutmann, Amy, and Dennis Thompson. 1996. *Democracy and Disagreement*. Cambridge, MA: The Belknap Press of Harvard University Press.

Habermas, Jürgen. 1991. *The Structural Transformation of the Public Sphere: An Inquiry into a Category of Bourgois Society*. Cambridge, MA: MIT Press.

Haefner, Klaus. 1984. *Mensch und Computer im Jahr 2000* (Humons and Computer in the year 2000). Basel: Birkhäuser.

Lazer, David, and Viktor Mayer-Schönberger. 2006. "Statutory Frameworks for Regulating Information Flows: Drawing Lessons for DNA Databanks from other Government Data Systems." *Journal of Law, Medicine and Ethics* 34: 366–374.

Mayer-Schönberger, Viktor. 1997. "Generational Development of Data Protection in Europe." In *Technology and Privacy: The New Landscape*, ed. Philip E. Agre and Marc Rotenberg, 219–241. Cambridge, MA: MIT Press.

Miller, Arthur R. 1971. *The Assault on Privacy: Computers, Data Banks and Dossiers*. Ann Arbor: University of Michigan Press.

Seltzer, William, and Margo Anderson. 2001. "The Dark Side of Numbers: The Role of Population Data Systems in Human Rights Abuses." *Social Research* 68, no. 2: 481–513.

Varian, Hal, and Carl Shapiro. 1998. *Information Rules: A Strategic Guide to the Network Economy*. Cambridge, MA: Harvard Business School Press.

Wilson, James Q. 2000. *Bureaucracy: What Government Agencies Do and Why They Do It*. New York: Basic Books Classics.

Index

Abernathy, Frederick H., 64
Abolishthebank.org, 208
Abreau, Elinor, 194
Accenture, 254n2
Access law, 130–131
Accountability
  agency and, 74–78
  rulemaking and, 107–112
  security issues and, 284–288
Activism. *See also* Online politics
  Battle of Seattle and, 186
  blogs and, 192–193
  civic debate and, 186–187
  cybergraffiti and, 209
  Denial of Service (DoS) attacks and, 208, 211
  globalization protests and, 208–211
  hacktivism and, 186, 208–211
  spam and, 208
Administrative Procedure Act (APA), 103–105
Agency, 9, 19, 88. *See also* Networks
  accountability and, 74–78
  bureaucratic expertise and, 101–102
  cross-agency collaboration and, 4, 25, 64, 70–87
  dyadic factors and, 265–267
  government regulation and, 101–102
  Grants.gov and, 65, 81, 83–87
  hierarchical models and, 76–77
  integration and, 65–66
  interagency cooperation and, 30, 34, 36, 81, 86–87

legitimacy and, 107–112
lending information and, 283
novelty and, 262–264
rulemaking process and, 102–107
security issues and, 284–288
systemic factors and, 265–266
Aggregation, 267–268
Air pollution, 101
Algesheimer, Rene, 243, 246
Allen, Barbara, 78–79
Allen, Thomas J., 266
Ambrose, Stephen E., 262
American Customer Satisfaction Index, 46
American Institute of Architects, 169
American Water Works Association, 117
Anderson, Margo, 285–286
Anti-Capitalist Convergence, 208
Apache Web server, 196
Apple, 194
Applegate, Lynda, 64
Area 51, 233
Armstrong, Michael, 59–61
"Around Ground Zero: A map for walking in Lower Manhattan after September 11" (Kurgan), 154–155
Asch, Solomon E., 270
Ash Institute for Democratic Governance and Innovation, 215–218
a16.org, 209
Assembly
  analytical challenges and, 147–152
  deliberation and, 159, 161–162
  demonstrations and, 162–169